THE HISTRIONIC MR. POE

LONDON: GEOFFREY CUMBERLEGE
OXFORD UNIVERSITY PRESS

EDGAR ALLAN POE

BY EDOUARD MANET

From the collection of The Baltimore Museum of Art

This unpublished portrait etching probably was intended to illustrate an edition of
Poe's Tales, as translated by Baudelaire.

THE HISTRIONIC
MR. POE

N. BRYLLION FAGIN

ASSOCIATE PROFESSOR OF ENGLISH AND DRAMA
THE JOHNS HOPKINS UNIVERSITY

BALTIMORE
THE JOHNS HOPKINS PRESS
1949

PRINTED IN THE UNITED STATES OF AMERICA
BY J. H. FURST COMPANY, BALTIMORE, MARYLAND

PREFACE

EDGAR ALLAN POE was a singer of songs and a teller of tales, and it is understandable that he should have inspired many rhapsodies in verse and prose. It is less understandable that he should have also inspired so many biographical and critical studies which are either unbearably heavy or merely thin air. To be sure, much of the patient and meticulous scholarship which, especially of late, has been expended on Poe has helped to destroy many of the myths and legends that had grown about his name, but even this mass of competent scholarship has not been able to dispel the weight of gloom, doom, and solemnity in which Israfel remains shrouded. Even the fanciful biographies, fictions, and scripts for stage, screen, and radio have been, for the most part, Condor-shadowed. It evidently was decided a long time ago that Poe's life was one of unrelieved tragedy and that anyone undertaking to write about him was therefore bound by the amenities to employ a tone of mournful seriousness.

Poe himself was, of course, largely responsible for this. He insisted on the tragic tone: in garb, word, voice, and exclamation point. But Poe, I have a notion, enjoyed his tone. Gravity and tragedy became him even more than mourning became Electra. One can almost see him laboring to achieve that tone, and glorying in the result of his labors. Poe was always, by his own testimony, a conscious artist.

18032

Some years ago Edward Shanks justified his writing of a book on Poe on the ground that Poe was "the man through whom was made America's first great contribution to the literature of the world." My own justification may be that Poe has himself become literature — myth, romance, poetry. To try to understand the nature of this myth, the personality of this romance, the texture of this poetry, seems to me an aim which needs no other justification.

The record of Poe's life and works is now fairly clear, thanks to the indefatigable labors of many scholars, to whom I am, of course, greatly indebted. Their contribution to this book is clearly indicated in the text, in the bibliography, and in the notes in the back of the book. I have also indicated what little known or, in some cases, completely unknown source material has fortunately come my way. Footnotes that are mere references to chapter and verse have been used sparingly, and even these I have thought it wise to separate from the text, because I am hopeful that at least some of my readers do not intend to write books on Poe. These readers, I am sure, will not resent the minor concession I have made to scholarship in the use of inconspicuous numbers to call attention to important documentation. Perhaps, after a while, they may come to feel about these numbers the way a Chinese theatre audience feels about the black-clad property men on the stage: they are presumed to be invisible and therefore they are.

One other hope I must express; it is that this book does not convey the impression that I have somehow succeeded in solving the riddle of Poe's personality and that, therefore, all other books on Poe henceforth become obsolete. All personality is complex and that of

Poe was more than normally so. Biographers who have claimed that he did not "love" his wife may be right; and so may be those who have claimed that he did. Medical writers have "proved" that he was a congenital dipsomaniac or that he suffered from a brain lesion; literary historians have found his work "great," morbid, adolescent, beautiful. Not one of these claims is *the* truth; all of them help us along toward it. They are the pieces that ultimately may fall into place to form the figure in the carpet.

Here, then, is one more piece. It presents another phase of Poe's personality, or a way of looking at it. The theatrical quality of much of his behavior in life has been casually noted by many writers on Poe, but it has not received the detailed attention it deserves. The numerous facets of its expression have never been brought together and placed under focus. I believe that greater recognition of this quality may to some extent dispel the almost intolerable gloom with which Poe has come to be associated in our minds. After all, the histrio may, like any mortal, suffer the slings and arrows of fate, but he has the gift of turning his suffering into a weapon of self-defense. By means of word and gesture and pose he achieves self-importance and exaltation. Seen thus, not a little of Poe's unhappiness appears to have been mere inflation, the swellings of high performance, in which art enlarged upon reality.

And if Poe's behavior in actual everyday life — cabbin'd, cribb'd, and confined — was not devoid of the compensations any artist derives from performing well, shall we overlook the even greater compensations derived from performing in the unconfined world of the imagination? For Poe's literary work was to a remarkable extent an expression of the same histrionic impulse. Many of his poems, stories, and essays are quite clearly theatrical performances. To admit this is not to reflect on their value as works of the imagination: art has many faces and many moods. It is no small tribute to Edgar Allan Poe to say that he was the master of a certain type of literature: and precisely because his own face and mood haunt his creations. No matter that the face is sometimes a tragic mask and the mood the ingenious result of stage magic. In the end, what he has bequeathed to us is none the less art, and art of a high order.

No literary study based on scholarship is completely one's own. I have already indicated my indebtedness to the large body of Poe scholarship, of which I have felt free to avail myself according to my need and judgment. I now wish to express my appreciation of the American Philosophical Society which approved the plan and intention of this book to the extent of helping to finance my researches. To the librarians of the Johns Hopkins University, the University of Pennsylvania, the University of Virginia, the Library of Congress, the Valentine Museum of Richmond, the New York Public Library, the Enoch Pratt Free Library of Baltimore, and the Maryland Historical Society I owe a special debt for their courtesy and cooperation. Mr. William H. Koester of Baltimore deserves the gratitude of all Poe scholars for making his fine collection of Poe material available for study and use. Other individuals to whom I am greatly indebted are Dr. John C. French, Librarian Emeritus of the Johns Hopkins University; Mr. Richard Hart, Head of the Department of Literature, the Enoch

Pratt Free Library; Dr. Thomas Ollive Mabbott of Hunter College; and Mr. H. L. Mencken. These gentlemen have read my manuscript, in whole or in part, and have been generous with wise counsel and constructive criticism. My thanks are also due to Mr. Gordon W. Wilson, of the Hopkins Library staff, for proofreading and to Mr. Abraham Feldman, of Temple University, for the preparation of the index.

N. BRYLLION FAGIN

Baltimore, Maryland
   March, 1949

TABLE OF CONTENTS

CHAPTER I

THE ONLY PROPER STAGE

" . . . as if the world at large were not the
only proper stage for the literary histrio."

A PECULIAR kind of fascination has kept Edgar
Allan Poe alive. It protected him during his brief
lifetime against the many frailties of his personality —
whether inherent or brought about by the conditions
under which he was obliged to live — and, for nearly a
century, it has protected his literary remains against both
inner frailties and the ravages of time. Scholars and
critics have passionately debated the merits of the man
and his poems, stories, and literary judgments, but the
very passion with which the debate has been conducted
is a tribute to this quality of fascination. The greatest
tribute, however, is the overwhelming testimony of his
contemporaries.

Throughout his so-called unhappy life everyone who
came in contact with this " saddest and . . . strangest
figure in American literary history " (1) was conscious
of this quality in the man. The " so-called " is prompted
by a feeling that Poe rather enjoyed his unhappiness,
and that some of his friends, especially the many literary
ladies who were drawn towards him, enjoyed it as much
as the " unhappy genius " himself. At any rate, Poe's
unhappiness was part of his fascination, like the glittering eye of Coleridge's ancient mariner. Other factors
were his general appearance — graceful, pale, and sad,

I

with "large, soft, dreamy eyes"—as one woman describes them (2)—or "magnificent" eyes—as one man describes them (3); his dress—habitually dark and, though often shabby, always immaculate—and one must not forget the Byron collar and the cane (4); his manner, restrained and aloof, even haughty; and his voice—that "rich, mellow and sweet voice," (5) which Poe evidently knew how to use effectively.

It is not a mere coincidence that Mrs. Clarke, the Richmond lady who remembered the richness and mellowness and sweetness of Poe's voice, should also have noted a resemblance between the great actor Edwin Booth and the Virginia poet. Mrs. Clarke did not, of course, stop to consider the possible significance of the resemblance. She merely felt the effect which both men produced upon her, and noted that in some subtle way it was similar in nature. It did not occur to her that both Booth and Poe were actors. But with the passage of many decades providing perspective, and with nearly complete knowledge of Poe's forty years of life, of his actions and reactions, purpose and pose—with all this before us, one is forced to conclude that Edgar Allan Poe, child of actors, was himself, both consciously and unconsciously, an actor. He had somehow, by a combination of circumstances, missed his true vocation and destiny. But if these circumstances deprived him of a stage in a theatre upon which to act, there was nothing to prevent his transforming "the world at large" into a stage (6) whereon he could strut and fret to his heart's content. Generously endowed by nature to play a richly romantic rôle, at a time when the romantic gesture was the fashion on the stage and in the drawing-room, he played it both in his life and in his writings, and played it to the hilt. His fascination was the unfailing fascination of the theatre.

2

The life of Poe has supplied countless biographers with material for articles and books ranging from pamphlet thinness to the 1,685-page bulkiness of Miss Mary E. Phillips's two volumes. Much of this vast outpouring of biographical effervescence has been inspired by legend rather than Poe's actual life; much of it is fiction rather than fact; yet behind most of it has been the laudable desire to establish the simple truth of a comparatively uneventful life. It is significant that "No biographer thus far, not even Mr. Woodberry, has succeeded in making very interesting the narrative portions of Poe's career." (7) This was written by John Macy in 1912, but the biographies that have come from the presses since then have not fared much better.

The trouble has been in the attempt of writers to treat Poe either as a hero or as a villain and to present his life as a series of tragic misfortunes or romantic adventures. The truth, however, seems to be, as Macy saw it, that Poe was an intelligible man whose life, stripped of the gaudy embroidery with which so many biographers — aided and abetted by Poe's fantastic posturings and inventions — have delighted to adorn it, was relatively unadventurous. It was neither colorful nor extraordinarily unfortunate, sad, or tragic. Charles Lamb began life in more unadvantageous circumstances; Charles Dickens knew greater poverty, at least in his childhood; Dostoievsky was more cruelly ravaged by spells of ill health; De Quincey, and probably Coleridge, imbibed more laudanum; and Robert Burns consumed more alcohol. In fact, the only exploits which deserve to be recorded with any flourishes in his biography are his writing of several beautiful poems, an equal number of excellent short stories, and some pieces of discerning and competent criticism.

At this late day, now that we have Professor Arthur Hobson Quinn's carefully-documented biography, it is no longer necessary for every writer on Poe, no matter how limited his intentions, to spread himself at great length in an attempt to disentangle the pertinent facts of the poet's life. They are comparatively few and, for the purposes of this study, may be summarized briefly.

Edgar Poe was born in Boston on January 19, 1809, the son of a mother who was apparently a good actress — a worthy member of a profession which had also been honored by her mother — and a father who was only a passably good actor. David Poe had been dedicated by his father to the study and practice of law in Baltimore, but had early " displayed a fondness for amateur acting," (8) had helped to found a Thespian Club, and had finally managed to join a professional acting troupe in Charleston. In 1806 he married Elizabeth Arnold Hopkins, a young widow who played "leads" in various theatres in Charleston, Richmond, Baltimore, Philadelphia, New York, Boston, and other theatrical centers. Three years later the young actress died in Richmond, while her company was playing at the local theatre, leaving her three little children not only motherless but also fatherless, for David Poe had disappeared sometime previously. Some biographers claim he had died in Norfolk; others, more cautious, deny that anything about his end is definitely known. For us it is important to know only that Edgar, the middle child — a " handsome curly-headed boy " with " big gray eyes " [1]— was adopted by Mr. John Allan, a Richmond merchant, and that the adoption was never made legal.

Edgar Allan Poe attended school in the city of his adoption, except for a period of five years when the Allans were in Scotland and England, and the boy was sent to schools there. In 1826, six years after the family's return to Richmond, Poe entered the University of Virginia, where he stayed but one year, because, having conducted himself like a " gentleman " — as such conduct was then fashionably interpreted — he accumulated large gambling debts which Mr. Allan resented having to pay. His relations with Mr. Allan had become tense and unhappy sometime before he went to Charlottesville; now, upon his ignominious return, they became intolerable.

Hence, on May 27, 1827, Poe was in Boston, the city of his birth, where, under the name of Edgar A. Perry, he enlisted as a private in the United States Army. Apparently he was a good soldier, for, in time, he rose to the rank of Sergeant Major, but upon the recommendation of his colonel, he was honorably discharged, so that, with Mr. Allan's aid, he could enter West Point, a place much more fitting — in the opinion of the colonel, Mr. Allan, and Poe himself — for a gentleman. Accordingly, in the fall of 1830, Cadet Poe began his studies at the military academy on the Hudson. Here, however, his career was brief. The gentlemanly life of a cadet proved rather expensive and Mr. Allan was somewhat

---

[1] This description is taken from Mary E. Phillips's *Edgar Allan Poe, the Man.* It was Poe's destiny to " charm " not only the ladies with whom he came in contact during his lifetime, but also many of his lady biographers in years to come. Miss Phillips, writing her two heavy tomes in our own century, was obviously under the spell at frequent intervals.

less than generous. It is also possible that Poe found the routine of the Academy not to his liking. But whatever cause or causes may have influenced him, he determined to have himself dismissed, and succeeded. At the end of January, 1831, he was courtmartialed on charges of neglect of duty and disobedience of orders, found guilty, and expelled.

The next four years he lived in Baltimore. His widowed aunt, Mrs. Maria Clemm, made a poor but fairly comfortable home for him. At the end of 1835, through the influence of John Pendleton Kennedy, a literary pillar of the time, he obtained an editorial position on the *Southern Literary Messenger* in Richmond. Here, feeling himself for the first time financially established, he settled down with his aunt and her daughter, Virginia, whom he married when she was only fourteen years old.

His position on the *Messenger* proved short-lived. Even though the publication prospered under Poe's editorship, Mr. T. W. White, its publisher, felt himself obliged to discharge an editor, who, though otherwise a likeable and reliable young man, could not be persuaded to abstain from excessive conviviality. A further and probably a more serious grievance of Mr. White's was that Poe "cramped" him from exercising his own judgment as to what articles should or should not be admitted into his periodical. (9)

Poe now decided to seek his fortune in New York. He contributed to various periodicals, while Mrs. Clemm tried to augment the family income by keeping a boarding house. But the efforts of neither proved remunerative enough, and in the summer of 1838 Poe took his family to Philadelphia, which was then, like

New York, a publishing center. Here, after a brief period of floundering, he obtained an editorial position on *The Gentleman's Magazine*, owned and edited by the ex-comedian William Burton. Later he associated himself with *Graham's Magazine*. Although his relations with Mr. Graham were cordial, he nevertheless soon tired of his position and resigned. He dreamed of establishing a literary periodical of his own, which he could edit in his own way, printing only the kind of material he approved and refusing to print material which he felt did not merit the honor of publication, but he failed to secure the necessary financial support for the enterprise. Thereupon he tried to obtain a government position in Washington, using all the " influences " at his disposal, and again failed.

In the spring of 1844 he was back again in New York. Once more he tried to earn a livelihood by contributing, as a free-lance, to newspapers and magazines, but again, in the end, he was obliged to seek the security of regularly paying editorial jobs. At least two periodicals — the *New York Mirror* and the *Broadway Journal* — found his services useful. In time he even came to own the latter publication, but it was not his dream come true, and it mercifully died for lack of financial energy.

In January, 1847, his wife died in their little cottage at Fordham. On October 7, 1849, Poe himself died, in Baltimore, where he had unaccountably been found unconscious several days before near an election polling place.

3

Assuredly Poe's life, thus presented in bare outline, does not add up to anything remarkable. It promises neither the romanticism of great deeds nor the exoticism of great strangeness, and it hardly suggests a fascinating "subject" for biographical lushness or dramatic exploitation. In fairness to Poe, it must be admitted that the brief chronology presented in the preceding section is incomplete. It fails to record, even in summary, the one phase of a "subject's" life which looms largest in modern biography: his experiences in love.

Poe's relations with women have been a rich source of material for many novelists, poets, playwrights and scenario writers, as well as biographers — both semi- and pseudo-scholarly — and psychoanalysts. The scribe who not so long ago labeled a motion picture as "The Loves of Edgar Allan Poe"[2] drew from the same storehouse of possibilities which imaginative persons all over the world have not only drawn from but added to with zeal and profit to themselves. Neither the purpose nor the scope of this book permits a detailed restatement of all the legends or even the facts of Poe's romantic entanglements. Nevertheless, since so much of his histrionic talent was expended on this area of the "stage," it is necessary to identify at least some of the female members of the cast.

The leading lady remains Virginia Clemm Poe, his cousin and wife. Susan Archer Weiss, after picturing the *Home Life of Poe*, came to the conclusion that his feeling for Virginia was, from beginning to end, merely "the affection of a brother or cousin for a sweet and lovable child" and that whatever "sentimental things he may have written concerning [his marriage], his whole conduct goes to prove its insincerity." (10) Joseph

---

[2] I cannot help sympathizing with the disappointment of the great masses of habitual patrons of Hollywood art, for the picture presented but two loves: one legitimate, ending in marriage; the other, not illegitimate and rather trivial.

Wood Krutch, under the spell of Freudian theory and methodology, came to a more startling conclusion; namely, that Poe's affection for any woman, including his wife, could not have been anything more than mental or Platonic, for Poe, Mr. Krutch believes, was impotent. (11) Which prompts Professor Quinn to dismiss Mr. Krutch's whole book with the terse yet delicate notation: "Based on a mistaken theory of Poe's physical constitution." (12) For Mr. Quinn is convinced that, at least just before his marriage, "Edgar Poe loved his little cousin not only with the affection of a brother, but also with the passionate devotion of a lover and a prospective husband." (13) There seems to be no reason to believe that this passionate devotion ever changed after Virginia became Mrs. Poe.

Poe himself is reported to have made conflicting statements, at various times, about his marriage. In a letter which has but recently come to light, a Massachusetts gentleman, Amos Bardwell Heywood, recounts one version of the marriage which he heard Poe tell. Mr. Heywood was the brother of "Annie," a married lady who for a while, after Virginia's death, was "important" in Poe's life. Sitting one evening in her home in Lowell, Poe said that for two years after his marriage he had been a husband in name only, occupying a chamber by himself. To be sure, during part of this time he had been travelling, alone, in Europe — a statement not borne out by any of the known facts. However, Poe, added Mr. Heywood, "spoke of his wife in a most eloquent and touching manner, the tears running down his cheeks in torrents." (14)

Next to Virginia, Sarah Elmira Royster deserves consideration among the featured players upon Poe's stage.

She was the Richmond girl who promised, when he left for the University of Virginia, to wait for him, but who proved too weak to resist the promptings of her practical-minded parents and the blandishments of the wealthy Mr. Shelton. When young Poe came back after less than a year, Elmira was Mrs. Shelton. Long years afterwards, with his wife dead and Mr. Shelton dead, Poe again returned to Elmira, perhaps with less passion but with greater prospects of success. They achieved a reconciliation and their marriage was impending, when Poe's sudden death eliminated her from the stage — except as a writer of reminiscences.

Another featured player was Sarah Helen Whitman, the Providence poetess and spiritualist, who floated daintily in silken draperies and filmy scarfs, exuding the odor of ether — which she imbibed for a heart ailment. She was a widow of forty-five when Poe met her. He addressed to her a whole series of bad literary letters, in which his love-making is painfully violent. He also wrote for her another "To Helen," a poem as unremarkable as the first one to bear the title was beautiful. The first one had been addressed to a lovely Richmond lady who had befriended Poe as a boy and had died early in life. Mrs. Whitman finally consented to marry the impetuous poet, but on condition that he promise to abstain from intoxicating beverages. Poe, of course, promised. But though the banns were proclaimed no wedding bells rang for them. . . .

Mrs. Jane Stith Stanard, the original inspiration of his earlier "To Helen," must be credited with having played the most gracious, most unselfish part in Poe's life. She was the mother of a playmate of his, and her kindness and sympathy bestowed upon a lonely boy of fourteen inspired him, he later wrote, with "the first purely ideal love of [his] soul"[3] and to the writing of his first undeniably distinguished poem.

Of the married ladies to whom he made presumably non-ideal love, only a few deserve more than a passing mention. In the end they all felt embarrassed by his attention; possibly their embarrassment and, in a few cases, downright surliness were a result of the irritating eye-liftings and mutterings of the paradoxical world which, though pretending to love a lover, persists in misunderstanding the beloved. Besides, the ladies Poe selected had reputations to uphold; and, in such cases, there are always husbands and loyal friends whose delight seems to be the safeguarding of these reputations.

One entanglement provoked a fair-sized scandal. Mrs. Frances Sargent Osgood was a Boston-born lady and the attractive wife of a New York artist; she was also a passably good poetess. Poe wrote favorably of her work, mentioned her in a public lecture, and sent her a copy of his "Raven" for an expression of opinion. He even called in person to hear her opinion expressed. She published some verses referring to him as Israfel. He dedicated to her several poems, including one he had written ten years before in Richmond to the daughter of editor T. W. White, and he composed especially for her a valentine which skilfully imbedded her name.

Mrs. Osgood was, however, imprudent enough to write at least one letter to this strange, irresistible swain

[3] " . . . the lines I had written in my passionate boyhood to the first, purely ideal love of my soul — to the Helen Stannard [sic!] of whom I told you — flashed upon my recollection. I turned to them. They expressed all — *all* that I would have said to you — so fully — so accurately — and so conclusively, . . ." — *The Last Letters of Edgar Allan Poe to Sarah Helen Whitman.*

which, in the opinion of another literary lady, Mrs. Elizabeth Fries Ellet, was indiscreet. Decidedly Mrs. Ellet should not have seen the letter, but there it was lying open on a table in Poe's cottage with no one else, at the moment, to read it or to see her read it. As a consequence, a committee of ladies consisting of the Misses Margaret Fuller and Anne Lynch soon called on Mr. Poe and, in behalf of Mrs. Osgood, requested the return of that lady's letters. With the precious bundle recovered, Mrs. Osgood deemed it wise to absent herself for a time from New York. She went to Albany; thence, to Boston, to Lowell, and to Providence;[4] but everywhere Poe followed her, until, back again in Albany, he was compelled by illness to abstain from further pursuit.

Mrs. Ellet herself deserves a few more words. When the propriety-minded committee called on Mr. Poe, he lost his poise to such an extent that he unguardedly exclaimed that Mrs. Ellett "had better come and look after her own letters." (15) Before that incident he had sometimes written favorably of Mrs. Ellet's talents as a versifier.

These were some of the principal players with whom Poe, either by choice or accident, performed. The list is far from complete. His biography is studded with names that have not been mentioned here.

"Annie," who has been referred to, was absorbing enough to merit greater detail. She was Mrs. Nancy Richmond of Lowell, Massachusetts, who inspired at least one good poem and a sheaf of strident letters, some of which he wrote at the very time he was wooing Mrs.

---

[4] It was during this trip to Providence that Poe first saw Mrs. Helen Whitman. ("I saw thee once . . . / Clad all in white . . . / Was it not Fate. . . .")

Whitman. He has left us a vivid pen-portrait of her in
"Landor's Cottage." Even the factual-minded Mr.
Quinn is led to psychoanalytic speculation. Poe, he concludes, loved "Annie" "as a man loves a woman, while
he loved Helen Whitman as a poet loves a poetess."
(16) Just how poets love poetesses is somewhat obscure, but that Poe's letters to Mrs. Richmond breathe
of the kind of love we generally attribute to a man for
a woman is unmistakable.

But what about the minor players — those who played
"bits" or mere "walk-ons"? That Richmond girl, Eliza
White, for instance. She was the daughter of the owner
of the *Southern Literary Messenger*, and the subject of
more than one poem by its youthful editor. Such a careful biographer as Professor Woodberry, after sifting the
evidence, is led to the speculation that Poe's "flirtation"
with Eliza may have contributed to his dismissal from
his first editorial position. (17) Another recipient of
his poetic effusions, at the time, is said to have been a
girl named Mary Winfree. To be sure, these poems
were later readdressed to other women, but that does not
invalidate the fact that Eliza had once contributed to his
performance or that Mary had once been an inspiration.
Then there was "Baltimore Mary" who as a young girl
had lived next door to Mrs. Clemm. When Poe returned
from West Point he fell in love with Mary (Devereaux),
courted her and proposed marriage — if the reminiscences of the same Mary as an old lady can be trusted.
(18) And there was his cousin Elizabeth Herring to
whom he addressed poems. Legend also mentions a
pretty Miss Kate Bleakley in Baltimore to whom ex-
Cadet Edgar Allan Poe wrote verses and letters. (19)
And always, in the last years of his life in New York,

there were "literary women" whose "pestilential society," he once wrote to "Annie" in one of his blue moods, he was determined to shun. . . . They were, he had discovered, "a heartless, unnatural, venomous, dishonorable *set*, with no guiding principles but inordinate self-esteem." (20) There were also the non-literary women, like Marie Louise Shew, to whom he made love. Mrs. Shew had nursed Virginia in her last illness and continued her ministrations to Poe himself when he went to pieces after Virginia's death. Poe addressed ardent poems to her and insisted on publishing a few of them, until the lady was obliged to make him understand that she was not interested in his amorous avowals.

The moot question as to which of these women Poe really loved or how much he loved any one of them cannot be answered here, if anywhere. That several of his best poems—"To Helen" (1831), "For Annie," "Annabel Lee"—were inspired by women cannot be denied; they indicate that Poe possessed not only the gift of song but also that of genuine and profound emotion. That most of his poems engendered by the same impulse are not of equally high quality is just as undeniable. But they do not indicate that in every such case no emotion had been experienced. More likely the emotion was different in nature.

Poe's letters to women make this clear. They are hardly a major contribution to epistolary literature. Generally, even at his mediocre best, Poe was a disciplined prose writer. In these letters, however, he is shrill, flamboyant, and graceless. Above all, their emotionalism is so highly charged as to be unconvincing. It is as though he felt at once too much and too little—too much as a writer and too little as a man. Their extravagant coloring conveys the impression of a species of emotional writing partaking of both Wertherism and surrealism.

No wonder many of Poe's biographers have been shocked. Woodberry felt that fortune had been kind in destroying much of this correspondence. (21) Mrs. Weiss charged Poe with "insincerity and dissimulation" when he wrote to Mrs. Whitman that he had loved her *for years*, during which time he had been unable to either see or hear her name "without a shiver, half of delight, half of anxiety." Yet that was the same period, complains Mrs. Weiss, when Poe was infatuated with Mrs. Osgood, and, moreover, when his wife — whom he claimed to have "loved as man never loved before" — was still alive. (22) And Quinn, incensed by Poe's revelation to his new Helen that he had done violence to his own nature in marrying Virginia, calls him a perpetrator of "deliberate falsehood." (23)

Yet Poe was neither insincere nor a liar — in the usual sense of these words. His affections for women were, as Harrison observes, (24) fleeting, but they were none the less intense. In this respect, "simulator" is a more appropriate description of Poe than "dissimulator." Some of his biographers have come close to an understanding of the true nature of his "love." Even Miss Phillips, whose analytical powers can hardly be called acute, realized that Poe was "an unconscious actor." (25) Woodberry, too, noted that Poe, even as a boy, "either was or affected to be the creature of impulse." (26) But are affectation and impulse always separable? Poe himself could not have been always aware of which came first, the genuine impulse or the affectation; in either case they soon became one and, for the time of duration, genuine. Stoddard must have sensed this when he remarked of the poet's sentiments for Mrs. Osgood that "Poe was enamored of her, felt or fancied that he was, which with him was the same thing." (27)

It was the same thing because Poe was a creative actor, one who throws himself into a rôle and proceeds to interpret it by tapping an emotional reservoir within him — which supplies him with the necessary artistic energy — and by shaping it into a unified creation. In Poe's case, the rôles, though varied, had a similarity of tone: the ardent, sad lover; the underprivileged, the misunderstood; the lover of beauty, of gentleness, virtue, womanhood. His identification with his own character-creation was at times so complete that art and life became interfused; the actor became the character. It was romantic art, and by modern naturalistic standards, short of convincing; but by the standards of the time, and by the standards of refined, "sensitive" ladies like Mrs. Osgood, "divinely beautiful."

4

Scholars and biographers sometimes forget that the person they have selected for study is significant primarily because of some outstanding contribution to the arts, the sciences, or to human history in general. This is especially true in the case of a writer like Poe. "The most casual reader," says Jacques Barzun, "will have noticed that whenever a romantic artist is talked or written about the facts of his life seem to outnumber and overwhelm the facts describing his work." (28) It is wholesome to be reminded that what the man did in his work is a greater — if not the sole — justification for adding another volume to the over-stocked shelves of the world than his merely having been a boy, a man, a husband, a lover, a pessimist, an optimist, a neurotic, a kindly soul, a boor, or a gentleman.

Poe was an artist, a creative writer. With that as a center all other facts about him become relevant and important: they may have contributed to the development, or stunting, of his talent. It is because his poetry still lives, his short stories still give pleasure, and his literary theories still have enough vitality to provoke discussion that Edgar Allan Poe is of contemporary interest. Edmund Wilson, writing in 1943, has called attention to the same obvious but often neglected fact. "In any presentation of American writing," he says, "it is still necessary to insist on his value. In the darkness of his solitary confinement, Poe is still a prince." (29)

Just how early Poe began to write has never been definitely established. That his first attempts were in verse is certain. Joseph H. Clarke, his Richmond schoolmaster, remembered a manuscript volume of verses Mr. Allan had brought him one day for a critical examination and advice. The ten-year old Edgar had given these verses to his "father" with the request that they be published.[5] Of some of his earliest published poems Poe himself remarked that their date of composition was "too remote to be judicially acknowledged." (32) More important is the certainty that, from his schooldays onward, there was never a question in Poe's mind that he was destined to be a poet; that he was as much of a dedicated spirit as Wordsworth ever claimed to be. Mr. John Allan might be practical enough to disapprove of poetry as a

[5] Mr. Clarke's recollection of dates was not very reliable. (30) Poe must have been somewhat older at the time. This does not however impair the value of the aged teacher's recollection that the verses consisted "chiefly of pieces addressed to the different little girls in Richmond, who had from time to time engaged his youthful affections." (31)

3

vocation — as he had disapproved of "strolling players" as worthy progenitors of offspring — but the boy knew his own calling and never betrayed it.

Excluding the brief time spent, under duress, in Mr. Allan's tobacco warehouse, Poe never earned one cent in any other way except by writing — unless the time spent by Mr. "Perry" in the United States Army be credited to Poe's attempt to earn a livelihood. Unless, also, we are willing to accept the unsubstantiated rumors of his having been employed as a professional actor in Boston and as a common laborer in a brick-yard in Baltimore. (33) His monetary returns from his writing were extremely modest, yet even in the year of his death he could write to a friend: "Depend upon it, Thomas, Literature is the most noble of professions. In fact, it is about the only one fit for a man. For my own part, there is no seducing me from the path. I shall be a *littérateur* at least all my life; nor would I abandon the hopes which still lead me on for all the gold in California." (34)

His first published volume appeared soon after he left Richmond to seek his fortune in the North. It was *Tamerlane and Other Poems*, a thin little book printed in Boston in 1827. With it he achieved neither fortune nor fame, for the critics of the period hardly suspected that this pamphlet of juvenile verses marked the appearance in American literature of a poet of stature, one destined for world renown and popularity.[6] Perhaps, if

---

[6] "It can be safely said that the works of Edgar Poe are better known than the poetry of Longfellow or of Whitman. . . ." — Horace Gregory in *Partisan Review*, May-June, 1943. "Without any question, the most significant thing which can be said about Poe is simply that his work has been read, or at least read at, by more Americans than has any other among our native classics." — Joseph Wood Krutch in *The New York Times Book Review*, August 6, 1944.

the critics noticed the volume at all, they felt resentful of the young author who obviously possessed little modesty and less humility. "We will not say," he wrote in the preface, "that he [the author] is indifferent as to the success of these poems . . . but he can safely assert that failure will not at all influence him in a resolution already adopted. This is challenging criticism — let it be so." (35) It was not until many, many years after the poet's bones had been mouldering in his grave that the little book "By a Bostonian" acquired the dignity of a collector's item, making fortunes for the few rare souls who have accidentally stumbled upon copies in neglected attics and junk-shops.

The second volume was published in Baltimore in 1829 and was entitled *Al Aaraaf, Tamerlane, and Minor Poems.* Here Poe's habit of perpetually reprinting earlier poems — sometimes after but minor revisions; at other times, after complete rewriting — becomes established. All through his writing career the artist in Poe was to labor toward the achievement of the inevitable form for his poems and, later, his stories. Critical reviews of this second book were few and inconclusive, ranging from a comparison of the meter of the leading poem with a "pile of brick bats" to a comparison of the youthful author with Shelley. Perhaps, however, not the least achievement of the volume was in impressing Poe's relatives that there might, after all, be something of value in scribbling verses. One hitherto aloof member of the family was moved to credit "Edgar" with possibilities: "*Our* name," he exclaimed, "will be a great one yet." (36)

A few months after Poe's expulsion from West Point, in 1831, his third book appeared, this time under the imprint of a New York publisher. It bore the modest title, *Poems by Edgar A. Poe.* The modesty suggests the possibility that the poet had by now acquired a measure of self-assurance. The book was dedicated to the United States Corps of Cadets, whose subscriptions may have encouraged the New York publisher to undertake the venture. The only notice, says Woodberry — with a slight exaggeration — Poe received "was from the laughter of the cadets, who were disappointed because the little green volume of dingy paper had not turned out to be a book of local squibs." (37)

And yet this "dingy volume" contained some of Poe's best poems, poems that in years to come would be quoted and recited in most of the world's known languages. It contained "Helen," "Israfel," "The Doomed City" (later to become "The City in the Sea"), and "Irene" (to become, after many revisions, "The Sleeper"). That such poetry could pass unnoticed is a commentary on the state of literary taste and judgment in America at the beginning of the fourth decade of the nineteenth century.

But even more than the maturing of a first-rate original poet was passed over in silence. That little green book also marked the emergence of a first-rate literary critic, gravely needed in American letters at the time. In a prefatory letter addressed to "Mr. B." — probably his publisher Elam Bliss — Poe enunciated certain theories on the nature of poetry which he was later to sift and refine. It matters little that some of these theories were derived from others, notably Coleridge; everything he touched became peculiarly his own as it passed through his keen intelligence. In this letter Poe expressed an aesthetics, at once classical and romantic, which he was soon to apply effectively. "In American criticism," a professor of classical learning was to state one hundred and eleven years later, "Poe set the fashion; . . . and much of the classical thinking of later critics . . . has one root in the classics, and another in Edgar Allan Poe." (38)

The reception accorded his first three volumes of verse evidently convinced Poe that the writing of prose might prove more profitable. He therefore turned to the short story. From Baltimore, where he soon found himself living with his relatives, he sent five stories to *The Philadelphia Saturday Courier*. They were all published, but not one of them — not even the powerful Gothic tale "Metzengerstein" — was deemed worthy of the $100 prize which the periodical had offered for the best short story submitted.

He was more fortunate when, sometime later, he submitted six short stories to the *Baltimore Saturday Visiter* and carried off the prize of fifty dollars with his "The Manuscript Found in a Bottle." Moreover, the judges — including no less a literary figure than John Pendleton Kennedy — in announcing the award confessed that they had been equally well impressed with all six of the stories, and expressed a hope that all of Mr. Poe's stories would soon be published in book form.

That book had to wait until 1840, when a Philadelphia publisher brought out the *Tales of the Grotesque and Arabesque* in two volumes. In the meantime Poe's stories had appeared in numerous periodicals, both obscure and popular. Among the twenty-five tales in the Philadelphia collection were such indubitable masterpieces as "The Fall of the House of Usher," "Ligeia" and "William Wilson." Poe had become the master of the American short story.

In the meantime also he had had published in New York — and in London — his only attempt at novelwriting, *The Narrative of Arthur Gordon Pym* (1838).

Two other collections of short stories followed the *Tales of the Grotesque and Arabesque*. Several of these later stories introduced a new type of short fiction, the tale of "ratiocination" or the detective story. In them Poe created a new kind of hero, a Frenchman named C. Auguste Dupin, a man of keen, perceptive mentality — a man apparently like Edgar Poe himself — who by ingenious logical deductions and inferences solved crime puzzles which eluded the unimaginative mentalities of the professional sleuths. As a foil — or "stooge" — Poe created a subsidiary character, a man who followed the great detective around, asking questions and receiving wise answers, and sometimes whole lectures on the simple yet mysterious operations of logic. The two characters have since become better known in world literature, under the names given them by Sir Arthur Conan-Doyle, as Sherlock Holmes and Dr. Watson.

One other important contribution Poe made to the short story. In 1842 he published in *Graham's Magazine* a review of Hawthorne's *Twice-Told Tales* which has become, according to Professor Fred Lewis Pattee, the historian of the American short story, "the leading document in the history of the form." (39) In it he formulated a comprehensive theory of the technique and aesthetic bases of what was to become the most popular form in American fiction.[7]

---

[7] Teachers of creative writing and writers of textbooks on the short story should be forever grateful to Poe for writing that review. It has become the heart of their teachings. It might be interesting to inquire to what extent Poe can be blamed for the machine-made short story which finds its way in such appalling numbers into our popular magazines, both the "slicks" and the "pulps" — but that is another story.

That review was part of a larger contribution which Poe made to literary criticism in general. By the time it appeared Poe had already established himself as one of our leading critics. His quill was prolific and he turned out reviews and literary essays so numerous that he was in danger of being forgotten either as poet or as story-teller and remembered only as a critic.

The appearance, in 1845, of another collection of *Tales*, and still another volume of his poems, containing "The Raven," somewhat restored the balance.

This almost completes the record of Poe's literary activity—almost though not quite. For in addition to these three main types of writing, in each of which he achieved fame if not fortune, Poe also from time to time digressed into various other fields. Thus he once wrote a book on conchology—mostly a rewriting of another's work. He solved cryptograms and perpetrated journal-istic and pseudo-scientific hoaxes. Altogether he did a prodigious amount of hack work. It paid little, but it paid. . . . And toward the end of his life he published *Eureka*, which he called a "prose poem" but which might be described with equal justice as a philosophical treatise or "scientific" dissertation. It was his most am-bitious undertaking, his Book of Truths—a turgid dis-closure of his comprehension of the laws and destiny of the universe. Critics to this day are baffled by it and differ widely on its value. Poe himself believed that *Eureka* was his *magnum opus* and would be read "two thousand years hence." (40) He dedicated it to Alex-ander von Humboldt, whose *Cosmos* had influenced some of his own philosophical reflections.

5

Edgar Allan Poe was a highly gifted writer. His stories are imaginative and his poems are musical. In both *genres* he was impressively romantic. The effect of his work upon the imagination is vivid and haunting. Yet to attribute the extraordinary impression he has left behind him solely to the qualities of his work would be erroneous. Shelley was imaginative and romantic; Keats was vivid and musical; but their fascination is purely that of the excellence of their work, and is confined to lovers of poetry. Only Byron somewhat approximates Poe's appeal, and it is significant that Poe as a youngster was strongly stimulated by the dramatic character of Byron's personality and writings. He felt impelled not only to emulation in verse, but also to a successful imitation of Byron's swimming exploit: six or seven miles (41) against the tide in the James River — duplicating the British poet's feat of swimming across the Hellespont.[8]

It is Poe's personality which has remained the inexplicable yet tangible core of his appeal. He was and still is a tantalizing mystery. Our emotional or critical attitude toward his work seems to have only a slight and remote connection with our warm curiosity. Even if we perceive some justice in Henry James's carefully-shaded self-congratulation — "An enthusiasm for Poe is the mark of a decidedly primitive stage of reflection" (43) — we nevertheless do not abandon Poe. No more than Yvor

---

[8] For an illustration of Poe's careful study of Byron, the reader is referred to Roy P. Basler's "Byronism in Poe's 'To One in Paradise.'" — *American Literature*, May, 1937. Lest, however, I may seem to overemphasize Poe's indebtedness to the English romantic bard, it is well to remember Edward Shanks's observation that Poe was not too successful as an imitator: at least in the better of his early poems his "own natural genius warps his imitative intent." (42)

Winters did when he publicly confessed several years ago, for himself and his friends, that Poe had long passed casually, with him and with them, "as a bad writer accidentally and temporarily popular." A psychologist might accept the act of confession itself as a disclosure of preoccupation.[9]

Poe's "temporary" popularity need not detain us. Edmund Wilson, Horace Gregory, Malcolm Cowley, Van Wyck Brooks, Professor Matthiessen, and others [10] have recently taken care of that. Whether there was — and still is — an element of the "accidental" in Poe's popularity is largely a matter of semantics. If the sum total of physical and psychological equipments, aptitudes, and patterns of behavior which constitute personality be merely accidental to a writer's work, then Poe's appeal has been "accidental." But we are still baffled by the man, and the attempts of some of the best minds to explain him have intensified rather than lessened our interest. Was Poe Griswold's scoundrel or Baudelaire's saint, one of the holy army of martyrs? Was he Lauvrière's congenital degenerate or Hanns Heinz Ewers's dreamer "beautiful in body and mind"? (44) Was he the satanic genius, the poet of hell, who like Lucifer, fell from sheer intellectual pride, or was he a great spiritual writer? [11] We shall probably never know

[9] Mr. Winters's interpretation of his impulse toward confession deserves quotation, at least in a footnote: "the fact of the matter is, of course, that he [Poe] has been pretty effectually established as a great writer while we [Mr. Winters and 'most' of his friends] have been sleeping." — *American Literature*, January, 1937.

[10] Among the "others" may be included the anonymous writer of an editorial in the Baltimore *Sun* (January 18, 1946) who began with the caption "Despite Poe's Critics, People Keep Right on Reading Him" and ended with the statement, "The more the termites nibble, the sounder and bigger his reputation seems to grow."

[11] The following titles suggest the range of opinion: "The Satanic

the answer. Poe will continue to haunt us and to raise questions. Perhaps all we shall ever know definitely is the indubitable fact noted by a reviewer of Harrison's *Life*, away back in 1903, that "Edgar Allan Poe is the most interesting and picturesque figure in American letters."

That reviewer, Jeannette L. Gilder, justified her use of the adjective "picturesque" by adding, "because of his weaknesses and misfortunes." (46) She was partly right. Poe's weaknesses and misfortunes have contributed to his picturesqueness. The element of pathos, if not tragedy, always hovered above him, like a dark halo: Orphaned as a child; sent to the university, but, alas, for one brief year; dismissed from West Point; deserted by the girl he loved; yoked to a child-wife, frail, consumptive, who died leaving him ill and lonely; and always poverty trailing him like a lean beast throughout his life; and, the crowning stroke of fate, his death — alone, unknown — in a charitable institution. Add to that his "weaknesses" — a predisposition to alcohol, a sensitive nervous organism, instability, irritability, inordinate pride perpetually wounded, physical pain necessitating the anodyne of alcohol or opium.

But add also Poe's unerring sense of romantic effectiveness. Consciously or by intuition he turned his weaknesses and misfortunes into assets. His letters teem with laments and complaints, with bitter outcries against

Streak in Poe's Genius," *Current Literature*, January, 1910; *Great Spiritual Writers of America*, by George Hamlin Fitch, 1916; " Three Interesting Sinners," by Newman Flower, *The Bookman*, October, 1926. I wonder, however, what Poe's own reaction would have been to the eulogy of an eminent Virginia educator: " I have always been an admirer of Poe, not only as our greatest literary genius, but as a ' good, safe household poet.' " (45)

an unjust fate, with proud defiance of a callous world, and with almost rhapsodic indulgence in self-pity.

"I am in the greatest necessity," he writes to Mr. Allan, after leaving that gentleman's house following a quarrel; "not having tasted food since yesterday morning I have no where to sleep at night, but roam the streets — I am nearly exhausted . . ." (47) Two years later, as a soldier stationed at Fort Moultrie, he writes: "I have thrown myself on the world like a Norman conqueror on the shores of Britain &, by my avowed assurance of victory, have destroyed the fleet which could alone cover my retreat — I must either conquer or die — succeed or be disgraced." (48) Three weeks later he follows up this letter with one at once more proud and more abject: "There is that within my heart which has no connection with degradation — I can walk among infection & be uncontaminated. . . . My father do not throw me aside as *degraded* I will be an honor to your name." (49) After his dismissal from West Point he again appeals to Mr. Allan for assistance — for the last time, he assures him. "I feel that I am on sick bed from which I never shall get up." (50) He does, however, get up, and he does write again to Mr. Allan. Not, to be sure, to ask for any favors, but merely to express his gratitude for past favors, to call himself the greatest fool in existence, and to curse the day he was born. Also to add, ever so casually — merely by way of general information — that he is wretchedly poor. (51) And if a month later he writes once more — and this time definitely begging financial assistance — it is only because he is in the "greatest distress," having been arrested for a debt incurred on his brother Henry's account.[12] (52)

[12] At Professor Quinn's suggestion, two scholarly Baltimoreans, Mr.

If Poe managed, in one mood or another, to call attention to his misfortunes, he managed equally well, in one key or another, to dramatize his weaknesses. In 1835 he writes to his friend and benefactor, J. P. Kennedy, that he is suffering from a spell of melancholy which he is unable to account for, as his financial condition, at the moment, is rather good and the prospects of future prosperity are even better. He is wretched and knows not why. "Convince me," he pleads, "that it is worth one's while — that it is at all necessary to live." One tell-tale sentence slips into this letter: "I say you will believe me, and for this simple reason, that a man who is writing for effect does not write *thus*." This hardly requires the analytical powers of a M. Dupin to draw the obvious inference that Poe was aware of the possibility that his writing might produce an effect he did not intend to produce.

It is not, however, until thirteen years later, during his unsmooth courtship of Mrs. Whitman that he attempts to do something about this feeling that it is not at all necessary to live. He buys two ounces of laudanum, writes to "Annie" imploring her to come to his death bed, and then swallows "about half" the laudanum. The amount is not enough to end his life, but it is enough to make him deathly sick. In the hysterical letter in which, several days later, he tells her the story, he renews his request that she come to him. "I am so *ill*," he concludes; "so terribly, hopelessly ILL in body and mind, that I feel I CANNOT live, unless I can feel

---

Louis H. Dielman and Dr. J. Hall Pleasants, made a thorough search of all Baltimore jail records for the years 1831 and 1832, as well as the records of imprisonments for debt, but found no mention of Poe in any of them, nor of "any misdemeanor that appeared to fit the case," assuming that Poe was sentenced under a borrowed name. (53)

your sweet, gentle, loving hand pressed upon my fore-head." (54) [13]

To Mrs. Whitman, who insisted on his curbing one of his weaknesses before she would consent to marry him, he confessed: "I have absolutely no pleasure in the stimulants in which I sometimes so madly indulge. It has not been in the pursuit of pleasure that I have periled life and reputation and reason. It has been a desperate attempt to escape from torturing memories." Perhaps the medical comment of Dr. John W. Robertson, one of Poe's friendliest biographers, is the only one that can be made on this confession: "If there were 'memories,' they were of prenatal inheritance." (55)

To another correspondent, who had evidently asked him for an explanation of the circumstances — or the "terrible evil," as Poe had hinted — which had caused his "irregularities," Poe wrote of the anxious years during which his wife had been desperately ill. "But I am," he wrote, "constitutionally sensitive — nervous in a very unusual degree. I became insane, with long intervals of horrible sanity. During these fits of absolute unconsciousness, I drank — God only knows how often or how much." (56) The explanation sounded impressive. John H. Ingram, the most painstaking English biographer of Poe, was the first to unveil "this terrible mystery in the poet's life," and he was so startled that he felt as though he were committing sacrilege in publishing the letter. And Harrison was moved to exclaim: "This, then, was the form that gnawed relentlessly at Poe's heart for six years, and well-nigh drove him mad. . . ." (57)

It is not strange that Poe should have conveniently

---

[13] The italics and capitals are of course Poe's.

forgotten that these "fits" had been part of his history long before Virginia's illness; but it is strange that his sympathetic biographers should have apparently shared his lapse of memory.[14] Harrison, for example, prints Poe's letter to Dr. Snodgrass, written seven years before the great revelation, in which Poe replies to the accusations made against him by his former employer, William Burton. After pledging, "before God, the solemn word of a gentleman," that he is temperate even to rigor, he proceeds, with due candor, to inform Snodgrass upon what foundation Burton "has erected his slanders." He has never been, he repeats, in the *habit* of intoxication, but he admits that sometimes, during his stay in Richmond, when he was editing the *Messenger*, he, "at long intervals," gave way to the temptation held out on all sides by the spirit of Southern conviviality. "My sensitive temperament," he explains, "could not stand an excitement which was an every-day matter to my companions. In short, it sometimes happened that I was completely intoxicated." (59)

Poe obviously believed his passionate assertions each time he made them, and he died believing them. On his last visit to Richmond he told his friend Dr. Carter that if people would not tempt him, he would not fall. He declared, "in the most solemn manner," that he *would* restrain himself. (60) Indeed, he was so confident that he *could* restrain himself that he took a pledge of total abstinence and became a member of the Order of Sons of Temperance, thereby gladdening the hearts of the

[14] There is something almost pathological in the attempts of scholars to prove that Poe drank, much or little, or did not drink. In this connection, H. L. Mencken's comment, somewhat over-vigorous and over-categorical as it may be, is apropos: "Strapped to the water-wagon, with a ton of Bibles to hold him down, he would have been precisely the same Poe." (58)

"best" people of Richmond, as one clerical gentleman later recalled. (61) Several days later he lay fatally ill in Baltimore. . . . What seems strange is that he made his biographers believe his explanations and avowals. That certainly is a tribute to the persuasiveness of his style, to his ability to make any moment vivid and complete.

6

Attempts to explain any creative gift are generally unconvincing, if not fatuous. In the case, however, of Poe's ability to present any moment as a complete experience, acquaintance with the whole history of the man can be very helpful. The concentration he managed to bestow upon any situation or mood is strikingly akin to that which one observes — or forgets to observe — in tense moments on a theatre stage. A gifted actor interpreting a part enters into his rôle with such intensity — even when controlled by artistic discipline — that each moment is a unique experience. There is no question of contradiction or affirmation of what has preceded; there is only an enactment of each scene, confrontation, or dramatic unit with such self-absorbed concentration as to render it roundly complete.

The resources of Poe for a successful career in the profession of his parents were very considerable. His heredity, temperament, mind, body, and voice would have been great assets to him had he been permitted to choose acting instead of literature as his profession. Such a choice was never his to make. The accident of his adoption by a petty Scotch merchant aspiring to become a Virginia gentleman deflected his life from a course which might have been the only logical one for him. The contempt with which a man of Mr. Allan's type —

who came into money soon after adopting the boy — looked upon "strolling players" early affected Poe himself and was always to wage war with his natural inclinations. Edgar Poe, reared to be a gentleman but unprovided with the means needful to maintain the life of one, could find only in literature an occupation tolerable to a tradition of genteel values. He followed it, but remained at heart as much of an actor as if he actually trod the boards. If we must find a split personality in Edgar Allan Poe, it is clearly discernible in the conflict between the gentleman and the repressed strolling player. Both were unhappy, because neither was permitted to function naturally, and each sought compensations and made adjustments: the gentleman by facing the world with insolent pride, by wearing his shabby attire with meticulous dignity, and by turning himself into a literary histrio; the player by turning the world itself into a stage.

That this conflict continued throughout his life there can be no doubt. In 1845 Anna Cora Mowatt, a New York lady accustomed to the highest social circles, found herself obliged, by a stroke of financial reverses, to professionalize her acting talents and, as a consequence, she also found herself the object of severe disapproval by certain members of her own class.[15] Among the voices that defended and encouraged her was that of the by then well-known literary and dramatic critic, Mr. E. A. Poe.

It was logical, of course, that he should defend her —

---

[15] Perhaps the worst condemner of Mrs. Mowatt was her own class-consciousness. "The idea of becoming a professional actress was revolting," she confessed. After eight years on the stage she was, however, able to tell "those who do not frequent theatres" that actors were *not* disreputable persons. (62)

and the acting profession as well — on general principles;
but his vehement defense contains a short passage — one
gratuitous autobiographic sentence — which shows special concern, as though the subject had long festered
within him, like a hidden wound: "We have no sympathies," he wrote, "with the prejudices which would
entirely have dissuaded Mrs. Mowatt from the stage.
There is no cant more contemptible than that which
habitually decries the theatrical profession — a profession which, in itself, embraces all that can elevate and
ennoble, and absolutely nothing to degrade. . . . In
the mere name of *actress* she can surely find nothing to
dread. . . . The theatre is ennobled by its high facilities for the development of genius — facilities not afforded elsewhere in equal degree. By the spirit of genius
we say, it is ennobled — it is sanctified — beyond the
sneer of the fool or the cant of the hypocrite. The actor
of talent is poor at heart, indeed, if he do not look with
contempt upon the mediocrity even of a king." Then
follows the tell-tale sentence: "The writer of this article
is himself the son of an actress — has invariably made
it his boast — and no earl was ever prouder of his earldom
than he of the descent from a woman who, although
well born, hesitated not to consecrate to the drama her
brief career of genius and of beauty." (63) The paral-
lelism — and the self-identification — is obvious. So is the
betrayal of the inner conflict: that touch about his
mother having been "well born" and the qualifying
"although."

For the seeds of this conflict one must go back to Poe's
childhood. He grew up to express pride in his actress
mother; but in the environment of the Allans, in the
private schools to which he was sent, and in the circle

4

of his early friends — themselves a product of nineteenth-century upper and middle-class Virginia — he heard but little that was favorable of acting and actors.[16] All of his biographers agree that Poe, especially as child and boy, was often hurt and humiliated because of his " low " lineage. At the Allan home the " memory of his outcast ancestry was not allowed to fade " so that the boy might remember his debt of gratitude to Mr. Allan and that " he was among ladies and gentlemen on sufferance only, that he did not belong among them and never could." (64) At school, things were no better. Mrs. Weiss cites the instance of one "sprig of an aristocratic family" who objected to associating with the son of actors and was in return lampooned by young Poe as " Don Pompiosa." (65) And Krutch, in trying to account for Poe's dislike of Boston, suggests that " it may be that in receiving these first wounds of the spirit "— the snubs and insults to which his schoolfellows had subjected him as the son of an actress — " he identified the place of his birth with its heritage of shame." (66) Quinn's summary is sufficient to speak for all the biographers: " There can be little question that Poe's heritage in the theatre did him little good in his social relations." (67)

Yet he could not escape that heritage; nor would the world which condemned him for it permit him to escape it. For it is the nature of the theatre to attract, and even the sober-minded and overly-respectable persons in

---

[16] A characteristic Richmond sentiment: " Those amusements are unlawful, which, if not in themselves absolutely sinful, have a dangerous tendency to sin. This will particularly include the diversions of the Playhouse. . . . For consider 1. *The Company* — of whom composed? Some virtuous characters, no doubt, are among them. But what a vast number of the most vicious and profane! Is not the Playhouse the very exchange for harlots? . . . 2. *The Players* — generally speaking, who are they? loose, debauched people . . ." — Quoted by Agnes M. Bondurant in *Poe's Richmond.*

whom it inspires distrust and disdain are affected by its "sinful" power. The suggestion of one biographer that Poe's earliest memories were of the stage onto which he may have been carried to enact the rôle of an infant seems far-fetched, although it is unquestionably true that much of his infancy was passed in the green-rooms of the various theatres in which his parents performed. It is equally true that as a little boy he enchanted the Allans and their guests by his acting. "At the age of six," says Woodberry, "he could read, draw, and dance; of more showy accomplishments (a chair, or else the long, narrow Virginia table, cleared for dessert, being his stage), his trick before company was to pledge their healths in sweetened wine and water with roguish grace, and his talent was to declaim, for each of which he had, perhaps by inheritance, an equal aptitude." (68) There is some doubt about his pledging "their healths," but there is none about his other accomplishments, including that of "spouting" verse, even at the early age of five. (69)

In the fashionable schools to which he was sent, both in Richmond and in England, he distinguished himself in declamation and debate. The boy of obscure parentage evidently knew how to make the most of his special gifts in competition with boys who had the advantage of social prestige. "Talent for declamation was one of his gifts," recalled T. H. Ellis, the son of Mr. Allan's partner. "I well remember a public exhibition at the close of a course of instruction in elocution . . . , and my delight when, in the presence of a large and distinguished company, he bore off the prize in competition with Channing Moore, Cary Wickham, Andrew Johnston, Nat Howard, and others. . . ." (70)

All through his later life Poe was to know the power to be derived from his talent. Declamation and elocution — as we shall soon see — were to be an important part of the glory that was Poe.

That the boy's successes gave him a feeling of superiority is probably true, but that they were, as is generally believed, bad for him is not so certain. The applause of his teachers and playmates at his performances and the enthusiastic approval of the home circle may have enhanced his innate pride, but to the born actor approval is the confirmation of his talent and helps to determine its direction. Had it not been for the hostility of his social environment toward the theatre Edgar Poe's dramatic powers might have found creative direction; as it was, they became distorted into mere sound and fury. There was no such hostility toward theatricality as one of the social graces; as such it was encouraged. It is not surprising, therefore, that the elocution and the grand pose never left the boy impelled to exhibitionism.

The episode of the Thespian Club is instructive. A group of boys from the Classical School founded a " Thespian Club." It may have been a coincidence, but it is worth recalling that Poe's father as a boy in Baltimore had been known to his friends as "a clever amateur actor and a boon companion of the Thespian Club." (71) Edgar's dramatic group in Richmond improvised a stage and gave performances for a small admission price, drawing audiences of forty or fifty for each performance. It introduced at least one good actor — Edgar Poe. "He was," reminisced Dr. Creed Thomas, who had been a fellow-Thespian, "one of the best actors." "He had undoubted talent in this direction," confirmed Col. T. H. Ellis. But while the audiences

might have been pleased Mr. Allan was decidedly dis-
pleased, and he forbade Edgar's "having anything to do
with these theatricals" — an action which was, records
Mrs. Weiss, "a great grievance to the boy." (72)

Beyond a very plausible likelihood there is no evidence that Poe ever again participated in dramatic performances. Ellis, whose information has proved correct
in other respects, believed that when Poe first went to
Boston, after leaving the Allan home, he tried to support
himself by turning professional actor (73); and Quinn
reports finding an item in the *Boston Courier* for April
24, 1827, announcing that the part of Bertrand in the
Foundling of the Forest would be played by "a young
gentleman of Boston, his first appearance on any stage."
(74) [17] We know that Poe was in Boston at the time,
arranging for the publication of his first book, to be
signed "By a Bostonian." It is also worth recording
that the late Mr. James H. Whitty once claimed having
seen a Philadelphia playbill listing Mr. Edgar A. Poe
as a leading actor in a benefit performance for a Philadelphia charity. [18]

But allowing for the possibility that these acting experiences are — like so many other rumors about Poe —
mere legends and hypotheses, it is nevertheless clear

[17] It is interesting to note that as far back as 1908 Padraic Colum, in
his introduction to the Everyman collection of Poe's *Tales of Mystery
and Imagination*, wondered that Poe, after leaving the Allan home,
"did not . . . try the stage; it would have fitted his temperament and
his gifts, but perhaps," he added, "the career of his parents had biassed
him against the theatre."

[18] Mr. Whitty told me of this playbill at his home in Richmond. He
was, at the time, a very old gentleman and in bad health. The possibility of the existence of such a playbill cannot be ignored, but it is
necessary to remember that there have been too many reminiscences and
statements regarding Poe by aged people whose memories were their
only source of evidence. So far, to my knowledge, no one else has seen
the playbill.

that not having the limited area of a theatre stage at his disposal did not stop Poe from exhibiting his talents. The curly-headed little boy who mounted Mr. Allan's dinner table to captivate the hearts of his audience by his declamation and general histrionic "cuteness" soon grew into the fifteen-year old Lieutenant of the Richmond Junior Volunteers who stood at the quay, sword in hand, welcoming General Lafayette. It was during the old General's triumphal tour of the United States in 1824, the same year in which Mrs. Stanard, "Helen," died, and whose grave the boy is said to have haunted, preferably at midnight. When the General went to church the next day, Sunday, "tradition has it" that Lieutenant Poe escorted him to the pew of Chief Justice Marshall. (75) One is not at all surprised to learn that at West Point Cadet Poe was also a Drum-Major.

Other forms of exhibitionism obtrude themselves. There was his "lifelong love of hoaxing." (76) John Mackenzie, a boyhood playmate of Edgar's, remembered that Poe "delighted in playing practical jokes" and in "masquerading." (77) There is Col. Ellis's reminiscence of the Christmas toy — a "hideous imitation of a serpent" — which young Edgar persisted in poking at little Jane Ellis until "it almost ran her crazy." (78) [19] There is the story of the Christmas ghost that appeared at the Gentleman's Whist Club meeting at the Ellis home. Behind its mask was young Edgar Poe. (79) And there is the story of the "slaying" of old K — a West Point professor, whose body hidden in a burlap sack turned out to be the bloody carcass of a gander dragged into the barracks as part of a little comedy. (80)

[19] It is rather surprising that this episode has been overlooked by the confirmed psychoanalysts. What an opportunity for injecting significant symbolism!

Poe's literary hoaxes, an ingrained element of his intellectual make-up, according to Harrison, (81) must be accepted as still another species of exhibitionism. Such fictions as "Hans Pfaall," "The Journal of Julius Rodman," "The Narrative of Arthur Gordon Pym," "The Balloon-Hoax," and "Mesmerism in Articulo Mortis" were passed off deliberately as news, actual adventure, and scientific investigation. His display of learning came pretty close to hoaxing: garbled quotations from obscure authorities; florid references to "great" names, often non-existent, and scholarly annotations of his own work, such as those appended to "Al Aaraaf." There are also his reviews; anonymous, like the one of Griswold's *The Poets and Poetry of America*, in which he takes the opportunity to mention "the brilliant career of Graham's Magazine under Mr. Poe's care, and its subsequent trashy literary character since his retirement" (82); or pseudonymous, like the one of "The Raven," under the mask of "Quarles" — very technical, very learned, and obviously intended to impress the reader as being very profound. His easy assumption of pseudonyms and aliases — E. A. Perry, Henri Le Rennet, E. S. T. Grey, Esqr., (83) Thaddeus K. Peasley (84) — needs no special comment.

These posturings and pretensions, combined with other forms of exhibitionism — such as most of his verses and epistles to ladies — undoubtedly helped to create the impression that he was essentially insincere, but a more understanding interpretation is decidedly possible. Professor J. Montgomery Gambrill, for instance — a trained historian — acknowledges the "basis of fact" underlying the accusation but does not overlook the extenuating circumstances. Poe, he says, "repeatedly furnished or approved statements regarding his life and work that were incorrect, he often made a disingenuous show of pretended learning, and he sometimes misstated facts to avoid wounding his own vanity." All this is true, of course, but, continues, Mr. Gambrill, "This ugly fault seems to have resulted from a fondness for romantic posing, . . . Perhaps, too, he inherited from his actor parents a love of applause, and if so, the trait was certainly encouraged in early childhood." (85) In the light of all that we now know of Poe's life — from his Richmond childhood to his death in Baltimore — there can no longer be any "perhaps" and "if so."

7

Although Poe was obliged to use the world at large as his theatre — and he was aware of the inescapable necessity fairly early — he nevertheless found himself unable to keep away from the real theatre and its peculiarly colorful people. His activities as playwright and dramatic critic are important enough to deserve extended treatment in separate chapters. But his relations with men of the theatre cannot be omitted from a consideration of either Poe the man or Poe the writer. They are significant in any possible interpretation of what Poe himself so aptly phrased as the "literary histrio."

It cannot be a mere coincidence that he should have been thrown together repeatedly with so many actors, playwrights, and elocutionists, and that some of his closest friends should have come from among them. It was as though the unindigenous Virginia gentleman, never quite accepted by the society [20] which by his early

[20] "His engagement to Mrs. Shelton [in 1849, just before his death] had made a vast difference in the way he was regarded even by the

conditioning he both respected and feared, found the theatre a place of light and warmth. Here at least he felt himself no alien, for here he found people whose easy camaraderie betrayed no moments of condescension, no tiny isles of frigid reserve. Like Mrs. Mowatt he might feel it necessary to defend the institution against his own unconscious contempt, but here, ultimately, was acceptance, congeniality, home.

One of the earliest of his friends in his Richmond boyhood was Robert Sully, whose father, Matthew Sully, had acted with Poe's mother. (88) Perhaps that knowledge influenced Edgar in becoming the protector of a delicate and sensitive boy against the tyrannies of his sturdier and more aggressive playmates. He would not allow the big boys to tease "Rob"; he also helped him with his lessons. (89) In later life, when Poe was a member of the circle of artists, actors, and writers meeting at a hotel in Philadelphia, Thomas Sully, Robert's uncle, painted a portrait of Poe draped in a cloak which "savored of Byron." (90)

Poe's relations with John H. Hewitt are difficult to characterize. They were friends, says Whitty (91); acquaintances, says Quinn. (92) Certainly they were at one time rivals, for it was Hewitt who under the name of "Henry Wilton" carried off the poetry prize offered by the *Baltimore Saturday Visiter.*[21] And it was Hewitt who likened the measure of "Al Aaraaf" to a pile of

Mackenzies [who had adopted his sister Rosalie] who, from having ignored him, now overwhelmed him with attentions and apologized for not accommodating him in their mansion." — Una Pope-Hennessy. (86)

Poe's elation over this belated acceptance of him by Richmond society is betrayed in a letter to his mother-in-law: "I have been received everywhere with enthusiasm." (87)

[21] Poe's entry, "The Coliseum," was rated very high by the judges, but since he was to be awarded the short story prize the judges felt that the poetry prize should go to another contestant.

brick bats. It was also Hewitt who left us an account of a fight he had had with Poe on the streets of Baltimore. (93) Besides being a poet and journalist, Hewitt was also a playwright, a composer of operas, and a member of a theatrical company organized by his father. (94)

Poe was a comparative newcomer in Baltimore when he became one of the group of young writers and artists meeting at the Seven Stars Tavern, all of them "knights of the quill, brush or stage." Poe, it is said, became "very popular with these littérateurs, both because of his pleasing manners and his singular elocutionary charm." (95) One of the group was T. S. Arthur, whose *Ten Nights in a Bar-Room* was to prove a forerunner of *Abie's Irish Rose*, *Tobacco Road* and *Life with Father* in its appeal to American theatre audiences. Another was Lambert A. Wilmer, whose *Merlin* dramatized Poe's early romance with Elmira Royster.

Little is known of the literary and theatrical coteries to which Poe may have gravitated when he returned to Richmond to work on the *Messenger*. It seems worth recording, however, that he soon found himself scribbling verses into Eliza White's album, the same Eliza White who in later life became a "well-known Shakespearean reader" and visited Poe at his home in Fordham. (96)

I have already mentioned the fact that during his residence in Philadelphia Poe was a member of a coterie that included many actors and playwrights. Quinn believes that William Burton, ex-comedian turned editor and publisher, "probably invited Poe to the dinner parties which he is reputed to have given at his home." (97) Hervey Allen has "no doubt" that the "theatrical

Mr. Burton . . . occasionally arranged to take his young editor" to the Chestnut Street Theatre "to see Edwin Forrest rant and tear." (98) It is certain that the Grahams invited their "interesting, good-looking young editor" to their home, where, at weekly parties, he left the impression of "an elegant black-cloaked figure making actor-like entries on the scene." (99) All contemporary sources indicate that Poe in Philadelphia met with such prominent actors and playwrights as Burton, Forrest, Richard Penn Smith, James N. Barker, Robert M. Bird, and Robert T. Conrad, (100) some of whom became his friends. His friendship with Junius Brutus Booth was close enough to have inspired a story of the two of them returning on one occasion from the theatre in such "high-flown" condition that they indulged in perpetrating a practical joke at the expense of an offended Jew. (101)

But it was in New York that Poe found himself closer to the theatre than he had ever been before. Wherever he went, at Frank's Place in Barclay Street, (102) at the homes of Willis, the Hon. John R. Bartlett, Miss Anne C. Lynch, Mrs. Oakes Smith, or at the theatre, he met many playwrights and actors. In his poorer days, friends, such as the bookseller Gowans, supplied him with tickets; later, his editorial connections, especially as dramatic critic on the *Broadway Journal,* enabled him to keep up with the theatrical life of the city. A celebrity in his own right and an influential commentator with magazine columns at his disposal, he was invited to first nights and to theatrical supper parties. Playwrights, actresses, and producers "angled for his notice and appeared to hang upon his words." (103) By then he was also the famous author of "The

Raven," which no less an accomplished actor than James E. Murdoch was willing to recite in public.

The first reading of the poem was as theatrical as Poe could manage to make it. Alexander Taylor Crane, in his recollections of the time when he was employed as errand boy and mail clerk in the office of the *Broadway Journal*, remembered Poe's coming in with Murdoch one day and handing him the manuscript of the poem. Murdoch, "one of the finest elocutionists," then proceeded to charm the office staff. (104) Sometime later Murdoch and a collaborator published a text-book on dramatic elocution, in which they included three of Poe's poems: "The Raven," "Annabel Lee," and "The Bells." (105) [22]

Another New York friend was Gabriel Harrison, whom Poe discovered in a general store on the corner of Broadway and Prince Street. Harrison was a playwright, an actor, and a founder of the Brooklyn Dramatic Academy. He was famous for his *Othello* to Lester Wallack's *Iago*. His acting, it is said, was characterized by perfect enunciation and magnetic power of voice and manner. (106) Long after Poe's death Harrison continued to write to Mrs. Clemm and to refer to "dear Eddie." His recollections, published toward the end of the century, testify to the friendship that had existed between him and the poet. (107) [23]

The opportunities with which New York provided Poe were many. It is not at all surprising, for instance,

[22] Poe managed to work into a review of "Mr. Murdoch's Lectures" a pre-publication announcement of this text-book. "We shall look with much interest," he wrote with apparent casualness, "for a work on Elocution which we understand he is preparing." — *Broadway Journal*, II, 31 (April 26, 1845).
[23] Harrison was also a painter and has left us an interesting portrait of Poe.

to learn that the first book publication of "The Raven" was in a text on elocution, written by George Vandenhoff. Poe, as Professor Mabbott — the discoverer of this fact — states, "was, by March, 1845, a well-known public figure in New York and was always friendly to actors. Vandenhoff, like his father, was an actor primarily." (108) How well acquainted Poe was with Vandenhoff we have no way of knowing; but we do know that Poe thought well of his acting talent, for in the *Broadway Journal* of April 12, 1845, Poe praised Vandenhoff's performance as Creon in the *Antigone*.[24]

That he was well acquainted with such a personality as John Brougham we know from the testimony of William Winter: "My old friend John Brougham, the comedian, who knew him [Poe] well." (109) Brougham, before coming to New York had been a prominent Irish playwright and actor and had played at Covent Garden with Mme Vestris. (110) We also know that Poe was equally well acquainted with the playwrights Samuel Woodworth and George Pope Morris. Woodworth was the author of popular successes such as *The Forest Rose*, "One of the longest-lived American plays before the Civil War." (111) Morris, besides being well-known as a journalist and the author of the celebrated "Woodman, Spare That Tree" — which Poe considered a composition "of which any poet, living or dead, might justly be proud" — had achieved fame as a playwright some years before Poe came to New York. (112) Poe's friendship with Nathaniel Parker Willis, Morris's journalistic partner, and himself a playwright of note, is too well known to need more than a mention.

[24] For what Poe thought of the other players in the cast, and of the production in general, see Chapter III.

Nor is more needed to be said here of Poe's relations with Cornelius Mathews, author of *The Politicians* and *Witchraft*. Mathews's testimony regarding Poe's theatre habits also happens to shed an interesting light on Poe's practices and theories of composition and consequently will be discussed in a later chapter.

Of the numerous ladies whom Poe met the record of those connected with the theatre is scanty. We know that he met and admired Mrs. Mowatt, both as a playwright and actress. His presence at the Park Theatre on the opening night of her comedy, *Fashion*, reads like a dramatic homecoming, for it was at the same Park Theatre that both his mother and father had often acted. (113) Several of the ladies with whom his relations were more than casual or merely social were playwrights as well as poets. Mrs. Osgood wrote *Elfrida*, in which the hero is strikingly suggestive of Poe. Mrs. Ellet wrote *Teresa Contarini*. And "Stella" (Mrs. S. D. Lewis) wrote *Sappho of Lesbos* which, when published in 1876, she dedicated to her "devoted friend Adelaide Ristori, the greatest living *tragédienne*." (114) [25]

This is not by any means the complete record of Poe's relations with the theatrical fraternity; it is sufficient, however, to warrant the conclusion that it was more than accident that threw him together with all kinds of

[25] " The play was put on the stage in London in 1868 and afterwards was given on the Athenian stage in a modern Greek version." — David M. Robinson, *Sappho and Her Influence*, Boston, 1924.

The lateness of both production and publication was fortunate for Poe: he did not have to review the play. He had, however — for a consideration — edited her earlier poems and written several reviews of them, (115) once going so far as to call her the " rival of Sappho." (116) It must be added — lest we assume that monetary considerations were the sole inspiration of such fulsome reviewing — that Poe had also once penned a sonnet to the lady which ingeniously spelled out her name — Sarah Anna Lewis. The poem was entitled " An Enigma."

theatre folk. He gravitated toward them naturally, and
they as naturally responded. The kinship was there to
begin with, and the atmosphere of the theatre brought
them together. Vachel Lindsay caught more of this
spirit of Poe than a hundred solemn, analytical critics:

> " This Jingle-man,[26] of strolling players born,
> Whom holy folk have hurried by in scorn,
>
> . . . .
>
> Of all the faces, his the only face
> Beautiful, tho' painted for the stage, . . ." (117)

8

Whether Poe's face was or was not " painted for the
stage," his voice was definitely pitched for elocution. We
have seen that all through his childhood and boyhood he
excelled in the arts of oratory and recitation. No small
part of his personal appeal must be credited to the impression he produced as a conversationalist, lecturer, and
reader. The impression was, of course, a result of his
whole personality — figure, dress, manner — but the share
contributed by his voice and delivery was extraordinarily
large.

It is dangerous, if not impossible, to abstract Poe's
voice from all the other elements that compounded his
appeal for those who heard him speak or lecture in
private or public. He " possessed," says Didier, " all the
qualifications that make a man shine in society. His
manners were graceful and refined, his voice was low,
musical, and exquisitely expressive, and there was about
him that air of unmistakable distinction, which ordinary
men cannot assume, and which few men ever have."

[26] The epithet is, of course an ironic repetition of Emerson's careless
jibe at Poe's expense.

(118) On the basis of the numerous reports left by ladies whose salons Poe graced with his magnetic presence, a more recent biographer evolves a picture of a romantic figure standing "by the mantlepiece talking and reciting poetry to a rapt circle. His buttoned frock-coat and black stock threw up the pallor of his face, his half-chanting voice, his restrained intensity was felt by all present, and whether it was Margaret Fuller . . . sitting on a sofa with Mrs. Oakes Smith, or Miss Lynch in the background, or Mrs. Osgood on a stool at his feet, all had their faces upturned to him like children listening to a ghost story." (119) The persistent mention of the quality of his voice, in all such reports and summaries, constitutes a powerful testimonial. It is like the chorus of references one reads in histories of the modern theatre to the voice of Max Reinhardt's star, Alexander Moissi, whose "gesanghafte Reiz der Stimme" seems to have been unforgettable. (120) The question as to whether Poe's voice alone, disembodied as it were, or unaccompanied by his other mesmeric graces, might have produced the effect described must remain unanswered.

That Poe knew how to use his voice — a "smooth baritone," low and deep (121) — to make its subtle qualities tell is amply clear. His powers as a conversationalist must have been considerable indeed, for one who most assuredly cannot be accused of having wished to pay tribute to Poe,[27] the notorious Rufus Wilmot Griswold himself, has added his enthusiastic impression: "His conversation was at times almost supra-mortal in its eloquence. His voice was modulated with astonishing

[27] Unless the very violence of Griswold's malice, rancor, and jealousy, with which his *Memoir* is permeated, are a form of tribute.

skill, and his large and variably expressive eyes looked repose or shot fiery tumult into theirs who listened, while his own face glowed, or was changeless in pallor, as his imagination quickened his blood or drew it back frozen to his heart." (122) Allowing for the Reverend's tendency toward metaphysical eloquence,[28] we still get an impression of a voice skilfully modulated and capable of profoundly affecting its hearers.

Griswold's tribute is glowing enough, but for a real understanding of the part played by Poe's vocal appeal in enhancing his popularity we must once again listen to the ladies. Mrs. Oakes Smith, at whose salon "no one received any more marked attention than Edgar A. Poe," candidly reported that "He did not affect the society of men" but "rather that of highly intellectual women with whom he liked to fall into a sort of eloquent monologue, half dream, half poetry. Men," she concluded, "were intolerant of all this, but women fell under his fascination and listened in silence." (124)

As a matter of fact, men too — as at least one of them, Bardwell Heywood, admitted — could hardly "listen to him one moment without being at once spellbound." But men were, generally, intolerant. When one evening during a discussion of vocal music at "Annie's" home, Poe, helping himself to ice cream, remarked in his usual categorical manner that males ought never to sing, and that females alone could make harmony, young Heywood had a strong inclination to throw a glass in his face. Men seemingly resented the poet's pontifical pronouncements and his rather unsubtle flattery of the gentler sex.

---

[28] Another example of Poe's power of metaphysical communication is recorded by Mrs. Gove: "so good a talker was Poe, that he impressed himself and his wishes, even without words, upon those with whom he spoke." (123)

5

And Poe's not affecting the society of men was very likely a result of his awareness that his social technique was far from effective with them, whereas it — monologue and all — made him irresistible to women. Mrs. Osgood, for one, confessed that she could listen to him for hours "entranced by strains of pure and almost celestial eloquence." (125)

The best-balanced record of the poet's conversational gifts — during the years when he was most fashionably in demand — was left by Mrs. Whitman, who, in spite of the ether atmosphere in which she floated, nevertheless possessed an underlying hard-headedness. After recalling the drawing-room exploits of such accomplished verbalists as Walter Savage Landor ("the best talker in England"), Oliver Wendell Holmes, John Neal, Margaret Fuller, Orestes Brownson, Bronson Alcott, and Emerson — to all of whom she had had occasion to listen — she comes to the conclusion that "Unlike the conversational power evinced by these was the earnest, opulent, unpremeditated speech of Edgar Poe." (126) Unpremeditated it may have been, but hardly without the speaker's consciousness of its effectiveness. The impulse to impress, to charm, seems to have been always with him. Even when he addressed only a few casual callers, mere boys, who one day in Richmond came to pay their respects to the famous author whose work was appearing regularly in their beloved *Southern Literary Messenger*, he seemed to them "to be talking . . . to a peopled atmosphere." (127)

An important attraction at the salons where he was "lionized" was his readings of his own poems, and not infrequently of the poems of Byron or some other romantic bard. Here his talent for declamation, which had served him so well ever since childhood, shone in its fullest glory. Had Poe actually been a professional actor, there can be no doubt as to the kind of actor he would have been. In spite of his known dislike of Edwin Forrest, (128) Poe too would have been a ranter, a flamboyant declaimer of sonorous lines. The acting style of the day favored the Forrests, and although Poe as a dramatic critic anticipated — as we shall see later — a quieter and more natural style, he was temperamentally close to the inflated stage of his time. His acting, however, would have had at least one difference from that of the established ranters: his modulated voice and his gentlemanly dignity would have sufficiently shaded the purple impulse to make the purple effect seem less starkly violent. Instead of Forrest's bull-like roar the audience would have heard tones that ranged from whispering softness to the musical cry of despair.

And this was essentially what happened in his performances as a reader. We have glowing tributes to "the beauty of his readings and recitals in parlor and hall" (129); they not only give us an impression of the effect but are detailed enough to help us understand his technique. There is always, of course, the necessity of sifting the facts from the generalities, of discounting the personal "raves," of extracting the bits of objective statement from the mass of vague poetic description and mystical emanations.

At the University of Virginia, we are told, his "little room on West Range was often filled with a . . . select audience of his most particular friends who, spell-bound, scarcely breathed while they eagerly listened to some story . . . that he had just written and that he read with his whole soul thrown into every action and in-

tonation of his voice — now loud and rapid, like the mad
rush of many waters, and now sinking into a scarcely
audible whisper. . . ." (130) At this time his technique may have been unconscious, merely the intuitive
changes of expression to accommodate the nuances of
the narrative. And it may have been instinctive when
later in Baltimore he repeated the famous speech of
Cassius, for the benefit of a young girl, Mary Poitaux,
who in her old age still remembered "how his flashing
eyes and mobile mouth expressed the various passions
of scorn, contempt and anger." (131) And it surely was
instinctive when in the office of Mr. Latrobe, one of the
judges that awarded to him the short story prize offered
by the *Saturday Visiter*, he told the projected story of
"Hans Pfaall." Mr. Latrobe's recollection of the incident is vivid enough. Poe described for him the imaginary voyage to the moon and in the course of his recital
became "so excited, spoke so rapidly, gesticulating
much" that his listener was "carried along" as "a companion of his aërial journey." After that Mr. Poe the
gentleman, having regained his self-control, apologized
for Poe the actor, for the latter's excitability, "which he
laughed at himself." (132)

But there was nothing unconscious or merely instinctive about his technique at public recitals in his socially
popular years. "The Raven" was the piece most generally in demand, and his manner of setting the stage for
its reading indicates that the effect he wished to create
was definitely preconceived. "He would," recalls one
lady, "turn down the lamps till the room was almost
dark,[29] then standing in the centre of the apartment he

---

[29] If the reading took place during the day, he would "shut out the
daylight and read by an astral lamp."

would recite those wonderful lines in the most melodious of voices; gradually becoming more and more
enthused . . . he forgot time, spectators, his personal
identity. . . . To the listeners came the sounds of falling
rain and waving branches; the Raven flapped his dusky
wings above the bust of Pallas, and the lovely face of
Lenore appeared to rise before them. So marvelous was
his power as a reader that the auditors would be afraid
to draw breath lest the enchanted spell be broken." (133)
It was by means of such theatrical expedients that he
made people feel that to hear him repeat "The Raven"
was "an event in one's life." (134)

A more moderate estimate of Poe's power as a reader
is that of Howard Paul, whose uncle, T. C. Clarke,
employed Poe on the staff of *The Saturday Museum,* in
Philadelphia: "His voice, though not especially melodious, possessed a peculiar charm, guided as it was by a
dramatic instinct, and, of course, by rare intelligence.
In his recital of 'The Raven' there were weird, fantastic
touches that remind me of some of Henry Irving's tones
in his rendition of the part of *Mephistopheles.* It is not
every author that can give dramatic effect to his own
creations." (135) Mr. Paul's tribute to the dramatic
instinct which guided Poe's voice may actually have
been a tribute to a conscious art which was never entirely
free from artifice. It is nonetheless clear that Poe was a
master of "weird, fantastic touches" — vocally as well as
in writing.

Those were the days of the lyceum, and Poe began
to capitalize on his declamation talents by giving public
lectures. His first lecture — on "The Poets and Poetry
of America" — was given in Philadelphia, at the William Wirt Institute, in 1843. (136) The same lecture

—with some changes and additions—was repeated a
year and a half later in New York. The impression he
produced upon the several hundred listeners can be
gauged from Willis's reactions printed in the *Weekly
Mirror*: "He becomes a desk—his beautiful head showing like a statuary embodiment of Discrimination; his
accent drops like a knife through water, and his style is
so much purer and clearer than the pulpit commonly
gets or requires, that the effect of what he says pampers
the ear." (137)

One such lecture—and reading—was given in Boston. It was the famous, or notorious, one which incensed
some of the "frogpondians" because Poe had not
bothered to write a new poem for the occasion but had
chosen to palm off his youthful "Al Aaraaf" instead.
Responding to the vociferously shouted demand of the
disappointed audience he also read "The Raven." His
"melancholy performance" that night was supercili-
ously attacked by the editor of the *Transcript*,[30] but perhaps Thomas Wentworth Higginson's description, being
at once the reactions of an intelligent boy and the
recollection of a mature man of letters, is more illuminating: Poe's voice, in reading "Al Aaraaf," had at one
point become softened until it "seemed attenuated to
the finest golden thread . . . every syllable was accen-
tuated with . . . delicacy and sustained with . . .
sweetness." Walking back to Cambridge from that lecture, young Higginson and his comrades felt that they
had been "under the spell of some wizard." (139)

[30] Poe was not one to accept in silence any public criticism. The
editor of the *Transcript* at the time was a lady, Cornelia Wells Walter.
Hence the "melancholy" performer chose to retort by calling her a
"pretty little witch." To which rather gentlemanly appellation she
replied by calling him "a wandering specimen of the Literary Snob,
continually obtruding himself upon public notice. . . ." (138)

That the wizard was a disciplined performer, an actor who knew his "lines" and "business," and was not above indulging in subtle "asides" for personal advantage, is shown by an incident during his lecture in Providence. That evening he drew a large audience. He read "The Raven" and other selections and then, as a closing number, began to recite Pinckney's "A Health." Mrs. Whitman — whom Poe was just then trying to induce to marry him — was seated directly in front of him. As he read the lines beginning "I fill this cup, to one made up of loveliness alone" he looked down into the eyes of the lady, and, says the narrator of the incident, Dr. Harry L. Koopman, "You can imagine the emphasis he gave, and how dramatic it was." (140)

Another incident is still more indicative of the skilled actor's presence of mind which enables him to take advantage of the moment and to improvise dramatic climaxes as opportunity presents itself. Mrs. Weiss recalls that one evening as Poe was reading "The Raven" at the Archer home in Richmond, the colored servants had stationed themselves outside the window and were listening. "As the speaker," Mrs. Weiss narrates,

became more impassioned and excited, more conspicuous grew the circle of white eyes, until when at length he turned suddenly toward the window, and, extending his arm, cried, with awful vehemence: "Get thee back into the tempest, and the night's Plutonian shore!" there was a sudden disappearance of the sable visages, a scuttling of feet, and the gallery audience was gone. (141)

Some dissenting impressions of Poe's skill as a reader must be noted. They are by men and refer to a lecture given at the Exchange Hotel in Richmond, in the last

year of his life. Bishop O. P. Fitzgerald found in Poe's
reading an absence of elocution. "There was not a trace
of any such thing in his delivery. Not a gesture was
made by him from first to last. His voice was without
any conscious inflections in the usual sense of the word."
(142) Similarly Professor B. L. Gildersleeve retained
the impression that Poe "did not read very well. His
voice was pleasant enough, but he emphasized the
rhythm unduly. . . ." (143) Both of these dissenting
voices are supported by the editor of the Richmond
Examiner who reported the event as a disappointment,
because "Mr. Poe . . . did not make his own 'Raven'
an effective piece of reading." (144)

The explanation of Poe's failure on this particular
occasion might lie, of course, in the simple fact that
performers are not always at their best. This might have
been an "off" night for the histrio; it might have been
one of those nights when a performer is uninspired,
"dry," even bored, and consequently not "giving." Mrs.
Weiss's detailed description of the reading of "The
Raven" at the home of her parents certainly supports
this probability. She notes that in the course of his
reading "the speaker became more impassioned and
excited," until "he turned suddenly toward the window,
and, extending his arm, cried with awful vehemence:
. . . " That time he was fully aware of his audience
and his performance; he was "giving" — in his customary and, for him, normal way.

Another explanation of his unimpressive performance,
as reported by the two gentlemen, suggests itself. The
lecture was given in the music hall of the fashionable
Exchange Hotel. Poe stepped upon the platform to con-
front an audience of *thirteen* persons, including the

janitor. Few performers can be at their best under such circumstances and Poe was certainly not one of them. (145)

But there is still another, and more fundamental, explanation. Professor Gildersleeve's touch about Poe's undue emphasis of the rhythm supplies the cue. And the testimony of another gentleman, the novelist John Estèn Cooke, who along with Gildersleeve was present on that auspicious occasion at the fashionable hotel, makes this second explanation even more plausible. Cooke, like Gildersleeve, found Poe's "sing-song" objectionable, although, unlike Gildersleeve, he was thrilled by the "wonderfully clear and musical voice." (146) When we recall that Poe's very definition of poetry was "the rhythmical creation of beauty," we are not at all surprised by his habit of stressing metrical values. When we recall further that in his first review of *Fashion* he chastised the actor who read the prologue for not stressing the meter of the lines, we know that his own practice in reading verse agreed with his theory. "It is pure irrationality," he exclaimed on that occasion, "to recite verse, as if it were prose, without distinguishing the lines." (147)

To most people of that elocutionary era this "rational" way of distinguishing the lines was natural and attractive. One lady, for instance, a Mrs. Trumbull who heard him lecture at Lowell, found that his illustrations were "rendered with pure intonation and perfect enunciation, marked attention being paid to the rhythm. He almost *sang* the more musical versifications." In his reading of Byron's "Bride of Abydos" that evening he measured "the dactyllic movement perfectly as if he were scanning it." To her the effect seemed "very pleasing." (148) If Poe read the same way at Richmond, which is more than likely, the two young men, Gildersleeve and Cooke, did not find the effect pleasing, for they apparently belonged to the dissenting few to whom public scanning, or almost singing, of verse did not seem an attractive way of conveying poetic values.

9

In the light of these characteristics and abilities of the man, the circumstances of his life, and the nature of the reaction of the "world" upon which he played, the "mystery" of Poe becomes considerably less mystifying. In one way, the time and the man met. The age of Romanticism supplied an appropriate setting for his histrionic personality and his particular form of art. The description of the German romantic actor of the period which appears in Karl Mantzius's *History of Theatrical Art* is, in most respects, as vivid a sketch of Edgar Allan Poe as if the Danish historian had had the American literary histrio "sitting" for him: "A strange being, with long, wild hair, black if possible, framing a pale, emaciated face; deep, melancholy eyes under dark, contracted brows, and a bitter, sorrowful smile on his quivering lips; his form . . . moving among his fellow men now with ostentatious, gloomy remoteness, now with hollow, rather scornful mirth." (149) This is Roderick Usher, and the numerous "I's" of Poe's other stories; it is, except for the wild hair, Poe himself.

But in another way, the time for Romanticism is never completely at an end. The appeal of a Poe has always been that of an unfortunate, lonely, remote, misprized genius. "In those days," Mantzius goes on to say, speaking of the heyday of Romanticism, "there was a universal passion for 'genius,' and 'genius' was scarcely thinkable without its external attributes of mystery, suffering, and contempt for the world." Those days have more or less persisted, and so has the interest in Poe. Certain realists of today may demur; they may find little in Poe that has survived from an age of rant and pose and ecstatic gloom. When several years ago Dumas Malone placed Poe fifth on a list of the most important literary figures America has produced, the *Saturday Review of Literature* objected editorially. "Poe," it commented, "is important chiefly as a vested interest of professional scholars . . . hardly anyone would put him on such a list, hardly anyone would call him, except as a historical figure, a first-rater." (150) The "hardly anyone" is easily debatable. That he is far from being merely a historical figure the preceding pages, I hope, have helped to prove. And if it is true, as the editorial statement admits, that Poe "has been more widely and more exhaustively studied than any other American writer" it has not been so much because he is a vested interest of the scholar as because he is still a living American writer whose power and influence have grown rather than diminished with the passing of time.

To be sure, Poe *is* a historical figure. More than any other literary artist he represents the expression of our abiding attraction to the misty mid-region of Weir. Like O'Neill's Dion Anthony, in *The Great God Brown*, Poe was born with ghosts in his eyes and he was brave enough to go looking into his own dark. Possibly many of us sense this bravery in Poe, although we may call it weakness. Possibly many of us — strong in puritanism and common sense and balance as we are — also sense our kinship with his other "weaknesses" and applaud his ability to have enjoyed them, as a man and an artist. Walt Whitman, no mean actor himself, felt an "indescribable magnetism about the poet's life and reminiscences as well as the poems." (151) That life and those reminiscences, as well as the poems and the magnetism, still exist; and not only for professional scholars but for the world at large. Poe continues to exist by virtue of the power he holds over us, a power which is not unlike that which Shaw's Candida felt in the boy-poet Marchbanks when she sent him away into the night.

It is true that Poe "appealed to sentimental women by his figure, his history and his actions, and to kind-hearted women by his suffering" (152) and that, as Arthur Hopkins once remarked, he has had more posthumous sweethearts than any other American writer.[31] But it is also true that Poe "has furnished mysteries enough for two generations of essayists and biographers, not to list romancers." (153) Three generations is now more exact—and many of the essayists and biographers have been men of sound intellectual astuteness.

It is, as a matter of fact, the work of these men—and of a few women, too—with its painstaking scholarship animated by eagerness to understand and clarify— that has made it possible for Poe to emerge finally neither as a demon nor as a saint, but as a comprehensible human being who happened to be, within his limited field, a great artist. The key to his humanity as well as artistry seems to have been his talent for acting.

Mrs. Weiss noted that in "all Poe's accounts of himself, and especially of his feelings, is a palpable affecta-

[31] The remark was made at a party in Baltimore after the opening of Sophie Treadwell's play, *Plumes in the Dust*. The play failed, like all the plays thus far written on the life of Poe.

tion and exaggeration, with an extravagance of expression bordering on the tragic and melo-dramatic: a style which is exemplified in some of his writings, and may be equally imaginative in both cases." (154) The applicability of his style to both his emotional life and his artistic creation is not a coincidence. The actor in dress and manner, in love and despair, in school, editorial office, and drawing-room, was also the writer creating parts for the declaimer and handsome, mysterious sufferer. Bishop Fitzgerald remembered him as "distingué in a peculiar sense — a man bearing the stamp of genius and the charm of a melancholy that drew one toward him with a strange sympathy." (155) And that was precisely the rôle Poe had selected for himself. That he was supremely successful in this chosen rôle is evidenced by the almost universal impression he produced, an impression carefully intended and achieved.

The autobiographic nature of much of Poe's writing needs no elaborate proof at this time. His "heroes" are so often portraits of himself that one is justified in comparing the original with them. Roderick Usher, it has already been mentioned, strikingly resembles Poe; William Wilson is undeniably Poe — or as much of him as Stevenson's Mr. Hyde is of Dr. Jekyll or O'Neill's "Loving" is of John Loving (in *Days Without End*). Harrison noted long ago that in "Eleonora" Poe drew "his own silhouette out of the cloudland of memory and self-analysis." It is the silhouette of a dreamer, poet, madman; an "ardent lover, the remnant of an ancient race, feverishly enamored of the Beautiful," a "solitary deluged with poetic visions. . . ." (156) Much of all this he undoubtedly was; much of it he believed that he was; all of it he wished others to believe that he was.

A good deal of his sadness was genuine. He was, in Longfellow's phrase, "a sensitive nature chafed by some indefinite sense of wrong." (157) What was mainly wrong was that he was a strolling player with no theatre, an actor with no bookings, or very few. In spite of various attempts in modern scholarship to show that he was not entirely aloof from the social, political and cultural ideas of his time, he wrote singularly little about the broad problems that agitated either his country or his world. Here and there he expressed an idea on slavery, on democracy, on government, or on a more restricted topic, such as the need of an international copyright law. But it would be easy to show that his ideas were the conventional views of the intrenched Southern aristocracy, to which he was a poor relation — although he would not acknowledge it. (158) He felt that as an Allan and a Poe and an Arnold[32] he belonged to a superior class that was entitled to make the rules of government; all others belonged to the "rabble," whose power in our democracy he resented.

For the most part, however, he refused to be interested in problems that, according to his aesthetic creed, did not concern the artist. Had he allowed himself to be tainted by the "curse" of didacticism his range might have been wider and his life less self-centered. Professor Parrington's conclusion that "Aside from his art he had no philosophy and no programs and no causes" (159) is, in the main, justified, if we add the word "social" before "philosophy." Poe's art was intensely personal, centripetal; his intellect played upon a cosmos whose core was Edgar Allan Poe. Mallarmé's belief that Poe

---

[32] He liked to believe that his grandfather Poe had really been a "General." His mother's maiden name was Arnold and he liked to pretend that he was related to General Benedict Arnold.

was killed by a soulless, unimaginative public, the "rabble," is but a blind worshipper's belief. For the truth is that no one killed Poe. He functioned well enough as the human being and writer that he was by heredity, environmental conditioning, education, and the general circumstances of his life. Norms of success differ, but since Poe himself attached so much importance to fame — and yearned passionately for it[33] — is it possible not to conclude that his brief hour upon the stage was reasonably successful? Even Parrington, whose general attitude toward Poe is not overly friendly, is obliged to record that "as an aesthete and a craftsman he made a stir in the world that has not lessened in the years since his death, but has steadily widened." (161) And it was as an aesthete and craftsman that Poe wished to be known, although, like many another person, he also thought himself a monstrously clever fellow in other respects: as a philosopher, for instance; and as a mathematician, and as a generally erudite gentleman.

But the weakness of exhibiting versatility and cleverness, universal as it is, assumes an intense coloring in the actor, and becomes a strength. Poe *was* good at mathematical deductions; his show of erudition *did* impress people; and even his philosophical speculations, such as those so loudly proclaimed in *Eureka*, combined as they were with a strain of poetry, added to his attractiveness. If his acting enveloped him in a sort of solitude, as though he were always on the other side of the footlights, behind a proscenium, he nevertheless enjoyed being on display, and he enjoyed the very aura

[33] " I love fame. . . . I would drink to the very dregs the glorious intoxication. . . . Fame! glory! — they are life-giving breath and . . . blood. No man lives unless he is famous." — Poe to Mrs. Mary Gove. (160)

of aloofness. To be sure, psychologically, there may have been another reason for his intrenching himself behind a proscenium. One who does not feel too secure in the midst of a confident self-assured society finds in isolation, in distance, a measure of protection. The principal reason, however, remains: he enjoyed both his isolation and the elevated platform.

Very likely he was often lonely up there on the boards of the world. Behind the actor's mask was the face of a hurt little boy who craved understanding and sympathy and warmth. He found all three in his dear "Muddie," the simple, uncritical Mrs. Clemm, and in "Sissie," his girl wife. Now and then he also found it in one or another of the numerous sentimental ladies who were attracted to him. Mostly, however, women loved him — as Margaret Fuller, writing to Mrs. Browning, remarked — more "with passionate illusion which he amused himself by inducing than with sympathy." (162) This is acute, except that "amused himself" is much too light a phrase for Poe's need to be loved.

That he has greatly "amused" us, for over a century, is the one important fact. A critic of the type of W. C. Brownell may have been temperamentally incapable of doing full justice to a writer like Poe, but he was right in attributing the growth of Poe's legend to "largely romantic" reasons. (163) Some of these reasons have been within us rather than the poet, but the center of all of them has nevertheless been a romantic personality endowed with indubitable gifts and able, like all good actors, to exhibit them arrestingly. This offspring of stage performers was richly equipped to continue their tradition. He was denied the opportunity of following their profession, but he could not help practicing their art.[34] Handsome in face, figure, and bearing, the possessor of a melodious voice and a volatile, sensitive temperament, he also received an education and training which enhanced and refined his natural gifts. He was early taught dancing, drawing, recitation, oratory, and music,[35] everyone of which arts he practiced for his own amusement and that of his friends and public. Besides being of use to him in the drawing-room, they also, especially drawing, music, and oratory, profoundly affected his writing.

And that writing was for him as much a form of acting as his public "lectures" or his public challenge to decipher any or all cryptograms. It was also, like all creative art, a form of rich living. Something happened to Edgar Poe when he knew that eyes were upon him, something akin to what happened to Henry James's nobleman who functioned creatively only in public. Poe, to be sure, also had a "private life," but even at his writing table the consciousness of an audience is ever present, and influences the rhythms and patterns, the very idiom and intonation of his work. For, essentially, the one great quality Poe brought to his life and art is the peculiar histrionic ambivalence to feel vicarious experience as though it were his own and to feel his own experience as though it were vicarious. That sense of "dream within a dream" is not mysticism but part of

[34] It may be interesting to add that Poe's brother, William Henry Leonard, also "recited in private and was proud of his oratorical powers." (164)

[35] For a study of the "Ciceronian and forensic" Southern tradition to which Poe belonged by breeding and education, see Herbert Marshall McLuhan, "Edgar Poe's Tradition," *Sewanee Review*, January-March, 1944. For Poe's musical accomplishments, both as a performer (on the flute) and as inspirer of composers, some as notable as Debussy and Rachmaninoff, see May Garretson Evans, *Music and Edgar Allan Poe*, Baltimore, 1939.

6

the actor's aloofness from the rôle which fascinates him, an aloofness which enables him to recreate that fascination for the benefit of others.

A lady poet like Mrs. Whitman remembered Poe's

> " Unfathomable eyes that held the sorrow
> Of vanished ages in their shadowy deeps," (165)

but a leading representative of the acting profession understood him more profoundly. On May 4, 1885, a monument to Poe was unveiled at the Metropolitan Museum of Fine Arts in New York. It was Richard Henry Park's "Angel of Sorrow." Among the speakers at the ceremony was Edwin Booth, great romantic actor himself, and son of Junius Brutus Booth, who had once been Poe's boon companion. "The stage," said Edwin Booth in tribute to Poe, "will always live in him as one of her children. The gypsy blood that runs in her veins ran also in his veins, and in the exuberance of his imagination she sees the power and the freedom of her own wild spirit." (166) Booth's prophecy has been fulfilled: the stage still lives in its strange poet-offspring. For, in the final analysis, it is the histrionic quality of Poe's exuberance of imagination which explains his contemporaries and posterity alike.

Chapter II

THE PROOF OF DRAMATISM

"A closet drama is an anomaly — a paradox — a
mere figure of speech . . . The proof of the
dramatism is the capacity of representation."

WHEN a shrewd judge of literary talent advises
a young writer to turn his hand to the writing
of farces for the stage, the compliment implied in his
advice cannot be lightly dismissed. Surely John Pendleton Kennedy must have had good reason for assuming
that Poe might be successful in producing farces, "after
the manner of the French Vaudevilles," good enough to
sell to New York theatrical producers.[1] It may be that
Kennedy, having received from Poe a pitiful letter,
written in a mood when he was obsessed by "villainous
blue devils," merely wished to console him and to direct
his mind toward a cheerful form of creative activity.
Yet the fact remains that Kennedy believed Poe capable
of writing successful theatrical pieces. (1)

On an earlier occasion Kennedy had dissuaded Poe
from concentrating on the writing of a tragedy — presumably *Politian* — and turned him to drudging upon
whatever might make money. (2) And while at the

---

[1] Early in our own century, a more discerning student of Poe
hazarded a similar guess but with one important difference. "Poe
could have done perfectly," wrote Padraic Colum, "a form of work
which perhaps he had no models for at the time — the 'thrill' of the
French vaudeville." — Introduction to the Everyman's Library edition
of *Edgar Allan Poe's Tales of Mystery and Imagination.*

time Kennedy suggested attempting some farces Poe was financially in a more flourishing state, it is reasonable to assume that Kennedy did not entirely ignore the material benefits his young friend might derive from such an undertaking. The fact that Poe evidently did not follow Kennedy's advice — for no farces attributed to his authorship have thus far been discovered — does not minimize its importance. Is it possible that Kennedy judged Poe's ability on the basis of previous work which has been lost to us? Perhaps he had read early attempts at playwriting, possibly some of the "skits" with which Poe is said to have amused his fellow-cadets at West Point. They are said to have been clever satires of certain professors at the Academy. (3) We are not, of course, in a position to estimate their stage-worthiness; nor do we know that they were in dramatic form.

We can, however, venture a judgment as to Poe's flair for playwriting in general, based upon those of his writings which are available to us, and upon our knowledge of the man himself. On this basis one is tempted to say, almost with certainty, that creating drama for the theatre was not among the many talents with which Poe was gifted. Actors usually make but indifferent playwrights, and Poe, as we have seen, was essentially an actor. Now and then dramatic history provides an exception: Molière, for instance, to take a classical example; or Noel Coward, to come to our own day. Shakespeare and David Garrick seem to indicate the more normal record: a minor actor may become a great playwright; a great actor may become a minor playwright. This is explainable by the fact that the true talent of the actor lies in his ability to animate a character which is but half alive in the script. His technique calls for enlargement, amplification, and direct appeal. Contrary to popular belief, the actor never quite loses himself in his rôle; the greater he is the more he projects himself along with the character he represents. The playwright, on the other hand, employing a strictly objective medium, exists only as a living breath behind the work he has handed over to the producer; the greater he is the less he permits himself to be visible. In comparison with the actor he is usually a shrinking violet.

That Poe was no shrinking violet hardly needs to be stressed. He was first and foremost a Romantic poet, and few, if any, of the Romantic poets of his age were either reticent or self-effacing. Poe least of all was the type who could forget himself long enough to construct a play about characters who might take the center of the stage in their own right, thinking their own thoughts, speaking their own language, and feeling their own emotions. On the contrary, he was the kind of creator who insisted on being visible. He left no writing, with the exception of some pieces of literary and dramatic criticism, which is even approximately objective. Certainly he left no such play, not even a tragedy.

For it would have been logical for a poet with a gift for tragic eloquence to aspire to the mantle of his greatly admired forerunner, the lofty creator of *Cain* and *Manfred*. That is why the judgment of a seasoned playwright like Robert Montgomery Bird, who — according to contemporary testimony — was willing to collaborate with Poe in the writing of a tragedy, deserves more than a passing mention. Dr. Bird was a Philadelphia writer whose plays, notably *Pelopidas* and *The Gladiator*, were highly successful. (4) That such a man should honor Poe with either a bid or the willingness for collaboration indicates faith in Poe's potentialities as a writer of tragedy. The young editor of *Burton's* or *Graham's* — for we do not know just when the project was conceived — was, of course, clearly marked for tragedy. He carried the tragic air about him wherever he went; it was in his pale face, in the haughty carriage of his head, in his very gait. And as for eloquence, surely one could expect that to gush forth from a man whose very utterance was a carefully-modulated declamation. It is unfortunate that the scenario which Poe is reported to have sketched out for the collaboration has been lost. (5) The "scheme" itself, we are told, "never got beyond outlines and much talk." (6) Nevertheless the scenario might have added to our information upon which to test the opinion of Monsieur Hughes — the first man to translate part of *Politian* into French — that Poe "could have supplied the lack of an important American dramatist, had he turned his attention more to that field." (7)

2

As it is we have *Politian* as Poe's sole contribution to the American drama. And we have several pieces — essay, story, skit — in dialogue form. Of these pieces three are complete "dialogues." They are interesting as poetic prose, as philosophy, as mysticism, but they are hardly significant as drama. The best of them, "The Conversation of Eiros and Charmion," makes good reading only in the last pages when the dialogue has ceased and Eiros alone holds forth. The first part, the "conversation," is brief and serves merely to introduce Eiros's monologue — or Poe's essay — on the destruction of the world. The one strong moment is the vivid word-picture of the last minutes of expiring mankind. This is effective but hardly dramatic.

"Eiros and Charmion" is prefaced by a quotation from Euripides; "The Colloquy of Monos and Una" by one from Sophocles. Both pieces are reminiscent of Plato's dialogues, but are far from Platonic in mood. Instead of the Greek calm we have, especially in "Eiros," overcharged description and erudite speculation verging on melodramatic pedantry. The "Colloquy," like "Eiros," begins as a dialogue but soon turns into a monologue in which Monos tells the story of his own death and his sensations in the after-life. Professor Quinn calls this piece — "which is not meat for babes" — a short story, but it would hardly meet Poe's own requirements, as stated in his famous review of Hawthorne's *Twice-Told Tales*, of what a good short story should be. It may, like *Eureka*, have depths of thought and imagination, emotion-colored ideas about life and death and immortality and even, as Quinn suggests, about Jacksonian democracy, (8) but — unless one is specially interested in Poe's ideas on these subjects — it is, alas, not a little dull.

The dialogue on "The Power of Words" is the only one that does not degenerate into a monologue. It continues as a conversation to the very end. The two speakers, Oinos and Agathos, discuss God, creation, and the soul's thirst for knowledge. The setting is again "Aidenn" or the realm of disembodied spirits, but the contours of Aidenn are nowhere disclosed, not even in the vaguest of outline. The sense of place so essential for any dramatic presentation is completely lacking. The conversation is quiet and intellectual, with overtones of poetic prose. Of action in the dramatic sense there is no hint.

What is striking about all three of these pieces is that Poe's use of dialogue is only a device for the expression of ideas, of certain pet theories. It suggests the classroom or lecture platform rather than the stage. Even Plato's discussions have more naturalness, and the typical medieval colloquy has greater casualness and simplicity. The speakers — for they can hardly be called "characters" — are not differentiated; not one is individualized by manner, diction, or specific — if not idiosyncratic — idea. The only theatricality these dialogues possess is in the shadowy figure of Poe himself behind the principal expounders, Eiros, Monos, and Agathos; it is he rather than they who does all the talking, exhibiting his abstruseness, ingenuity, philosophical comprehension, wide reading, and magnificent self-confidence.

Two other bits of dialogue deserve consideration. They are parts of the short stories "Mesmeric Revelation" and "Three Sundays in a Week." Here Poe gives some indication of talent for the writing of stage dialogue. He manages to convey a sense of both place or scene and progression. His stage directions, in brackets, add gesture and tonal shadings. And although the speeches, especially in "Mesmeric Revelation," tend to grow long they show some attempt at restriction to character and situation.

"Mesmeric Revelation" purports to be an account of an experiment. The narrator, Poe himself, hypnotizes a certain Mr. Vankirk and proceeds to interrogate him on the nature of God, matter, motion, etc. Mr. Vankirk's responses are profoundly oracular; they do magnificent justice to the ideas held, and expressed elsewhere many times, by Mr. Poe. The questions and answers are recorded as a dialogue between "P." and "V." They begin succinctly enough:

P. Are you asleep?

V. Yes — no; I would rather sleep more soundly.

P. [After a few more passes.] Do you sleep now?

V. Yes.

P. How do you think your present illness will result?

V. [After a long hesitation and speaking as if with effort.]
      I must die.

P. Does the idea of death afflict you?

V. [Very quickly.] No — no!

Thus they continue, almost as in a modern psycho-
analysis, as recorded by some of our contemporary
pseudo-Freudian playwrights, until the examiner raises
the question of "What, then, is God?" and the patient becomes verbose and sententious. From then on
Mr. Vankirk has exchanged places with the brilliant
author, who delivers himself of a learned monologue—
except for a few distracting interruptions intended to
maintain the fiction of the dialogue form—in a deeply
solemn manner which, if spoken on the stage, might
be appropriate for a dead-pan cartoon of a certain kind
of pedant. One sample will, I believe, suffice:

The matters of which man is cognizant escape the senses in
gradation. We have, for example, a metal, a piece of wood, a
drop of water, the atmosphere, a gas, caloric, electricity, the
luminiferous ether. Now, we call all these things matter, and
embrace all matter in one general definition; but in spite of
this, there can be no two ideas more essentially distinct than
that which we attach to a metal, and that which we attach to
the luminiferous ether. When we reach the latter, we feel an
almost irresistible inclination to class it with spirit, or with
nihility. . . .

"Three Sundays in a Week" is a whimsical story
about an old gentleman who promises two young lovers
that they will have his consent to their marriage when

three Sundays come together in a week. In the conversation (in play form) with which Poe ends the story such an occurrence is contrived and the promise is kept. Herschel's *Treatise on Astronomy* (9) and an article on circumnavigation which appeared in a Philadelphia paper (10) provided Poe with his dénouement. The story is not particularly noteworthy; it is one of Poe's attempts at humor which, somehow, nearly always miss fire, like those of an essentially serious person unbending to tell an anecdote and feeling ill at ease. What is noteworthy is the management of the dialogue, among five characters, each distinguished by characteristic diction and general tone. Their speech is economical and relevant to the plot; moreover, it is lively and, for Poe, ordinary enough to sound realistic. The stage directions — *Jumping up eagerly; After a pause*, etc. — indicate that the writer saw his characters in a definite place, behaving in a definite way, and saying the things that under the circumstances they might or would say.

Altogether, however, Poe's dialogue is far from impressive. His tendency to "talk" is too dominant for the necessary give and take of stage conversation. His lack of objectivity results in monotony of phrase and idea; on the rare occasions when he tries to report objective dialogue — as in his use of Negro dialect ("The Gold Bug"), Irish ("Why the Little Frenchman Wears His Hand in a Sling"), and German ("The Angel of the Odd"), — his ear fails him. No doubt he had sufficient ability, and knowledge and love of theatre, to learn the art of writing good dialogue, but the discipline of subordinating himself and his own type of mentally-passionate eloquence to the seemingly independent projections on the stage was not his.

3

Yet, there is *Politian*, Poe's one serious attempt at drama. Whether he intended it for the stage is not definitely known. Quinn believes that Poe thought of it simply as a poem, (11) because nowhere in his letters does he express a desire to have the play produced. Yet the revisions, including a rearrangement of scenes, indicate at least an unexpressed hope that the manuscript might some day receive a stage production. There is also Poe's view that "a 'dramatic poem' is . . . a flat contradiction in terms . . . a man of true genius [and Poe never denied that he was such a man] . . . has no business with these hybrid and paradoxical compositions. Let a poem be a poem only; let a play be a play and nothing more." (12) However, during the poet's lifetime only several scenes of *Politian* were published; other scenes appeared later; and the whole of what now constitutes the almost completed play, carefully edited by Professor T. O. Mabbott, was printed in 1923. Ten years later, and almost a hundred years after its writing, the play was produced by the Players of the University of Virginia, first in Richmond and a month later in Baltimore.

The effect of this romantic tragedy in the modern theatre can be fairly judged by the review it received in the Baltimore *Sun*. Dramatic critics are not, of course, infallible, yet Donald Kirkley's reactions deserve recording in more permanent form than the files of a daily newspaper. This is what Mr. Kirkley wrote in his column on February 19, 1933:

"Politian," produced last night at Catherine Hooper Hall, Goucher College, for the first time in the city in which it was written one hundred years ago, showed what a bad playwright Edgar Allan Poe was, and what a good company of actors exists at the University of Virginia.

The Virginia Players revealed a mastery of all the branches of stagecraft which certainly would have brought out whatever hidden treasures might have lurked in this minor work of a major American poet.

The effort was a commendable one, fulfilling the highest function of that valuable branch of the theatre which is amateur in the best sense of that much-abused word.

" Politian " turned out to be a poorly constructed and inadequate play, judged even by the standards of Poe's own time. By the standards of today it is no more than a quaint example of the florid romanticism and artificial heroics of a period in American literature which, happily, has vanished. Such phrases as " the grave untimely yawning for a ruined maid " and *Politian's* request that Castiglione " arise and die " have become faintly ridiculous. " I cannot pawn my honor," says Castiglione. " Wed a wanton? Never — no, never! "

These inflated phrases might be overlooked, but there are other faults, such as skimpy characterization, feeble attempts at humor and the failure of the plot to get well under way until many scenes have unfolded. Also one looks in vain for occasional lines of living poetry, until the final scene.

It is well that Poe's reputation does not depend on the quality of the poetry in the first ten episodes. Only in the Coliseum soliloquy, which deserves to be better known, does his genius manifest itself.

The fact that the critic liked the production adds weight to his impressions of the play. At least in this case the playwright could have had no comeback in the usual way on the grounds that his work was mutilated in production. We shall see later that Poe as a critic of drama in time came to hold views of plot construction, dialogue, and characterization not unlike those of Mr. Kirkley. Undoubtedly his ideas of what constituted a good play had developed largely *after* his youthful attempt at playwriting, yet he republished several scenes of his play in his own magazine in 1845, (13) after he had delivered himself of such opinions as that "A closet-drama is an anomaly — a paradox . . ." and that "There should be no such things as closet-dramas." (14) At any rate, it is very likely that had *Politian* been produced in 1845 Mr. Poe of the *Broadway Journal* might have condemned it even with greater gusto than Mr. Kirkley — provided, of course, that the author of the play was not Mr. Poe. Playwrights are not, however, critics, any more than critics are playwrights. Mr. Poe the critic advocated realism on the stage and excoriated American writers of drama for using the wrong models, yet his own play is definitely indebted to the Byron school of Romantic tragedy. *Politian* is no more realistic than a play by Sheridan Knowles whom Poe denounced with unbridled severity.[2]

And yet Poe based his tragedy on one which had actually taken place in real life. He found the story in newspaper and other accounts of the murder of Solomon P. Sharp, a prominent Kentucky lawyer and political figure, by Jereboam Beauchamp, another Kentucky lawyer. Sharp had seduced Anne Cooke, who a few years later married Beauchamp on condition that he revenge her dishonor. On November 7, 1825, Beauchamp fulfilled the condition by killing Sharp, and, together with his wife, was convicted for murder. (16) The couple then attempted suicide, but only the wife was successful. Beauchamp lived on until July 7, 1826,

[2] " . . . this . . . dramatic feeling he has manifested in the most preposterous series of imitations of the Elizabethan drama, by which ever mankind were insulted and begulled. Not only did he adhere to the old plots, the old characters, the old stage conventionalities throughout; but, he went even so far as to persist in the obsolete phraseologies of the Elizabethan period . . ." (15)

when he was executed. The case received wide publicity and attracted the attention of many American novelists, poets, and playwrights. Poe, in reviewing Charles Fenno Hoffman's novel *Greyslaer* (1840), felt that the "incidents might be better woven into a tragedy." (17) (Was he thinking of his unfinished *Politian* as just such a tragedy?) Later, in a review of William Gilmore Simms' *Beauchampe* (1842), he expressed a belief that "No more thrilling, no more romantic tragedy did ever the brain of poet conceive than was the tragedy of Sharpe and Beauchampe." (18) Still later, in another comment on the same novel, he was of the opinion that the facts in the case, or the historical truth, had "hampered and repressed" the natural strength of the novelist. (19)

Presumably it was to get away from the facts, to permit his imagination to soar, that he had placed the action of his play in Renaissance Rome. Politian, the young hero, is no less a personage than the Earl of Leicester, an infinitely more romantic character than a Kentucky lawyer named Jereboam Beauchamp. The villain is Castiglione, son and heir of a Duke and named after the famous author of *The Book of the Courtier*. The prosy Mr. or Col. Solomon P. Sharp could hardly have dreamed of a greater transformation. Anne Cooke becomes "Lalage," a name possessing the requisite liquid sounds in which the poet-elocutionist luxuriated: Ulalume, Ligeia, Lenore, Annabel Lee. (20) The other characters bear equally exotic names: Baldazzar, Jacinta, Alessandra, San Ozzo, etc.

With this remote setting and these strange names Poe sought to escape being hampered and repressed by the facts upon which he based his play. But the romantic tragedy he intended did not come to life. It has much sound and fury but its significance as drama is slight. Others have been inspired to playwriting by newspaper melodrama. Ibsen was able to create *A Doll's House* out of intrinsically less dramatic material. Dreiser based his novel *An American Tragedy* on the accounts of a contemporary murder case, and when dramatized — especially by Erwin Piscator — the novel became a stageworthy play. Maxwell Anderson found his *Winterset* — perhaps the most successful of modern poetic tragedies — in a study of the Sacco-Vanzetti case. All these writers and many others managed to create work which left far behind the factual germ out of which it grew. Poe's *Politian* still remains the Kentucky murder case — theatricalized; it is neither great drama nor great poetry; and it is decidedly not a stageworthy play.

The reasons for Poe's failure are fundamental to any understanding of the nature of his peculiar talents. Mrs. Weiss, recalling her memories of Poe, remarked that his insight into " personal character was quick and intuitive, but not deep." It struck her that " in knowledge of human nature he was, for a man of his genius, strangely deficient." (21) I am not sure that on the basis of all the evidence we now have, we can accept these statements as absolutely accurate judgments, yet the characters in *Politian* — the one tragedy Poe has left us — are so weak and unconvincing as to suggest that Mrs. Weiss's impressions deserve our respect. Not one of the principals is realized as a person. All make their costumed entrances, speak their labored eloquence, and make their exits. They pass out of memory or, at most, remain vague puppets. If, as the eminent critic, Mr. Poe, said categorically of the characters in Nathaniel Parker Willis's *Tortesa the Usurer*, that they were nobody, nothing, or less than nothing, (22) then what would Mr. Poe — assuming that he would be consistent — have said of Castiglione, Lalage, Politian, or Baldazzar?

The meagerly motivated villain, Castiglione, is a good illustration of the weakness of Poe's characters. Castiglione is neither a coward nor without a sense of honor, and there are lines in his speeches which suggest that he still retains his love for Lalage, yet he persists in his "dishonorable" course. He defends Lalage against the aspersions of his friend San Ozzo, in a passage that is theatrically effective and humanly understandable:

> you do her wrong — unmanly wrong
> Never in woman's breast enthroned sat
> A purer heart! If ever woman fell
> With an excuse for falling it was she!
> If ever plighted vows most sacredly
> Solemnly sworn perfidiously broken
> Will damn a man, that damned villain am I!
> Young, ardent, beautiful and loving well
> And pure as beautiful, how could she think —
> How could she dream, being herself all truth
> Of my black perfidy? (23)

To which San Ozzo replies with heavy cynicism:
> Exceeding fine!
> I never heard a better speech in my life.
> Besides you're right — Oh! honesty's the thing!
> Honesty, poverty, and true content,
> With the unutterable extacies
> Of butter, verily, gingerbread, and milk and water. (24)

And that is sufficient to restore Castiglione's peace of mind and leave him to soliloquize that

> After all I don't see why
> I should so grieve about this little matter
> This every-day occurrence. (25)

The man who but less than thirty lines before ardently defended the purity and truth of Lalage and called himself a black villain and his behavior toward her black perfidy, now, but a minute later, left alone on the stage and facing only his conscience — and the audience — dismisses her tragedy and his deed as "this little matter." The fact that he wishes that he were not

> Castiglione but some peasant hind
> The humble tiller of some humble field

so that he might "dare be honest," does not remedy the faulty motivation. If, as he confides to himself and the audience, "Di Broglio's haughty and time-honoured line" will not permit his marrying the "lowly born" Lalage, there is still no need for him to dismiss his "black perfidy" as a "little matter," and to further neutralize his one plausible reason for rejecting her by such lines as

> Castiglione wed him with a wanton!
> Never! — oh, never! — what would they say at the club?
> What would San Ozzo think?

But it is futile to subject Poe's characters either to the test of verisimilitude or to that of dramatic consistency. In the main they are derivative, indebted to the very models which Mr. Poe so bravely and pontifically condemned.[3] The numerous similarities Professor Mabbott's scholarly researches have discovered between *Politian* — characters, lines, moments of mood and thought — and such plays as *Hamlet, Romeo and Juliet, Othello, King John, Macbeth, King Lear, Antony and Cleopatra, The Tempest, As You Like It, The Maid's Tragedy,*

---

[3] "The first thing necessary is to burn or bury the 'old models,' and to forget, as quickly as possible, that ever a play has been penned." (26)

*Antonio and Mellida, The Duchess of Malfi, All for
Love,* (27) and many others are striking enough. In
writing his play the young Poe had his eye neither on
the characters in the Kentucky tragedy nor on any
imaginary beings whom his poetic brain conjured, but
on the stock characters in the many romantic plays he
had read and seen. Dame Pope-Hennessy's conclusion
that *"Politian* is a feeble imitation of the Cenci-Fazio
type" (28) is justified. It is definitely an imitation, and
certainly feeble.

4

A few other weaknesses of this play are equally illuminating. The man who as a literary and dramatic critic
chastised many storytellers and playwrights on the score
of lack of sound structure was himself unsuccessful in
his one attempt to construct a dramatic plot. If, as he
insisted — in italics — plot is *"that in which no* part can
be displaced without ruin to the whole," (29) then
Politian is without plot. It would be possible, for instance, to omit all of Scene VIII, the long soliloquy of
Jacinta, Lalage's villainous maid, without causing the
slightest injury to the whole. If it was meant to be a
contributing episode toward the dénouement it is out of
all reasonable proportion and inconsequential. If, on the
other hand, it was intended merely as a minor digression,
for the sake of comic relief, then it is indeed — as one of
Poe's French editors has expressed it — the work of an
"icy humorist." (30) [4] Moreover, the scene adds to the
general sense of inactivity of the plot. That Poe was

---

[4] The expression used by M. Woestyn is "humoriste à froid," which
is a French idiom equivalent to "sham humorist." Nevertheless, as
applied to Poe, a more literal translation seems appropriate and justified.

aware of the "talkiness" of this scene is indicated by his efforts to inject some "action" into it. Jacinta carries a bandbox; looks at a watch; kicks the bandbox "to and fro"; other servants — Ugo, Benito, Rupert — cross and recross the stage; and finally Ugo inadvertently treads upon the bandbox and Jacinta strikes him. But all this activity is unrelated to the plot, immaterial and un-imaginative digression.

When there is action — relevant or irrelevant — it is managed so badly as to be almost absurd. In the scene in which San Ozzo mocks Castiglione's melancholy he promises to send him sackcloth and ashes. He exits and, almost at once, the sackcloth and ashes are delivered. The timing is weirdly inept. Between San Ozzo's exit and the fulfillment of his jest, poor Castiglione has time to recite but twenty-three lines of iambic pentameter. The audience cannot fail to realize that the props were ready off-stage even at the moment San Ozzo conceived his amiable little notion.

Politian's greatest weakness still remains the dialogue. The numerous asides and interminable soliloquies in-deed support the views of the more mature and eminent Mr. Poe. They do "utterly" destroy "verisimilitude." But the soliloquizing of his characters is in itself not half as preposterous as what they say and how they say it. Mr. Kirkley found such phrases as "the grave untimely yawning for a ruined maid" and "arise and die" faintly ridiculous. What shall we say of such time-honored clichés as Politian's avowal of love on "bended knee . . . Thro' good and ill — thro' weal and wo . . ."; of his challenge to Castiglione, "Draw, villain" and of the latter's reply, "Ha! — draw? — and villain? have at thee then at once"; and of Castiglione's "Strike thou home (*baring his bosom*). Here is no let or hindrance to thy weapon — Strike home"? We can only agree with Mr. Edward Shanks that Poe "was clearly a poor hand in dramatic dialogue." (31)

The publicity used in advertising the performance of *Politian* in Baltimore featured this quotation: "If Poe had lived in a European center he might have become one of the world's greatest dramatists." (32) The "might" seems to me hardly warranted. He might no more have become a great playwright than Sheridan Knowles, or Wordsworth, or Coleridge, or his admired Byron became one. *Politian* is a closet drama, and as such it suffers from all the ailments to which this *genre* is heir. These ailments have been perfectly described by T. S. Eliot (who has himself nevertheless managed to create poetic drama which is at once good poetry and effective theatre): "It is not primarily lack of plot, or lack of action and suspense, or imperfect realization of character, or lack of anything of what is called 'theatre,' that makes these plays lifeless: it is primarily that their rhythm of speech is something that we cannot associate with any human being except a poetry reciter." (33) Poe, we have seen, was exactly that. As a critic he was not in a position to indulge his talent; as a playwright the temptation was too great. At any rate, what he produced in *Politian* is no better than what he once accused another poet of having produced: "a theatrical world of mere verbiage, somewhat spaciously bedizened with a tinselly meaning." (34)

5

But if *Politian* does not represent a great contribution to dramatic literature, it is nonetheless of considerable importance in helping us to understand Poe as a man and an artist. For it is, more than many of his poems and stories, a piece of self-revelation, an act of confession, and its failure as an actable play is due largely to his inability to forget himself.

Who is Politian, besides being a fictitious substitute for the Kentucky lawyer Jereboam Beauchamp? He is first and foremost the hero in a poetic tragedy written by a young Virginia gentleman who aspired to literary fame. But even before the noble youth ascends the stage to speak the lines written for him by the as yet unrecognized young genius, he begins to assume the lineaments of the author. We today cannot fail to recognize in the young hero the characteristic bearing, tone, and gestures of young Edgar Allan Poe. Politian is, says Duke Di Broglio,

>   A man quite young
> In years, but grey in fame. . . .
> . . . Rumour speaks of him as a prodigy
> Pre-eminent in arts and arms, and wealth,
> And high descent . . .
> No branch, they say, of all philosophy
> So deep abstruse he has not mastered it.
> Learned as few are learned.

The Duke's niece, Alessandra, and Castiglione, her betrothed, have heard other rumors: that the young man is "Gay, volatile and giddy," that he is "As one who entered madly into life, Drinking the cup of pleasure to the dregs," or that "He is a dreamer and a man shut out From common passions." (35)

Politian is, in short, the kind of mysterious hero Edgar Allan Poe imagined himself to be. He is, to be sure, also a bit of Byron and many bits of heroes encountered in the romantic melodramas which cluttered the stages of England and America in Poe's time. But essentially he is strikingly like the heroes in many of Poe's short stories — melancholy, brave, learned, brilliant, aloof, satanic, perhaps more than a little mad, noble, contradictory, misunderstood. Mr. Hervey Allen believes that the description of the hero in "The Fall of the House of Usher" is a pen-portrait of Poe himself and might be labelled "Self Portrait of the Artist at the Age of Thirty." (36) It would be difficult to label the sketch of Politian. No doubt it is, in part, a self portrait of the artist a little less than a decade earlier; but it is also, in greater part, a picture of the kind of hero the artist imagined himself to be — either then or in the future. Professor Mabbott has noted Politian's resemblance to the hero in Poe's early short story "The Assignation":

Ill-fated and mysterious man! bewildered in the brilliancy of thine own imagination, and fallen in the flames of thine own youth . . . squandering away a life of magnificent meditation in that city of dim visions, thine own Venice. . . . Who then shall call thy conduct into question? who blame thee for thy visionary hours, or denounce those occupations as a wasting away of life, which were but the overflowings of thine everlasting energies? . . . the graceful person of a very young man, with the sound of whose name the greater part of Europe was then ringing. (37)

One may add similar resemblances with the heroes in other stories, especially "Ligeia" and "Eleonora." The source from which Poe may have derived his plots matters little; his leading character is always a person who in many ways is what Poe was, thought himself to be, or wished to be. To be sure, the tendency to make himself the hero of his own work was not unique with Poe; most of the writers of the romantic school — Chateaubriand, Byron, Shelley, to name but a few — shared it;

in fact, the performance of these writers supports Irving Babbitt's definition of the Romantic impulse as a man's "expansive eagerness to get his own uniqueness uttered." But no one, not even the author of "Epipsychidion" and "Alastor" — as one British critic noted away back in 1901 — had such a gift for "arabesquing" and "transcendentalizing" himself as Poe. (38)

The contradictions in Politian's nature which the other characters perceive are part of the duality which Poe himself was to treat in "William Wilson" and which Poe's biographers were to point out again and again: the flashes of gaiety and spells of melancholy, his great charm and, at times, equally great insolence, his "normality" and "abnormality," his haughtiness and self-immolation. He who passionately longed for fame could, in a moment of despondency, exclaim through Politian's lips "Speak not to me of glory! I hate — I loathe the name; I do abhor /The unsatisfactory and ideal thing." It is not only love which impels the noble hero to contemplate the possibility of going down into the dust "unhonored and forgotten"; it is also revulsion from that same world which has, alas, proved unappreciative of the true greatness of his creator.

The best lines in the play, the soliloquy in the Coliseum, were among the earliest written, since they were the poem he entered in the *Baltimore Saturday Visiter* contest. If it be true, as H. W. Wells thinks, that they "were apparently to be the heart of . . . *Politian*," they are also apparently the heart of young Edgar Poe. The lines were undoubtedly suggested by Byron's lines on the same subject in *Manfred* and *Childe Harold*. But while, continues Mr. Wells, "The sight of Rome invigorated and redeemed Byron's heroes; the dream of it

unnerved Poe." (39) The young man who as a boy had
been brought "home" to "the glory that was Greece
and the grandeur that was Rome" now brooded upon
the transience of fame. He asks:

> These crumbling walls, these tottering arcades,
> These mouldering plinths, these sad and blackened shafts,
> These vague entablatures, this broken frieze,
> These shattered cornices, this wreck, this ruin,
> These stones, alas! these grey stones are they all,
> All of the great and the colossal left
> By the corrosive hours to Fate and me? (40)

Perhaps, since the lines were written in Baltimore,
where Poe was living in a tiny house in great poverty,
he was contemplating not only the impermanence, and
hence the futility, of the fame that someday might be
his but also the state of material glory that once was his
in the home of Mr. Allan in Richmond.

In the end, unnerved as he might be for the moment,
fame still remained the spur. His belief in himself, in
his genius, led him to hear prophetic voices. The boy
who had written to Mr. Allan that "Since I have been
able to think on any subject, my thoughts have aspired
. . . to eminence in public life" (41) never died in
Poe. The grey stones of the Coliseum, Politian re-
assures himself, are not all that is left of the great and
the colossal:

> "We are not desolate, we pallid stones,
>   Not all our power is gone, — not all our Fame,
>   Not all the magic of our high renown,
>   Not all the wonder that encircles us,
>   Not all the mysteries that in us lie,
>   Not all the memories that hang upon
>   And cling around about us as a garment
>   Clothing us in a robe of more than glory."

No, the stones of the Coliseum were not desolate. Nor was Poe. In one way or another the glory that was Rome spoke to him, and his desolation, of which he wrote constantly, was pretty much of a myth. Like the myth of his visit to Rome, which he encouraged the world to accept. At a meeting of the Humanitas Association held in April, 1945, an Italian writer, Filippo Donini, expressed his conviction that judging by "The Coliseum," Poe had never visited the Eternal City. The poem is general and bookish in its description of local color. The only objects not found in Byron's or Lamartine's lines on the ruins are a bat and some canes and thistles, and these are objects which are certainly not difficult to imagine as invading any ruins. Poe, concludes the reporter of the meeting, Pietro Paolo Trompeo, "has truly demonstrated that he has never put his foot in Rome." (42)

But it really matters little whether the lines on the Coliseum were based on direct observation, derived from other poets, or completely invented in Baltimore. They are part of the poetry that was Poe. They are also part of the drama that was Poe, and for this reason they are part of the feebleness of what was intended to be the drama of *Politian*.

6

It was M. Hughes who hazarded the surmise that Poe might have become an important American dramatist. Our study of *Politian*, its dialogues, and, in fact, Poe's handling of dialogue in general — even in his short stories — makes the surmise implausible. M. Hughes himself supplies one reason — the principal one — for doubt. "Edgar Poe," he remarks, apropos of one of

Politian's speeches, "endows the characters he has placed on the stage with his own personal sensations and sentiments." (43)

In other words, Poe never left his characters alone. Very likely he never actually saw them, except as projections of himself. Living himself in a vague world of fancy and inarticulate desire, he permitted his imaginary personae to float in a similarly vague world, speaking rhythmically high words and noble phrases, and doing little except analyzing their souls. For a playwright all this is fatal. Except in fantasy, stage characters must be recognizable people, bearing a resemblance to our friends and neighbors, walking a substantial earth, acting and reacting upon each other in a manner which recalls common experience. Even the dreamy creations of a Maeterlinck — upon whom Poe is said to have exerted a strong influence (44) — have more substantiality than Poe's shadowy evocations.

D. H. Lawrence once remarked that Poe never saw anything in terms of life, (45) and while Lawrence's opinions on American literature were often tinged with malice, they were sometimes — as in this case — singularly acute. Poe seemingly had no ear for the speech of real people, nor did he seem to have either the curiosity or the patience to observe real people. Instead, he observed himself, patiently, everlastingly, fascinatedly. His characters are endowed not only with Poe's thoughts and emotions but with his physical characteristics and stage mannerisms as well. What is worse: after writing the "sides" for them, he pushed his Politians, Castigliones, Ushers, and "I's" aside, and walking onto the stage, stopped where the light was brightest — or romantically dimmest — and proceeded to deliver the lines himself. The very patterns of the speeches are in the elocutionary idiom of Edgar Poe, the actor rather than the playwright.

In the final analysis, Poe failed as a dramatist for the same reasons that Byron failed. It is worth recalling Baudelaire's description of Poe as "a Byron entangled in an evil world." (46) Entangled he certainly was, but more with himself than the world. Had he read Macaulay's essay on Milton, especially the short digression in which the great Victorian attempted to explain Byron's shortcomings as a playwright, he might have profited by it. For Macaulay saw clearly that

The business of the dramatist is to keep himself out of sight, and to let nothing appear but his characters. As soon as he attracts notice to his personal feelings, the illusion is broken. The effect is as unpleasant as that which is produced on the stage by the voice of a prompter or the entrance of a scene-shifter. Hence it was, that the tragedies of Byron were his least successful performances. . . . In all the characters, patriots and tyrants, haters and lovers, the frown and sneer of Harold were discernible in an instant. (47)

It is possible, however, that Poe may have read these words of Macaulay — whom, incidentally, he admired both as a critic and stylist (48) — and could not profit by them. The species of egotism to which dramatists of the type of Byron and Poe succumb is not affected by logic or reason. It is an overmastering impulse to exhibit the ego, and only by yielding to it does such a writer-actor live, breathe, and feel himself truly creative.

And, in truth, he is creative; if not as a great dramatist then as a great lyrist. The very entanglement with self which prevented Poe from creating a great — or even an acceptable — drama was his inspiration and strength as a poet. Rémy de Gourmont had good reason for calling him " le plus subjectif des poètes subjectifs." (49) In his lyrics he could dream, brood, lament, and exclaim all he wished. Mere overflow of the ego cannot, of course, produce poetry. The gift must be there. In Poe's case, as in Byron's, it was. But it was not the gift of the dramatist. He was totally incapable of obliterating himself, of losing himself completely in other lives, of hearing the accents of other people, of recording experience — real or imaginary — except his own. In the end, the romantic histrio smothered the playwright.

CHAPTER III

SCHOLARLY GENTLEMAN

"How absolute is the necessity now daily grow-
ing, of rescuing our stage criticism from the
control of illiterate mountebanks, and placing
it in the hands of gentlemen and scholars."

THERE is a story to the effect that one cold night
in December of 1844 Cornelius Mathews went to
the Park Theatre and found himself seated next to Mr.
Poe. Mathews, with a modicum of encouragement, told
the distinguished poet, story-teller, and critic about a
new play, *Witchcraft*, upon which he was then at work,
and Poe, "in his low, melodious voice," suggested that
the fourth act might gain in effectiveness if a raven, that
bird of ill-omen, were to flit across the stage over the
head of the hero's mother, who is suspected of being a
witch. (1)

This story — even though it contains a dubious account of Poe's scribbling away on "The Raven" under a
lamp post, on the corner of Bleecker Street and Broadway — is important because it is one of the few definite
records we have of Poe's physical presence in a theatre.
Unless we accept as further evidence his vivid description of the interior of a theatre, during a performance,
in such a story as "The Spectacles." A few months
after his meeting with Mathews Poe became a professional dramatic critic and was, of course, in attendance
at various New York theatres on opening nights. He

93

wrote his judgments of the new plays — in the positive, summary manner traditional with the craft — for the *Broadway Journal*, a weekly of less than a thousand circulation.

It is not easy to account for the qualifications of dramatic critics, neither in Poe's day nor, for that matter, in our own. We are, however, justified in entertaining a few assumptions. One is: that anyone who undertakes to inform the theatre-going public on what is occurring in the theatre is himself part of that public; that, in other words, he is familiar with the practices, habits, customs, and "climate" of the theatre; that, in brief, he has been himself an habitual theatregoer. To be sure, other qualifications are necessary, but without a direct knowledge, a store of vivid memories, of the living stage nothing else is of great significance.

Did Poe bring to his task as dramatic critic such knowledge, such a store of memories? Was a love of the theatre, of its color and stimulation, of the variety and intensity of experience it provides, part of his equipment? We know that he respected the art of acting. We remember his eloquent defense of Mrs. Mowatt's appearance on the stage and his pride in his mother's career. We remember his attempt at playwriting. And we have his numerous reviews of published plays to testify to his life-long interest in drama as literature. But none of these offers us more than an inkling of how much of the living theatre of his day Poe actually knew.

Although it is not likely that, as a child in Richmond, he was taken to see theatrical performances, we know that he was taught dancing and dramatic recitation, with which he was expected to entertain special company in the Allans's drawing-room. We also know that as a school-boy he founded a Thespian Society which met and gave performances at 6th and Marshall Streets. Whether the active professional theatre in Richmond, especially after 1820, "inspired the play-acting of Poe and his boyhood friends," as Miss Bondurant suggests, cannot be proved, (2) but the probability is strong that as Poe grew older he took advantage of the fashion among the best people and visited the local theatre. The best families supported it, as was indicated the evening of the great fire, December 26, 1811, when seventy-two persons, among them Governor Smith, lost their lives. "The family of John Allan, who had recently taken Edgar Poe into his home," writes Miss Bondurant, "was spending the holidays out of town. Otherwise they, too, might have suffered from the fire." (3) A new theatre was built in 1819, and here a lover of drama might have seen the most popular plays of the day presented by actors and actresses well-known in both England and America. (4)

After Poe left home to enter the University of Virginia his chances of seeing plays were, if anything, improved, because now he was at last free of Mr. Allan's supervision. Nor is there any reason to assume that he did not visit the theatre in Boston, where he spent some little time waiting to get his first volume of poems published and where he finally enlisted in the United States Army, unless poverty prevented him. The same obstacle existed during his West Point days, and throughout the rest of his life in Baltimore, Philadelphia, and New York. Yet his writings, and those of his friends, record specific instances of his attendance at the theatre, especially in the latter two cities. These do not necessarily prove that he was an habitual patron, but they at least indicate that, whenever his financial circumstances permitted, the call of the theatre found him responsive.

I have already noted the large number of playwrights and actors among Poe's friends. These often supplied him with theatre passes. It can therefore be said that in at least one respect he possessed the necessary equipment for the profession of dramatic critic: the ability to pass the box-office.[1] But no matter how he got in, the theatre was no unexplored country to Poe, for, as one Philadelphian who had had occasion to observe him expressed it: "Poe was a play-goer" and "admired the drama." (5)

2

Play-going and admiring the drama are not, however, enough to make a dramatic critic. At least one other assumption becomes unavoidable. It is: that anyone undertaking to pass judgment on drama possesses a wide knowledge of dramatic literature. In Poe's case, this assumption appears to be justified the moment one dips into his writings. They bristle with references to playwrights, great and small; with apt quotations from plays, ancient and modern; and with allusions to plots and characters that are part of the history of world drama. It is true that Poe often pretended to more knowledge than he possessed, that he liked to quote from obscure, and sometimes mythical, writers, and that he made a little learning pass for much and profound erudition. But it is equally true that all his life he was an eager and persistent reader. Professor Killis Campbell's finding of areas of literature of which Poe apparently fails to reflect

[1] There still remains Col. T. H. Ellis's statement — mentioned in an earlier chapter — that Poe "was on the stage in Boston." If this be true, then, for a while at least, the box-office was no problem at all.

awareness (6) does not absolutely prove unawareness, for display of scholarship is not always an index of acquaintance with literature, nor of understanding or appreciation. Nor does Professor F. C. Prescott's surmise that Poe got some of his knowledge — and " perhaps most of his knowledge " — of Greek and later dramatic literature from A. W. Schlegel's *Lectures on Dramatic Art and Literature* (7) exclude the possibility that Poe had read and continued to read widely in the dramatic literature itself.[2] In the less scholarly mind these surmises and " perhapses " have become certainties. It was from Coleridge, says Dame Pope-Hennessy, that Poe learned to appreciate Schlegel's *Lectures*, and it was from the *Lectures* that he derived his allusions to Crébillon, Corneille, and other authors " whose works he had not read." (9)

Yet a man does not quote from one play (*Hamlet*) thirty-eight times without having read that play. And if ten years before he became a dramatic critic, in reviewing three volumes of Greek plays — " the whole of Euripides " — he spiced his observation with quotations from Schlegel, we are still not justified in concluding that he did not read some or all of the plays. The fact is that not even Poe, clever and presumptuous as he was, could have discussed the drama with such assurance and intimate detail as he shows in his numerous reviews, essays, brief notations, offhand comments and judgments, unless he had read it first-hand.

---

[2] In connection with the unflattering surmises regarding Poe's " borrowed " knowledge, it seems only fair, on occasion, to let the accused speak for himself; for instance: " I . . . hold Macaulay to possess more of the true critical spirit than Augustus William and Frederick Schlegel combined." — *Marginalia*. And again: " For much of all this [the *cant* in current discussion of dramatic principle], we are indebted to the somewhat overprofound criticism of Augustus William Schlegel." (8)

Thus he cites *The Clouds* of Aristophanes as an example of the antiquity of rhyming and the *Antigone* of Sophocles as an example of the dramatic crudity of the ancients. One of his short stories, "Thou Art the Man," begins with the sentence: "I will now play the Oedipus to the Rattleborough enigma"; another, "Eleonora," attempts to allay the reader's possible incredulity by urging him to "play unto its riddle the Oedipus"; and in still another place he subjects the *Oedipus* to a detailed analysis in an attempt to prove that it served as a source for *Lear*. He cites the *Eumenides* of Aeschylus and *Oedipus at Colonus* of Sophocles[3] as tragedies of happy termination. "The Colloquy of Monos and Una" is prefaced by a quotation from Sophocles's *Antigone* and "The Conversation of Eiros and Charmion" by one from Euripides's *Andromache*. He confessed himself to be an ardent admirer of Euripides, whom he thought "truly great," but only when compared with many of the "moderns." As compared, however, with his own immediate predecessors, Euripides fell short of true greatness. Aeschylus alone, whose *Prometheus* Poe believed to be immortal, and in whom he found verse most strictly married to music, seemingly had no disadvantageous comparisons; and both Sophocles and Euripides were echoes of him. Altogether he refers to Aeschylus thirteen times; to Sophocles, seven times; and to Euripides, six times.

Poe had much less to say of Roman drama. His abhorrence of imitativeness is well-known, and he considered the Roman playwrights the most imitative of all. Even Terence, he pointed out, was only Menander and "noth-

---

[3] Which, incidentally, he attributes to Aeschylus, thus indicating that he felt sure enough of his knowledge of the play to rely on his memory.

ing beyond," and the tragedies of Seneca — "a puerile writer" — were mere copies of Greek subjects.

Shakespeare and his Elizabethan and post-Elizabethan colleagues loom large in Poe's awareness. Almost at the very beginning of his career, in his famous "Letter to B—," Poe held up to scorn the type of person who thinks Shakespeare a great poet, but who has nevertheless not read Shakespeare. He himself preferred to be among the "few gifted individuals who kneel around the summit, beholding, face to face, the master spirit who stands upon the pinnacle." Some years later, in a review of a book on the Elizabethan dramatists, he urged the procuring of a copy of this work by "every person who has a copy of Shakespeare, (that is to say, by the world at large.)" (10) When, in August of the year in which he became a dramatic critic, he reviewed Hazlitt's *The Characters of Shakespeare*, he displayed an acquaintance with the character creations of the greatest of English dramatists which he could have attained only by constant and close reading of the plays themselves. (11)

His analysis of Hamlet especially indicates long and profound thought. And no wonder. He had lived with the great tragedy of the Danish prince since his earliest childhood, a copy of the play having been bequeathed to him by his mother. (12) His review of Hazlitt's book is largely an attempt to differentiate between Hamlet the man, created by God, and the dramatic character, created by Shakespeare. It is significant that Poe should attribute the inconsistencies of the character to the playwright's impulsion to exaggerate: because it is one more illustration of Poe's habit to formulate theories based upon his own creative practices and impulses. Neither this idea about Shakespeare, nor the speculation on the

extent of the Bard's identification with Hamlet, is in
Hazlitt or Schlegel. But there are other betrayals of
Poe's intimacy with the play. Although such an allusion
as "out-Heroded Herod" (used at least three times)
(13) may be merely the employment of common cur-
rency, the ease with which phrases, lines, and names
from the play spring to his mind is unmistakable.

Besides *Hamlet*, the "Letter to B—" mentions the
Tempest, Midsummer Night's Dream, and some of their
characters: Prospero, Oberon, Titania. "Al Aaraaf"
contains a paraphrase of a line from *The Merry Wives
of Windsor*, and the short story "The Angel of the
Odd" contains a character who reminds Poe of Falstaff.
He is also reminded of Falstaff—"so life-like a character that it seems as if we had drunk canary with
[him] at the Boar's Head"—while reviewing Bulwer's
novel *Zanoni*. *Politian* reverberates with memories of
Shakespeare. Here we find a reference to Cleopatra and
her two attendants, Eiros and Charmian (whose names,
we have already noticed, he was to use as the title of a
dialogue). Here we find glory personified as "trumpet-
tongued," like the virtues which Macbeth heard plead,
like angels, against the murder of Duncan. Here we find
an imitation of the moonlight scene in the fifth act of
the *Merchant of Venice*. And here we find, in three
separate scenes, echoes of passages from *King John*. . . .
(14). In another short story, "Four Beasts in One," Poe
indulges in a quotation from *Twelfth Night*, three lines
apparently recalled from memory, for they are full of
tiny lapses from the original text. In a review of a
play by Willis he notes that an incident "seems adopted
from the 'Winter's Tale.'" (15) Another review, of
an obscure poet's work, calls attention to the lifting of a

scene from *Romeo and Juliet*. (16) Sometimes his assimilation of a Shakespearean character is so complete that he can discuss it in terms of historical accuracy, without even taking the trouble to identify the play in which it occurs. In a paper on Robert T. Conrad he compares the character of Jack Cade as treated by Judge Conrad in his popular tragedy *Aylmere* and by Shakespeare, presumably in the second part of *Henry VI*, coming to the conclusion that Shakespeare's account of the English rebel was historically unjustified. (17) There can be no question that he knew the plays of the master at whose summit he knelt, knew them minutely, reflectively, and appreciatively.

Yet, kneeling though he might be, he was no blind worshipper. "Your hero-worshippers," he exclaims in a comment on Carlyle's *Hero-Worship*, "what do they know of Shakespeare? They worship him — rant about him — lecture about him — . . . for no other reason than that he is utterly beyond their comprehension. They have arrived at an idea of his greatness from the pertinacity with which men have called him great. As for their own opinion about him — they really have none at all." (18) *He* apparently had an opinion and, high as it might be, it was his own. No better summary of his enthusiasm for Shakespeare is needed than his own statement — made in spite of his strange belief that *Lear* owed its plot to the *Oedipus* — that "If all the dramatists of antiquity were combined in one, they would not be found worthy to touch the hem of his garment." (19)

Equally unmistakable is Poe's knowledge of other Elizabethan and seventeenth-century dramatists. It colors his writing and thinking; it creeps into his pages in oblique allusions to, or direct quotations from, such plays as *Gorboduc*, Marlowe's *Faustus*, Peele's *David and Bethsabe*, Chapman's *Bussy d'Ambois*, Beaumont and Fletcher's *The Maid's Tragedy*, Webster's *Duchess of Malfi*, Marston's *Malcontent* and *Antonio and Mellida*, Shirley's *Example*, Milton's *Comus*, and Dryden's *Assignation* and *All for Love*. References to later English plays and playwrights are even more numerous. At the slightest opportunity his mind is ready to supply names, plots, and lines from eighteenth and nineteenth century English drama.

The number of non-English " moderns " of whom he shows awareness is no less respectable. In his early story, "The Assignation," the hero reads " Politian's beautiful tragedy, 'The Orfeo,' (the first native Italian tragedy)." Politian is, of course, Angelo Poliziano, the fifteenth-century poet and scholar. In at least two of his many discussions of plot he refers to the intrigue in which the plays of Cervantes and Calderon abound; in a third, he quotes a passage from Calderon; and in a fourth, he recalls the innumerable comedies of intrigue attributed to Calderon and Lope de Vega. Other references, scattered through his writings, are to Corneille ("The Man That Was Used Up") and Racine ("Pinakidia"), to Molière's M. Jourdain ("Murders in the Rue Morgue"), to Voltaire's *Brutus* and *Mort de Cesar* (*Marginalia*), Hugo's *Hernani* ("Masque of the Red Death") and *Cromwell* (*Marginalia*), to Crébillon, to Goethe[4] and Schiller. . . .

It is quite clear that Poe's knowledge of dramatic literature was considerable. The field is vast and it is only natural that certain areas should have remained

[4] One Germanic scholar has even accused Poe of borrowing from Goethe for a few scenes in *Politian*. (20)

unreflected in the writings of a man who did not, after all, devote himself exclusively or even mainly to drama. We cannot, however, be certain that because these areas have remained unreflected in his writings they also remained beyond his orbit of exploration or interest. At any rate, we are safe in crediting him with a knowledge of drama much wider than that possessed by the average reporter of Broadway entertainment in his day. And — what is more important — out of this knowledge he had evolved a philosophy of dramatic excellence and theatrical effectiveness by which to judge the product being offered the American theatre public in the year 1845.

3

What this philosophy of excellence amounted to was to become clear from his application of it to the living drama. He had apparently watched the state of theatrical reviewing for a long time, and had formed some definite ideas about its appalling shortcomings. Almost a decade before assuming his position as a molder of dramatic taste, he had insisted, in the pages of the *Southern Literary Messenger*, (21) on the necessity of rescuing American stage criticism from the control of illiterate mountebanks, and had advocated placing it in the hands of gentlemen and scholars. And now at last his own chance had come, the chance for a gentleman and scholar to show what could be done.

That his standards were high is obvious; they obliged him to be cantankerous and cruel; and they involved him in much unpleasantness and — like his literary criticism — made bitter enemies for him. Even when he wished to be kind, the result was sometimes unavoidably embarrassing. Thus he comments on a new play by, apparently, some friend whose name he thoughtfully withholds: "And this is the 'American Drama' of —! Well! — that 'Conscience which makes cowards of us all' will permit me to say, in praise of the performance, only that it is not quite so bad as I expected it to be. But then," he adds, "I always expect too much." (22) We may be sure that, despite the critic's thoughtfulness, the playwright was not grateful. And certainly no playwright could be expected to harbor the slightest inclination toward gratitude for a comment such as this: "L— is busy in attempting to prove that his play was not fairly d—d — that it is only 'scotched, not killed'; but if the poor Play could speak from the tomb, I fancy it would sing with the Opera heroine: 'The flattering error cease to prove! Oh, *let* me be deceased!'" (23) Poe's statement that he expected too much may not have been the whole truth, but it was true enough as a cause of his difficulties. He did expect much; and in the theatre of his day that was rarely to be found.

What the producers thought of the *Broadway Journal's* dramatic critic can best be judged from the actions of one of them. On April 7th Palmo's Opera House presented Sophocles's *Antigone* with music by Mendelssohn. Poe's review appeared five days later, and the next week his publication printed a scorching protest which it had received from the producer, W. Dinneford. The angry gentleman accused Mr. Poe of being ill-natured and unjust, and informed him that

In *Justice* . . . to MYSELF, I have withdrawn your name from the free list. I am always prepar'd to submit, as a caterer for public amusement, to any *just* remarks, though they may be severe, but I do not feel MYSELF called upon to offer *facilities* to any one, to do me injury by *animadversions* evidently marked by ill feeling.

Mr. Poe's reply, entitled "Achilles' Wrath," and printed in the same issue of the *Journal*, is that of a scholar — courageous in the defense of his right to independence of judgment — but hardly that of a gentleman. It begins by attacking the producer's luxuriously elegant style of living (at the Astor House), complains that the letter of protest was sent without payment of postage, and proceeds to derive amusement from Mr. Dinneford's "shockingly bad hand," bad punctuation, and eccentric underscoring. These betrayals of ill-temper are unfortunate, and detract from the substance of the reply, which, however, remains unimpaired. For in substance, Poe's reply constitutes a sort of manifesto, a brave, uncompromising declaration of the duty of the critic to remain uninfluenced in his judgments by considerations of self-interest.

We are not wasting words on this Quinneford [5] — it is the public to whom we speak — to the editorial corps in especial. We wish to call their attention to the peculiar character of the *conditions* which managers such as these have the impudence to *avow*, as attached to the privilege of the free list. No puff no privilege, is the contract. That is to say, an editor, when admitted to the theatre, is to be understood as leaving his conscience in the street. He is admitted not to judge — not to criticize — but to adulate.

Strangely enough, the review which provoked "Achilles' Wrath" is, for Poe, rather tame. It begins with a dignified expression of the opinion that the *Antigone* of Sophocles is inferior to any of the plays of Aeschylus,

---

[5] Although Poe here pretends that he is possibly misreading Mr. Dinneford's wretched signature, his deliberate use of this device for satirical purposes is typical. Thus he referred to Thomas Dunn English as "Thomas Dunn Brown"; similarly, he once referred to Dr. Griswold as "Dr. Driswold."

and that, in general, the idea of reproducing a Greek play before a modern audience is that of a pedant. The "insufferable baldness" of Greek drama, verging on the platitudinous, was not the result of a "studied and supremely artistic simplicity" but rather of artistic inexperience. Drama as an art form, Poe suggests, demands "the long and painful progressive experience of the ages," which the Greek playwrights had not had to the same extent as the "moderns." To make matters worse, the production at Palmo's is not at all in the Greek manner and tends to become a burlesque of the original. He was therefore not surprised to observe that while on opening night a "very respectable" audience was present, the second night brought only less than a hundred paying spectators. He then proceeds to praise one of the actors, Mr. Vandenhoff, as a capital "elocutionist" — which in Poe's vocabulary was a word of commendation and synonymous with "actor"[6] — to bestow some superlatives upon Mendelssohn for his music, and to condemn the execution of the choruses:

a large number of men are paraded upon the stage, scarcely one third of them singing correctly, while the other two thirds either do not sing at all, or vamp the words and music. . . . Indeed, the whole of the musical arrangements reflect but little credit upon Mr. Loder's reputation as an energetic and skillful conductor. (25)

It is true that, as Professor Percy H. Boynton once charged, Poe was a literary "swashbuckler, cutting and

[6] As in his comment on Mrs. Mowatt's performance in Bulwer-Lytton's *The Lady of Lyons*: "indeed all her movements evince the practiced elocutionist." — *Broadway Journal*, July 19, 1845. Incidentally, George Vandenhoff was the gentleman who included "The Raven" in a textbook on elocution, and was thus responsible for the first appearance of the poem in book form. (24)

thrusting, and strutting about a stage on which he played the villain to his complete satisfaction." (26) Still, there is no reason to assume that his judgments, even in the case of Vandenhoff, were not sincere. How seriously he took his task of reviewing plays is indicated by his reference to both the first and second night audiences. He apparently saw the play twice. And in the case of another play, Mrs. Mowatt's *Fashion*, he claimed to have seen it ten times, besides having read it in manuscript. Such an attitude toward current drama was unknown among American critics at the time, as it is uncommon today. Poe may have enjoyed his rôle of castigator, of stern judge and merciless exposer of sham and shoddy; he may even have mistaken, as Lowell suggested, his phial of prussic acid for his inkstand (27); but all this is unimportant beside the fact that he brought to stage criticism a sense of responsibility as well as dignity and scholarship. He had pledged himself to "honest and fearless opinion" (28) and, like the great reviewers in the British journals which he read regularly — Jeffrey, North, Hazlitt, Macaulay — he felt that severity was inseparable from honesty and fearlessness. But even if his method was at times ungentlemanly, it was wholesomely prophylactic at a time when puffery and sentimentality were rampant along Broadway.

4

The review of the *Antigone* production is a typical sample of Poe's "executionery" skill, but not of his method of critical procedure. Generally his reviews begin with a synopsis or sketch of the plot, continue with a statement of the dramatic principles by which the reviewer chooses to be guided, and end with an application of those principles to the play and production under review. The last step involves detailed analysis, comment, and judgment. While he abhorred the prevalent type of eulogy which passed for criticism, he was equally opposed to the purely impressionistic attack; his ideal was a judicious weighing of good and bad points, and more often than not he achieved his ideal.

It is in his synopses that Poe's training as "magazinist" makes itself felt. Each synopsis is clear, objective, and, despite seeming length, to the point. Even when he intends to tear the play down, the summary of the action is generally just and unclouded by his intention. All relevant details and complications are deftly and economically given, so that his discussion can be followed by a reader who may not have seen or read the play. Sometimes it would seem that the amount of space devoted to a retelling of the plot is out of proportion to the rest of the review. Thus his first report on *Fashion* (29) consists of seven paragraphs of synopsis and eight of comment.[7] But since so much of what he has to say revolves either around the plot or the action of the characters, his lengthy synopsis is a logical necessity.

It is both logical and necessary because for Poe — as for Aristotle — no play existed unless it had a plot. His definition of plot as a "construction" in which "*no part can be displaced without ruin to the whole*" we have already noted. Here his elaboration of the definition

---

[7] One device sometimes resorted to by present-day dramatic reviewers, in cases where they have no favorable comment to make and are not in a position to speak out unfavorably, is to devote the entire space allotted to them to a non-committal rehash of the plot. Poe, however, sooner or later always committed himself.

deserves our attention. It is "a building so dependently constructed, that to change the position of a single brick is to overthrow the entire fabric." (30) He believed this to be true of the novel as well as of the drama, and repeated his definition, in but slightly different words, on many occasions. "A plot," he wrote in an article on American drama, "is perfect only inasmuch as we shall find ourselves unable to detach from it or *disarrange* any single incident involved, without destruction to the mass." (31) He was consistent in his Aristotelian assertion that any literary composition must be an organic whole. And in consistently demanding that the dramatists of his day meet his definition he found himself obliged to pass adverse judgment on practically all the plays he reviewed. For the American theatre of 1845 was not the theatre of Ibsen, not even of Dumas *fils*; it was rather the theatre of Sheridan Knowles, Bulwer-Lytton, and Dion Boucicault.

Poe's first objection to Mrs. Mowatt's play is on the ground of the unoriginality of its plot. "Had it . . . been designed," he remarks, "as a burlesque upon the arrant conventionality of stage incidents in general, we should have regarded it as a palpable hit." And, indeed, his summary of the hoary complications *Fashion* utilizes reads like a page in the writings of our own contemporary satirist of Times Square antics, George Jean Nathan. "Their hackneyism," exclaims Poe, "is no longer to be endured. The day has at length arrived when men demand rationalities in place of conventionalities." (32)

In his second review (33) of this play he modifies somewhat his strictures on the score of unoriginality of plot. Now that he has seen several performances he is not quite sure that Mrs. Mowatt's "thesis" is not an original one. The idea of satirizing fashion *as* fashion, rather than specific fashionable foibles, appeals to him. He realizes, however, that this is a distinction too nice to be of any practical value, and that he can really let himself go only so far as to admit "some pretension to originality of plot," a mere shadow of originality, and even that vanishes in the presentation.

A more detailed development of his ideas on the subject of dramatic plot is embodied in his review of Nathaniel Parker Willis's *Tortesa, the Usurer*. Since this contribution to the *American Whig Review* (34) is part of a general survey of American drama, rather than a hasty report of a theatrical performance, Poe formulates his thoughts carefully. Again we have the detailed synopsis of the action, but we are warned that the story makes better sense in this form "than in the words of the play itself." For *Tortesa*, as a play, is cluttered with irrelevant intrigue, introduced for the sake of "action," "business," or "vivacity." Willis evidently did not know that "a mere succession of incidents, even the most spirited, will no more constitute a plot, than a multiplication of zeros, even the most infinite, will result in the production of a unit." A plot, Poe repeats, is an organic whole; it can be said to exist only "when no one of its component parts" is "susceptible of *removal* without *detriment* to the whole."

In other words, we are once more with Poe's favorite principle of unity. Only a unified plot is capable of imparting pleasure. Not that he would rule out all illustrative incident, or even digressive episodes; for in the hands of a skilful artist, such as Shakespeare, they become consequential underplots. In the hands of a Willis, however, they remain nothing but overloading, pure "fuss," and cause weariness and unintelligibility. Three-fourths of *Tortesa's* plot could be removed and not missed. Besides being, like Mrs. Mowatt, unoriginal and uninventive, Willis commits the even greater sin of permitting much of his hackneyed dramatic action to remain unmotivated. "In fact," concludes Poe, "the whole drama is exceedingly ill *motivirt*." This could not have happened had the author submitted his plot to the discipline of structure. For *every* plot, Poe tells us in "The Philosophy of Composition," if it is to be worth the name, "must be elaborated to its *dénouement* before anything be attempted with the pen. It is only with the *dénouement* constantly in view that we can give a plot its indispensable air of consequence, or causation. . . ."[8] Apparently neither Willis nor Mrs. Mowatt had the knowledge and skill to manage it.

And certainly not Longfellow in his feeble bid for dramatic attention. For his *Spanish Student* has no construction at all. It, of course, has other faults. Imitativeness is one; it constantly reminds us of something we have seen before. Bookishness is another; it abounds in literary allusions which require explanatory notes, and are objectionable because the drama, Poe reminds us, "demands that everything be . . . instantaneously evident"; notes to a play impress him only with the fact that their author is desirous of showing his reading. Then there is the matter of Longfellow's style, which is both tautological and ungrammatical. But these are ad-

---

[8] Another statement seems even more revealing of Poe's philosophy of composition: " I believe it is Montaigne who says — ' People talk about thinking, but, for my part, I never begin to think until I sit down to write.' A better plan for him would have been, never to sit down to write until he had made an end of thinking." (35)

mittedly minor faults. The major trouble with the
Spanish Student is that it is not a play at all. It may
have some merit as a poem, but as a play it does not exist.
In two final sentences Poe disposes of Longfellow's
dramatic effort tersely and neatly: "Let a poem be a
poem only; let a play be a play and nothing more. As
for 'The Spanish Student,' its thesis is unoriginal; its
incidents are antique; its plot is not plot; its characters
have no character: in short, it is little better than a play
upon words, to style it 'A Play' at all." (36)

   He knew of but one test for a play: that it be actable.
This is clear from the complimentary letter he wrote to
Sarah Josepha Hale in January, 1846. He has re-read
her *Ormond Grosvenor*, he tells her, and has become
confirmed in his first impression of the play's "vigor
and dramaticism. I not only think highly of this individual play, but deduce . . . that with earnest endeavor
in this walk of Literature, you would succeed far better
than any American in the composition of that rare work
of art, an effective *acting* play." (37) He then proceeds to advise her to curtail some of her dialogue.

5

   Poe has been accused of permitting at times personal
prejudice or expediency to influence his critical writings.
In the case of a few of his reviews of current books,
especially poetry, there is some truth in the accusation,
but it cannot apply to his writings on drama. Personal
motives did betray him once in a while to a digression,
or a *non sequitur* — as in his reference to Mrs. Ellet's
embonpoint (38) — but even in these cases the play he
was reviewing was, generally, bad and deserved the
castigation to which he subjected it. Certainly his charge

against Longfellow's characters cannot be ascribed to mere dislike of an eminent "Frogpondian." It is rather the expression of a judgment based on a cherished critical principle. Stage characters for Poe had to be human beings, consistent in behavior, plausible, "natural"; in other words, they had to be what we have since come to understand by the term "realistic." In this sense, Parrington's statement that Poe was the first of our critics is indeed true. For it was Poe who first rebelled against the conventional puppets with which the American playwright populated the stage. "There is not one particle of any nature," he wrote of *Fashion*, "beyond green-room nature in it. . . . Our fault finding," he added, "is on the score of deficiency in verisimilitude — in natural art — that is to say, in art based in the natural laws of man's heart and understanding."

These "natural laws" require, of course, that behavior on the stage be convincing, an end which a playwright can achieve only when his characters act in conformity with their natures. The weakness of Willis's characters is not only that they are negative — "The Duke is nobody; Falcone, nothing; Zippa, less than nothing" — but also that they are made to do things which violate their natures. The leading character, for instance, reforms in the end, without any preparation for such a change. The fact that the transformation is brought about by a dramatic twist which is older than the hills is reprehensible enough, but even more reprehensible is the lack of character motivation. "When," Poe says, "in the course of the *dénouement*, the usurer bursts forth into an eloquence virtue-inspired, we cannot sympathize heartily in his fine speeches, since they proceed from the mouth of the self-same egotist who . . . uttered so

9

many sotticisms . . . in the earlier passages of the play."

Poe cannot bring himself to accept violations of the principle of naturalism even where he obviously wishes to be generous. His sentiments toward Mrs. Frances Osgood are by now well-known and, as we have seen, involved him in embarrassing and unhappy situations. It was, therefore, only natural that he should begin a review of a work of hers with a tribute to her personal character, which is "one perpetual poem." But the work under review, *Elfrida*, bears the subtitle, "a Dramatic Poem, in five acts," and Poe could no more accept such an impossible combination from Mrs. Osgood than from Mr. Longfellow. Moreover, as drama — the embarrassed critic is obliged to admit — it is "faulty in the extreme," full of impossible situations and inconsequential incidents. And although the leading character is forcefully portrayed, the force displayed by the author is poetic rather than dramatic. Elfrida and the events narrated are not integrated to produce the singleness of effect which the good dramatist must strive for. "The object of poetry," Poe gently informs Mrs. Osgood, "is beauty"; while the object of drama "is the *portraiture of nature in human action and earthly incident*." (39)

Nor does the moral which the play attempts to preach redeem it as a work of art. Poe reminds Mrs. Osgood of the old adage that "there is a time for all things," and adds that it is not the office of drama — nor of poetry, for that matter — "to inculcate truth or virtue, unless incidentally." He then proceeds to lecture to the lady — and to the readers of *Godey's* — on the relationship between moral preachment and dramatic art. His lecture is so much a part of his persistent, almost single-handed effort to remove the "curse of the didactic" which afflicted the drama of his day — and, in fact, American literature in general — that the following quotation, lengthy though it be, seems unavoidable:

Now, the conveying of what is absurdly termed, "a moral," . . . should be left to the essayist and preacher. Those who uphold the value, in a moral point of view, of such absurdities as "George Barnwell," seem to us strangely paradoxical in their demands and expectations. "George Barnwell" is applauded for its "moral" — that is to say, for the impressiveness with which it conveys the *truth* that dissipation leads to crime and crime to punishment; but we are at a loss to understand how this truth, or how any truth can be conveyed by that which is in itself confessedly a lie. Does the fact that a dramatist *invented a fiction* that one George Barnwell was hung for robbing his uncle, tend to prove in any way that every man who robs his uncle will actually be hung? *It is not in the power of any fiction to inculcate any truth.* The truthfulness, the indispensable truthfulness of drama, has reference only to the fidelity with which it should depict nature, so far as regards her points, first, and, secondly, her general intention. Her arrangement or combination of points may be improved — that is to say, a greater number of striking points than are ever seen closely conjoined in reality, may, for artificial purposes be gathered into the action of a drama — provided always that there be no absolute controversion of nature's general intention. But all this is very different from the *inculcation of truth.* The drama, in a word, must be truthful without conveying the true — just as the brain, although the seat of sensation, is nearly, if not altogether, insensible itself.

It is clear that Poe was an early advocate of naturalism, of "fidelity" in depicting life on the stage; it is, however, equally clear that he was far from advocating the brand of naturalism which came into vogue some decades after Poe and has confined so much of the drama of our own day to photographic literalism. Poe never made the mistake of confusing the reality of art with that of life. "Arrangement," "combination," "artistical purposes"—these are terms which in the modern revolt against photographic sterility in the drama have become heated slogans. It is as if the critic of the 1840's, while leading a movement for a more naturalistic drama, one that would break with the conventions of Romantic melodrama and the theatricalities of Dion Boucicault, was at the same time adumbrating the many anti-naturalistic movements of the Twentieth century, the latest of which is being led, in the 1940's, by the Existentialist Jean-Paul Sartre.

It is only in the light of Poe's fullest statement of his critical criteria that we can begin to understand his enthusiasm for such a second-rate play as Bulwer-Lytton's *The Lady of Lyons*. Here was a tremendously popular melodrama which moved "rapidly and consequentially" and whose incidents were "skillfully wrought into execution." Its characters had the merit of being "natural," although, Poe admitted, they showed no marked individuality. Except one, Pauline, whom he defends against the charge made by other critics that she is weak, mercenary, and ignoble. What if she is? he asks. "We are not dealing with Clarissa Harlow. Bulwer has painted a woman." But the highest compliment he bestows upon Pauline is not that she possesses verisimilitude, but that she has been drawn with imagination, that she is a *creation*, one that would have done no dishonor to Shakespeare himself. (40) We may smile today at this implied comparison, but the fact remains that in the theatre of his day Poe could find but few examples of character portrayal combining dramatic skill with a semblance of reality.

The major trouble with the drama of the day, as Poe saw it, was its traditional imitativeness. Again and again he commented on the fact that while all the other arts had made an effort to retain some measure of originality and to develop new forms, the drama alone had remained stationary, "prating about Aeschylus and the Chorus, or mouthing Euphuism." This view he expressed most vigorously in an editorial article contributed to the New York *Evening Mirror* early in January, 1845, (41) under the title, "Does the Drama of the Day Deserve Support?" His answer was, of course, a categorical negative. Dramatic art being essentially imitative, one drama was apt to be fashioned too nearly after another; consequently, "there is less originality — less independence — less thought . . . less effort to keep up with the general movement of the time . . . more rank and arrant conventionality in the drama, than in any single thing in existence which aspires to the dignity of art." He would not admit that the drama had "declined"; it had simply not kept pace, like the other arts, with the spirit of the times.

He had but one remedy to suggest: The American playwright must discard all the old models. He must come to a realization that no public could be expected to continue supporting a drama teeming with absurd conventionalities and "monstrous inartisticalities." He must dare to bring his own thought to his craft, to apply "*principles* of dramatic composition founded in Nature, and in common sense." For "the common sense, even of the mob," Poe exclaims, "can no longer be affronted, night after night, with impunity."

More specifically, the two anachronisms of the soliloquy and the "aside," inherited from the Elizabethan theatre, must be abandoned. And it is with an attack on these, expressed in his most characteristic "magazinist" style, that Poe ends his editorial:

> If, for example, a playwright *will* persist in making a hero deliver a soliloquy upon the stage, such as no human being ever soliloquised in ordinary life, — ranting transcendentalism at the audience as nothing conceivable ever before ranted, short of a Piankitank candidate for Congress — splitting the ears of the house, and endangering the lives of the orchestra, the while that a confidential friend who holds him by the shoulder is supposed not to overhear a single syllable of all that is said: — if the playwright, we say, *will* persist in perpetrating these atrocities, and a hundred infinitely worse, for no better reason than that there were people silly enough to perpetrate them four or five hundred years ago — if he *will* do this, and will *not* do anything else to the end of Time — what right has *he* . . . to look any honest man in the face and talk to him about . . . "the decline of the drama?"

That he felt keenly on the subject is indicated by the fact that when he came to review *Fashion* some three months after the *Mirror* article, he continued to write in the same vein: "Will our playwrights never learn," he asked rhetorically, "that an audience under no circumstances can or will be brought to conceive that what is sonorous in their own ears at a distance of fifty feet from the speaker cannot be heard by an actor at the distance of one or two?" (42) And five months still later he began a marginal note in *Godey's* with the statement: "When I call to mind the preposterous 'asides' and soliloquies of the drama among civilized nations, the shifts employed by the Chinese playwrights appear altogether respectable." (43)

One cannot help recalling Poe's own play, *Politian*, which contains both soliloquies and "asides," and which he could have used as an illustration of all the absurdities against which he inveighed. Apparently in the decade between his attempt at playwriting and his work as dramatic critic he had thought much on the subject of the American drama and had evolved his naturalistic principles. Of the deeper possibilities of the soliloquy in dramatic technique he had no inkling. In spite of his intimate knowledge of *Hamlet*, he had overlooked its use by Shakespeare as a device for revealing the profoundest thoughts and impulses of character. There is not the slightest foreshadowing of its employment by, say, such a novelist as Melville, only half a decade later, in *Moby Dick*, in a way which, after Joyce, would become established as "the interior monologue." (44) And he surely did not envisage the possibility that three-quarters of a century later an American playwright, Eugene O'Neill, in *Strange Interlude*, would combine both the soliloquy and the "aside" into a new medium, adding a whole dimension to character portrayal on the stage.

For his own day, however, Poe was the critic the American stage needed at the moment. The fight for a realistic drama was just beginning, and required the services of a fearless, vigorous pen. Even Dion Boucicault, whose plays were one of Poe's pet aversions, had just made a contribution toward the "naturalizing" of the drama. His *London Assurance*—which Poe called "the most inane and utterly despicable of all modern comedies" (45)—had been produced with a ceiling over the stage, making the set look like a real room. Realism was beating behind the canvas walls, and plays with the breath and idiom of ordinary human experience were desperately needed. It seems strange that the man who in his own creative work showed all the tendencies toward a movement which we in our century have come to recognize as "Expressionism," the man who peopled his poems and stories with typically expressionistic forms, should, as a critic, champion realistic drama. Yet strange as it seems, it is nevertheless true that Edgar Allan Poe, the poet of Tamerlanes, Israfels, Conquering Worms, and misty mid-regions of Weir, was a capable *accoucheur* of the drama of commonsense and everyday life.

6

Poe's comments on production and acting were equally thoughtful and far in advance of the practices in the theatres of his day. He objected to the rectangular crossings and recrossings of characters on the stage; to their coming down to the footlights when important communications were to be made; to the reading of private letters in loud rhetorical tones. (46) In other words, he objected to the entire style of pre-naturalistic theatre. It was for this reason that he welcomed innovations in realistic staging; for, by creating the illusion of reality, such innovations sometimes succeeded in saving a bad play. "If," he predicted in his first review of *Fashion*, the play should succeed, "it will owe the greater portion of its success to the very carpets, the very ottomans, the very chandeliers, and the very conservatories" that made popular even such a play as Boucicault's *London Assurance.* He was discerning enough to differentiate between the dramatic qualities of a play and those imparted to it by an effective production. The fact that Boucicault's comedy had survived five hundred performances in a lavish mounting did not blind him to its insignificance as a play. (47)

Professor Odell, the annalist of the New York stage, has remarked that Poe reviewed *Fashion* with the effect of breaking a butterfly on the wheel. (48) The effect has evidently been greatly exaggerated, like the effect of dramatic criticism in general on the success or failure of plays in our own day. *Fashion* was a huge success in 1845, was revived professionally as recently as 1929, and is still being played from time to time in our community and college theatres. This, of course, constitutes no reflection on Poe's judgment, any more than the popularity of *Abie's Irish Rose*, a short while ago, was a reflection on contemporary dramatic critics, nearly all of whom felt that this stage confection could hardly be called a specimen of noble drama. Nor was the effect of Poe's other "animadversions" as catastrophic as we may be inclined to suppose. It is certain that *The Taming of the Shrew* has survived, in spite of Poe's belief that the whole design of Shakespeare's comedy was "not only unnatural but an arrant impossibility"—because, explained Poe, "The heart of no woman could ever have been reached by brute violence." (49) It would seem that this was spoken by the Virginia gentleman of the 1840's no less than by the dramatic critic. However, an imitation of Shakespeare's *Shrew*, produced at Niblo's under the title of *Katharine and Petruchio*, has not survived. The *Broadway Journal's* critic dismissed it as "absolutely beneath contempt—a mere jumble of unmeaning rant, fuss, whip-smacking, crockery-cracking, and other Tom-Foolery of a similar kind." (50)

That Poe's interest in theatrical production was not a sudden acquisition, in maturity, is indicated by some of the items he included in "Pinakidia," published in the *Southern Literary Messenger* as early as 1836. In one such item he noted Von Raumer's mention of an optical representation of the banquet scene in *Macbeth* by means of a shadowy figure thrown into the chair of Banquo. The idea had been conceived by Enslen, a German optician, and Poe mentioned it with approval because it could be "accomplished without difficulty" and because it produced an "intense effect upon the audience." In another item he took Voltaire to task for boasting of having introduced the Roman senate on the stage in red mantles and for having misunderstood the Greek use of masks. (51) It is logical to assume that Poe's interest in production methods and effects ante-dated the writing of "Pinakidia." Very likely it went as far back as his school-days, for surely the boy Edgar who had founded and directed a Thespian society could not have been without curiosity about ways and means of staging plays. From those early days to the days of his maturity his interest in production remained fresh and enthusiastic. As an established critic he testified that "the usual outcry against 'stage-effects,' as being mere-tricious, has no foundation in reason." (52)

For the mature dramatic critic, however, the play came first; then, the production; and, finally, the acting. He was ready to defend acting as a profession and as high art on every occasion, but no actor could hope to receive his commendation unless he possessed talent. "The actor of talent," he wrote in his famous defense of Mrs. Mowatt, "is poor at heart, indeed, if he do not look with contempt upon the mediocrity even of a king." (53) On the other hand, the actor of no talent, like Mrs. Mowatt's leading man, could expect nothing but contempt from Mr. Poe. "In Ruy Gomez," he wrote, "Mr. Crisp was intolerable." This referred to the leading character in Planché's *Faint Heart Never Won Fair Lady*. Mr. Crisp was intolerable because he had failed to understand the character he was presumed to represent. According to Poe, Ruy Gomez, "as designed by Planché, is a dashing, ardent, chivalric cavalier, urged to extreme audacity by the madness of his passion, but preserving through all a true dignity," while Mr. Crisp "makes him an impudent trickster — at times even a vulgar chuckling mountebank — occasionally a simpering buffoon." (54)

Lack of understanding, and, consequently, doing violence to the playwright's conception, was the unforgivable crime. The opposite was therefore deserving of the award of merit. The first of Mrs. Mowatt's virtues as an actress is that her "conceptions of character are good." This is indispensable but, of course, not enough. Mrs. Mowatt is also dowered with excellent elocution, with an expressive countenance, general beauty, marvellous self-possession, a queenly step, and a grace of manner which, in Poe's opinion, has never been equalled on the stage. Above all, she possesses the essential quality of enthusiasm — which is "an unaffected freshness of the heart, the capacity not only to think but to *feel*." (55)

This was his considered judgment after observing her acting a number of times. When he had first seen her, as Pauline in Bulwer-Lytton's *The Lady of Lyons*, he noted down minor qualities of physical and temperamental equipment for the stage. Her figure, slight but "eminently graceful"; her not unintellectual forehead; her grey, brilliant, and expressive eyes; her well-formed Roman nose [9] and energetic chin; her largish mouth,

_____

[9] Apparently a well-formed nose, "with the Roman curve," was for

brilliant and even teeth, and flexible, expressive lips; her radiantly beautiful smile, the like of which he did not remember ever having seen before; and, finally, her profusion of rich auburn hair. (56) That this appreciation of sheer physical beauty was not confined to the appeal of a particular woman is clear from Poe's remarks about other actresses, such as this comment about Miss Horne, one of the performers in *Fashion*: "She sets at naught all criticism in winning all hearts. There is about her lovely countenance a radiant *earnestness* of expression which is sure to play a Circean trick with the judgment of every person who beholds it." (57) And even more than feminine beauty, Poe, like all critics of acting, could not help appreciating the importance to an actor of an adequate physical equipment for his exacting career. Thus among the talents for which he admired his friend Murdoch — talents which included the comprehension of "the whole *rationale* of elocution," — he was careful to list the possession of physical powers which enabled Murdoch to give effect to his conceptions. Although Poe realized that this "best elocutionist in America" was "somewhat" deficient in naturalness, there was ample compensation in his "effective delivery and grace of gesture." (58)

    These laudatory comments run counter to the popular belief that Poe was *always* a bitter, mean, and can-

Poe an indication of more than energy; it also bespoke high-born quality, and was aesthetically beautiful. He used the terms "Roman" and "Hebrew" interchangeably. Thus the heroine of what he considered his best story, "Ligeia," is the possessor of a nose of such perfection as to remind him of "the graceful medallions of the Hebrews." And Roderick Usher, the hero of what critics generally consider his best story, is endowed with a nose "of a delicate Hebrew model." Usher, it is also interesting to note, is just as generally accepted as a self-portrait of the author.

tankerous critic, a belief based mainly on Griswold's spiteful Memoir.[10] They show a man with definite enthusiasms, with the capacity — in his own phrase — "not only to think but to *feel*." It is true, however, that his services to the American drama and theatre were perhaps greater by virtue of his indignant rejection of the cheap, the meretricious, and the mediocre. His vocabulary in dispraise of the talentless and unworthy was pointed and picturesque. We have already noted his dismissal of Mr. Crisp with the one massive word "intolerable." Similarly he polished off an actress at Niblo's with the one statement that "Miss Taylor spoke and stepped more like a chambermaid than a princess." (59)

And sometimes his keenest shafts were aimed not at the actors, nor at the production, but at the one element in the theatre which critics dared not then — nor often dare today — attack: the public. He was sure that Willis's *Tortesa* was a bad play but he predicted a successful run for it nevertheless, because it had many points "well calculated to tell with a conventional audience." (60) *The Honeymoon*, he remarked in another review, "is a wretched affair, which has been unluckily saved to the stage (for its sins) by a number of sparkling points well adapted to tell with audiences too ill-cultivated to estimate merit otherwise than in detail." (61) Or he wrote a dead-pan one-sentence review, such as this " At the Chatham, a vast number of

[10] See, for instance, *Poe as a Literary Critic*, by the Virginia novelist John Esten Cooke, a manuscript recently discovered in a private collection and published by the Johns Hopkins Press (1946) for the Edgar Allan Poe Society of Baltimore. This essay is obviously founded on Griswold, but revisions indicate that as more objective knowledge of Poe became available Mr. Cooke, an honest gentleman, felt impelled to tone down his earlier Griswoldian harshness.

people without coats [this review appeared in August], have been thrown into raptures by the representation of 'The Female Horsethief,' in which the leading character is one Margaret Catchpole, and the leading incident her riding *en homme* a very lazy and very stupid little horse." (62)

7

Poe's interests were wide and varied and his self-confidence was abundant. The theatre, as he understood it, included many artistic activities besides the production of drama. It included, at the lower level, vaudeville and the circus, and, at the higher level, music, ballet, and grand opera. Thus he reports that at Castle Garden the public is well entertained by Herr Cline performing on a tight rope. (63) At the same theatre, he reports on another occasion, "the chief attraction has been the admirable dancing of Mademoiselle Desjardins. Since Ellsler," he adds, "we have had no one more graceful." (64) Of another dancer he wrote: "I should not say, of Taglioni, exactly that she dances, but that she laughs with her arms and legs." (65)

We have seen that, in his review of *Antigone*, he did not hesitate to pass judgment on the music of Mendelssohn, the conducting of Loder, and the singing of the chorus. If, at times, he seemed modest enough to content himself with a general comment on the production of an opera, and to refer the reader to the music department for more specialized criticism — as in the case of *La Juive*, presented at the Park Theatre by a French troupe (66) — it was because there was a clear understanding on the *Broadway Journal* that Mr. Henry C. Watson was "in entire control of the Musical department." (67) Even Mr. Poe — or, perhaps, especially

Mr. Poe — must have known by this time that the toes of department heads — literary, theatrical or musical — were very sensitive. Yet he managed to wedge in a musical remark now and then, such as that Pico was singing at Castle Garden, "delightfully, of course." (68)[11]

Besides, there were other publications and other departments in which he could express his opinions, general and specific, on music. In at least two marginal notes he expounds his philosophy of indefiniteness as an essential element of "true musical expression." (70) In another note, contributed to the *Democratic Review*, he discusses the philosophy and science of music. He admits that his acquaintance with eminent composers is limited, but it is sufficient to convince him that few of the "so-called scientific musicians" know anything about acoustics and mathematical deductions. They look blank when such a well-informed person as himself happens to mention the mechanism of the *Sirène* or to allude to the oval vibrations at right angles. (71) In still another note, published in the *Southern Literary Messenger*, he quotes Mozart's death-bed statement that he "began to see what *may* be done in music" and remarks that "it is to be hoped that De Meyer and the rest of the spasmodists will, eventually, begin to understand what may *not* be done in this particular branch of the Fine Arts." (72)

[11] He had had a better chance as a book reviewer in this respect. When, for instance, half a decade earlier, he reviewed the *Memoirs and Letters of Madame Malibran* for *Burton's Gentleman's Magazine*, he spread himself on the subject of singing, discussing learnedly such matters as the range of Malibran's voice, embracing "three complete octaves, extending from the contralto D to the upper soprano D," and the effect of melodic transitions "from the *voce di petto* to the *voce di testa*." He pronounced the cantatrice unequaled as an actress because of her apparent absence of acting. (69)

It is important to add that for Poe music was related to acting in that it was essentially a collaborative, or public, activity. Much as he loved music — and he often referred to it as one of his "passions" — he did not believe that a musician, anymore than an actor, could derive the fullest satisfaction from performing, unless there was an audience to hear him. Coming upon a statement of Marmontel's that music is the only talent which an artist can enjoy by himself, Poe adds: "No more than any other *talent*, is that for music susceptible of complete enjoyment, where there is no second party to appreciate its exercise." (73)

It was this "second party" which Poe found essential to the well-being, to the very existence of the artist — musical, literary, or dramatic. This view was undoubtedly a reflection of Poe's own habit as an artist: before he himself could function creatively he always envisaged an audience. In a way, it was an audience which was the real instrument upon which he played. He had played upon it as a boy Thespian, as a lieutenant in the Richmond Volunteers, as an orator at the University of Virginia, as a Drum-Major at West Point, and as a literary histrio afterwards. He now played upon it as a dramatic critic, as a lecturer at Lyceums, and as an elocutionist in literary salons. It may be said of him with justice that all of his creative activities partook of the theatre and colored his principles and philosophy of art.

For the theatre has no existence without an audience. And not alone for the performer — who has only a public life, in the Henry Jamesian sense — but for the listener as well. Half of the latter's pleasure, Poe pointed out, is derived not from the performance but from his consciousness of being part of an audience. Poe illustrated his point by means of an incident which had occurred at the Park Theatre when an eccentric gentleman found himself the solitary occupant of box, pit, and gallery. Had he been permitted to remain he would have derived "but little enjoyment from his visit," said Poe. "It was an act of mercy to turn him out." (74) And without audience response, participation, effect, Poe's own work is not completely understandable. He once wrote a little essay on the art of conversation, an art of which, we have observed, he was a proficient practitioner. "To converse well," the little item begins, "we need the cool tact of talent—to talk well the glowing *abandon* of genius." There is no question as to which qualification he believed himself to possess. Nevertheless he was aware that his own talk was not always the performance of genius. That was apparently when his particular audience at the moment was not cooperating. Perhaps this offers an explanation, partially at least, of the contradictory reports about him we have received from his contemporaries: on the one hand, enthusiastic testimony of his sparkling conversation, of his brilliance and warmth; on the other hand, no less authentic but equally positive testimony of his aloofness and sullenness. "Men of *very* high genius," he wrote in his short essay, "talk at one time *very* well, at another *very* ill:—well, when they have full time, full scope, and a sympathetic listener." (75) The last was obviously essential to a performer like Poe.

8

But to return to the scholarly gentleman who aspired to rescue American stage criticism from the hands of those who were neither scholarly nor gentlemen. A modern essayist has characterized Poe as "the Mencken and Nathan and Burton Rascoe of his day all mixed together in one hell's brew." (76) This is clever and contains a certain amount of truth, but it is not entirely fair to Poe. He was, like the three gentlemen mentioned, a severe critic with a sharp style; in some instances, he may even have justified the complaint of his friend and admirer, Dr. Thomas Holley Chivers, that he, Poe, used the tomahawk instead of the pruning-knife, with which he not only lopped off redundant limbs but eradicated the entire tree. (77) Poe, I am sure, like the three modern critics of tomahawk-wielding propensities, might have countered that, in some instances eradication of the entire tree was precisely what was needed. At any rate, as a dramatic critic Poe was in many ways a prophet and a champion of the type of drama and theatre we have, at their best, today, and his dramatic reviews were indeed, as one historian of American literary criticism has noted, "easily seventy-five years in advance of his time." (78)

He believed in realistic drama, containing plots whose plausibility could be tested by experience in real rather than stage life. He demanded characters that should be human beings rather than stage puppets. He advocated the abandonment of outworn dramaturgic traditions and models which no longer had any validity for a theatre which had changed both physically and intellectually. At a time when our native drama was held in contempt by critics and public alike, he preached the doctrine that "to Americans the American drama is the special point of interest," (79) and if the American drama today is accorded the critical dignity of being accepted as a reflection of American life, no little credit is due to the vision and courage of the plain-speaking Mr. Poe.[12]

Another and perhaps keener type of vision was required to foresee the ultimate emergence of a type of stage vehicle which, Poe predicted, might have to be designated merely as "a play," because the older classifications — "tragedy, comedy, farce, opera, pantomime, melodrama, or spectacle" — would no longer apply to it. He welcomed this phenomenon in anticipation, believing that such a play would be able to "retain some portion of the idiosyncratic excellencies of each" of the other *genres*, while introducing "a new class of excellence as yet unnamed because as yet undreamed of in the world." (81) One is justified in assuming that Poe would have greeted heartily such "a play" as Chekhov's *Cherry Orchard*, which the author called a comedy but which the public insists on accepting as a tragedy, or Maxwell Anderson's *Knickerbocker Holiday*, which the author called a musical comedy but which the public thinks of as a serious drama.

He insisted on acting based on direct observation of nature rather than on hackneyed theatrical routine. Had he been able to he would have cleared the temple of tricksters and pretenders. He believed that acting was "a profession which . . . embraces all that can elevate and ennoble," (82) and if the American actor today finds himself respected as the practitioner of a dignified art, we must again grant a certain measure of credit to the "atrabiliar" Mr. Poe.

---

[12] Of the obligation on the part of the American critic to be plain-spoken, Poe's own words are a sufficient justification: "It is folly to assert, as some at present are fond of asserting, that the Literature of any nation or age was ever injured by plain speaking. . . . As for American Letters, plain-speaking about *them* is, simply, the one thing needed." (80)

Here too — in the art of acting — his clear vision enabled him to foresee future developments. In fact, he adumbrated some of the theories, now widely practiced in the theatres of the world, of Constantin Stanislavsky. The great charm which Mrs. Mowatt's acting had for him he attributed to her naturalism and to her ability to speak and move with "a well-controlled impulsiveness as different as can be conceived from the customary rant and cant — the hack conventionality of the stage." (83) His vocabulary of acting values — "naturalism," "well-controlled," "seeming impulsiveness" — reads as though it appeared in *My Life in Art*, which John Gielgud has called the modern actor's Bible.

Critics of Poe have found many shortcomings in his poetry, fiction, and literary essays; they have accused him of overestimating his creative powers and accomplishments. Only a few of them, however, have taken the precaution to examine his dramatic criticism. They could not fail to be impressed with his services to the American stage. He once remarked that the business of the critic is "so to soar that he shall *see the sun*, even though its orb be far below the horizon." (84) Here at least, in the field of dramatic criticism, he did not overestimate himself. In the light of both what preceded him and what followed him, it is clear that when Mr. Edgar Allan Poe, son of strolling players, but proud gentleman of Virginia nonetheless, walked along Broadway he saw the sun.

CHAPTER IV

RED PAINT AND BLACK PATCHES

"Most . . . poets . . . would positively shudder at letting
the public take a peep behind the scenes, at . . . the
cock's feathers, the red paint and the black patches, which
. . . constitute the properties of the literary *histrio*."

A QUARTER of a century ago George Moore invited to his home in London two of his literary
friends, John Freeman and Walter De La Mare, and
proceeded to expound to them his theory of "pure"
poetry, which he defined as "something that the poet
creates outside of his own personality." (1) The result
of their discussion was an anthology which begins with
John Skelton and ends with Swinburne. It is significant
that Poe is represented by no less than six poems, a
number exceeded only by Shakespeare, Blake, and
Shelley. Almost seventy years before Mr. Moore's anthology another British editor, James Hannay, published
a volume of poems — all by Poe — prefaced by an introduction in which he stated that, in his opinion, Poe
wrote "sheer" poetry, a species which borrowed "nothing from without, as didactic poetry does." (2) One
may question both theories which inspired these seemingly contradictory judgments and yet, as applied to
Poe, find them helpful.

According to Moore the outstanding characteristic of
Poe's poetry was objectivity; according to Hannay, it is
a lack of didacticism. Apparently they are speaking, at

least to some extent, of the same thing; and while "pure" and "sheer" are not precisely synonymous, the adjectives represent an attempt to convey the idea that Poe's poetry is not dependent on topicality, morality, opinion, or so-called philosophy. Like music, it is content to merely be. Perhaps we get closer to the meaning of these terms by recalling A. E. Housman's belief that the function of poetry in general is "not to transmit thought" but only "to transfuse emotion." "The Haunted Palace," for instance, appeals to Housman as one of Poe's best poems only "so long as we are content to swim in the sensations it evokes and only vaguely to apprehend the allegory." (3) In short, although it is almost impossible to separate the content and form of a poem — the thing said from the manner of saying it — Poe's poetry, at its best, is all form.

The achievement of form is not easy. With Poe the process was a conscious one. There is, as an example, the difference between the formlessness of "Al Aaraaf," an early "philosophical" poem, and the structural firmness of "The Raven" or "The Bells," both written in the Forties. Allowing for Poe's propensity to exaggerate when he claimed that he wrote "Al Aaraaf" when he was only ten years old, (4) we must nevertheless accept the poem as having been composed when he was in his 'teens, when his mind, like that of any talented young poet, was teeming with ideas. His sense of form had not yet matured; his theories of poetry had not yet become crystallized. The poem strives to convey a "meaning" or, what is more likely, a host of meanings. These remain diffuse, unorganized, unsubordinated to the less tangible meaning of the poem as a whole. Twenty years later he has learned to begin with the

preconceived effect he wishes to produce, rather than
with ideas; he labors to achieve totality of impression,
poetic coherence. Form has become his " message " or
" meaning," and " ideas," as such, are no longer important.

And it is as form that his poetry has had its greatest
effect on modern literature. No one who has read the
studies of Léon Lemonnier and Camille Mauclair (5)
can fail to be impressed with the extent of Poe's influence on French literature; and no less impressive is even
such a brief glimpse of his influence on the literatures
of other lands as is afforded us by the papers contributed
to the symposium sponsored by the Edgar Allan Poe
Society of Baltimore several years ago. (6) All the
literary creations of Poe — his poetry, his fiction, and his
criticism — have helped to spread his enormous influence, but since, for the moment, I am concerned only
with his poetry, it is important to remember that it was
" le poète par excellence " whom Paul Valéry extolled
and that it was the American poet's lyrics which the
Russian Valery Brusov hailed as " one of the most marvelous phenomena of world literature," marvelous because they embodied " an unapproachable high in verbal
art." (7) For another Russian, the Symbolist poet Con-
stantine Balmont, Poe was " the adored singer of songs,
the most star-like of all troubadours of eternity." (8)
With less rhapsodic and more scholarly insight, Professor Pedro Salinas, a poet of note himself, attributes Poe's
influence on Spanish American poetry to his magic with
words and sounds. Poe was the man

who had changed rhythms and tones in English poetic language. And . . . the poets of Spanish America who were
attempting a like revolution in Spanish poetic language, saw in

Edgar Allan Poe the great figure of a revolutionary poet, of an innovator — perhaps the first spiritual conqueror of Europe, the first American poet to teach the old world a lesson in poetry. (9)

And even a carping critic of Poe, our own Ludwig Lewisohn, grants him the possession of one pure gift — the gift of verbal music. "The music of 'To One in Paradise,'" he remarks, "has an enchantment that no analysis can deaden or destroy." (10)

But what precisely was this gift? Hundreds of studies have been attempted of Poe's versification, of his rhymes, rhythms, stanzaic forms, his use of consonants and vowels, of tone-color and synesthetic effects;[1] the result has been to leave us, in the main, no wiser than before. Even so subtle an analyst as Paul Elmer More, despite his belief that Poe survived as "chiefly the poet of unripe boys and unsound men," found himself obliged to resort to such mystic phrases as "pure evocative quality" and "opiate magic" in commenting on certain lines and cadences. (12) It seems impossible, even for the most cautious critics, to escape Poe's "magic," "music," "enchantment" or "lulling cadences."

Yet it is evident that Poe's critics — both approving and disapproving — are also aware of a quality of coldness, dryness (the *sécheresse* to which Barbey d'Aurevilly called attention), or artificiality somewhere beneath or above the magic. Sometimes this quality creeps in between lines of great beauty, like little plots of sterile earth in the midst of a green field. Sometimes it perme-

---

[1] " . . . his employment of synesthetic effects has extended the sensuous appeal of poetry beyond any other device adopted, perhaps, in its history . . . it took genius to see the advantages of deliberately mixing [sense impressions], so that one could write of the 'grey rumble of the dawn' or the 'yellow cry of the beetles.'" — Oscar Cargill. (11)

ates a whole poem. During the discussion at George Moore's home Walter De La Mare raised the question of the possible inclusion of "The Bells" in the projected anthology. "A trick! A trick!" cried John Freeman, and the poem was rejected. Such "tricks" are many in Poe's slim corpus of poetic creations. Perhaps that was what Walt Whitman felt when he said that Poe's verses belonged among the electric lights of imaginative literature, brilliant and dazzling but without heat. (13) Unmistakably, they are the productions of a poet; they are also — and equally unmistakably — the work of a mechanician. Commenders and contemners alike have often observed this duality in the creativeness of Poe, and have commended or contemned to the extent to which they have been able to remember the one and forget the other. More often, however, they have labored under the necessity of explaining the "problem," of reconciling the two disparate elements, and of effecting a synthesis. In this they have not entirely succeeded.

Paul Elmer More was inclined to accept Poe's own account of the mechanical way in which he wrote "The Raven." Poe, he reasoned, was a person who combined nervous irritability with rigorous intellectual analysis; hence it seemed plausible that he could "put together" a poem, even one which is deeply emotional, "like a piece of calculated machinery." Poe's *conscious* logical analysis, Mr. More believed, "was present with him throughout the whole work of composition to an abnormal degree, now preceding, now accompanying, now following the more inscrutable suggestions of the creative faculty." (14) This is an appealing theory. Yet a thorough knowledge of Poe's life and character suggests other possibilities no less appealing. The most likely of these is that of Henry Seidel Canby who is convinced that while the theme of "The Raven" came from the poet's deepest experience, its form was nothing but technical trickery. "The Raven," Mr. Canby insists, "whatever its inception, was undoubtedly tuned up for the show-off of elocution by precisely the methods described in 'The Philosophy of Composition.'" (15)

2

One may be less positive than Mr. Canby that the methods which Poe described in "The Philosophy of Composition" were in every detail precisely those he used in creating "The Raven," and still find the suggestion about the technique of the poem illuminating. Not only "The Raven" but the essay as well was very likely "tuned up for the show-off" — not of elocution, in the latter case, but of the powers of ratiocination and artistic logic of the brilliant essayist. Each piece of writing was for Poe a separate performance and had its own laws of effect.[2] The grieving, elocuting hero of "The Raven" remains on the stage, seated in his violet-cushioned chair or standing before the purple-draped windows; the intellectually sharp and defiantly honest hero of "The Philosophy of Composition" — its author,

---

[2] Horace Gregory has called attention to another essay, "The Poetic Principle," which Poe used as a "lecture" or public performance. "It can be said that the lecture itself resembled a series of delicately timed dramatic entrances and scenes, each bringing to a close its moment of suspense by the recitation of an unfamiliar piece of verse. . . . Between the silent pauses of surprise — and perhaps an approving hand-clap from his audience — one almost hears Poe's *apologie pour mon vie* . . . though I suspect that Poe's eloquent use of . . . passionately abstract terms bewildered the ladies and their gentlemen who heard them. I am nearly certain that his utterance flattered their ability to understand and to applaud them. . . ." — *Partisan Review*, May-June, 1943.

"I" — stays behind the scenes, at least part of the time, but makes himself none the less visible. Both owe much of the effect they know so well how to create — and know that they are creating — to the same lights and shadows among which Elizabeth and David Poe had once lived. Note the gusto and the vocabulary of the following paragraph:

I have often thought how interesting a magazine paper might be written by any author who would — that is to say who could — detail, step by step, the processes by which any of his compositions attained its ultimate point of completion. Why such a paper has never been given to the world, I am much at a loss to say — but, perhaps, the autorial vanity has had more to do with the omission than any one other cause. Most writers — poets in especial — prefer having it understood that they compose by a species of fine frenzy — an ecstatic intuition — and would positively shudder at letting the public take a peep behind the scenes, at the elaborate and vacillating crudities of thought — at the true purposes seized only at the last moment — at the innumerable glimpses of idea that arrived not at the maturity of full view — at the fully matured fancies discarded in despair as unmanageable — at the cautious selections and rejections — at the painful erasures and interpolations — in a word, at the wheels and pinions — the tackle for scene-shifting — the step-ladders and demon-traps — the cock's feathers, the red paint and the black patches, which in ninety-nine cases out of the hundred, constitute the properties of the literary *histrio*. (16)

The delivery is quite clearly that of a histrio; and we need not inquire into the source of the images in the culminating part of the monologue. We are back again in the theatre.

And it is here that we can find the most convincing indication that Poe's duality was neither something mystical nor paradoxical, but a typical phenomenon which every talented actor has displayed, whether he has known it or not. A perfect instance has been left us by Feodor Chaliapin in his autobiography. The Russian basso — of whom it was sometimes said that had he lost his superb singing voice he might still have been one of the world's great dramatic actors — was at one time playing Sousanin in *A Life for the Tzar*; the moment came when he cried out: "I have been ordered to go, and must obey!" and a little later, holding his daughter in his arms, he sang:

> "Do not grieve, my dearest child,
> Do not weep, my dearest daughter . . . ."

Suddenly he became aware that tears were trickling down his cheeks. Chaliapin's comment on this occurrence is instructive:

At first I paid no attention to them, thinking that it was Sousanin who wept, but suddenly I was aware that, instead of the agreeable tones of my voice, a kind of plaintive bleating sound was issuing from my throat. I was horrified and immediately realized that it was I, Chaliapin, who was weeping for pity, that, too poignantly moved by Sousanin's grief, I was shedding futile tears. I pulled myself together in an instant and recovered my self-control. "Not too much sensibility, old man," said the critic in me; "leave your Sousanin to his own sorrows, and sing and act as well as you can. . . ."

Chaliapin was one of the geniuses of the stage who think deeply about their art and understand its processes. His own summary of the actor's duality is fully as instructive as his recollection of the embarrassing moment:

Here the actor is confronted with an extremely difficult problem: he is faced with the necessity of being two people at the same time. . . . When I am singing, the character that I am creating is always present in my mind. It never for an

instant leaves me. I sing and listen, I act and take notice.
I am never alone on the stage. Two Chaliapins are always
there. One of them plays his part, the other watches him
play it. (17)

It is safe to say that there were always two Poes, one
playing his part as poet, as story-teller, or as critic, the
other watching him play it. What appeared to Paul
Valéry as the combination of "a sort of mathematics
with a sort of mysticism" was in reality a form of art
which the best stage histrios have practiced since the
theatre began. Poe, being conscious of the process involved, and being, in his own way, honest, plainly admitted it, even flaunted it. He brought "The Raven"
to its completion, he said, "with the precision and rigid
consequence of a mathematical problem." (18) Moreover, no one, he believed, could appreciate thoroughly
a work of genius who is himself without the constructive ability—"the faculty of analysis"—to get a full
view of the artist's proposed effect, "and thus work it
and regulate it at will." (19)

Poe, as his short stories testify, was a master of décor,
and this mastery did not desert him when he wrote
poetry. In considering the locale for the action of "The
Raven"—which is really a little drama, or monodrama,
in verse form—he discarded the idea of using a forest
or a field, because he felt that "a close *circumscription
of space*" was "absolutely necessary to the effect of in-
sulated incident." Such a setting, he knew, had "the
force of a frame to a picture." (20) It was, perhaps,
statements like the last one which had led Robert Sully
to forming the opinion that Poe had "an eye for dramatic, but not for scenic or artistic effect." Except in
"The Raven," Sully could find nowhere in Poe's poems

a subject for a picture. (21) As a matter of fact, however, Poe had an excellent eye for scenic effect; only it was the effect produced by stage scenery. The picture frame he spoke of in his "Philosophy of Composition," whether he was conscious of it or not at the moment, was the proscenium of a stage, which he immediately proceeded to fill with functional and decorative furniture, properties, and "action" — a door and latticed window for tapping and rapping, a fireplace with the glow of dying embers, rustling purple curtains, a bust of Pallas, "quaint" tomes necessitating a quietly ornate table on which to recline, a velvet-covered chair, a lamp, strange, improbable shadows on the floor, and a rug which would permit tinkling foot-steps to "register."

It is necessary to recall for a moment the little story about the meeting of the young playwright, Cornelius Mathews, with Poe at the Park Theatre with which I began the preceding chapter. According to Mathews, Poe advised him to incorporate into the play he was then writing a scene showing a raven flitting across the stage over the head of the hero's mother. Mathews rejected the advice, for reasons on which his story is silent. A plausible supposition would be that he may not have found it relevant to his projected play. Poe, however, may have been right and the scene he suggested might have proved very effective. He knew the truth which so many young playwrights only discover, if at all, after much fumbling: that drama has its own logic and relevance. The appearance of the raven — while not so organic a bit of symbolism as Chekhov's sea gull — might have heightened the tone of foreboding and terror. Perhaps it would have been only another "trick," a product of Fancy rather than Imagination, in the Coleridgean sense. Nevertheless, for a play about witchcraft, it might have been right; it might have added a touch of stage magic.

And it is as the master of just such magic that Poe becomes comprehensible. We may inveigh, as one critic does, against his "glaring defects"; we may call him "vulgar, affected, sentimental, and trite"; we may describe his poetic properties as "fashionable furniture and bric-a-brac"; but we are compelled to admit that his "symbolical raven lasts." (22) And it lasts because the poem is precisely what W. C. Brownell, another of Poe's severe critics, once called it: a star performance. (23)

3

No less lasting have been the symbolical bells. Admittedly the most "mechanical" of Poe's poems, "The Bells" has been generally accepted as an experiment in onomatopoeia, an experiment so successful that Stoddard, who was usually no more friendly to Poe than Brownell, was moved to declare that he considered this poem the most perfect example of Poe's power of words, "if not, indeed, the most perfect example of that kind of power in all poetic literature." (24) Another editor called it a "melodious *onomato-poem*, the most perfect imitation in word, sound, and rhythm, in suggestion, in exquisite mimicry, of its theme ever written." (25) The encomiums have been many and fervid. And so have been the detractions.

The latter have been confined mainly to pointing out the poem's lack of substance and the artificial manner in which it was conceived and executed. The story of its origin, at the home of Mrs. Shew who suggested the then ringing bells of the neighborhood as the subject of a poem is too well known to need repetition here. Poe immediately wrote the first draft, which he later revised and enlarged. The structure, consisting of four stanzas, each centering around a particular set of bells — the silver bells of sledges, the golden wedding bells, the brazen alarum bells, and the iron bells of death — is simplicity itself. In fact, it is so simple that some thirty years ago an English professor proved to his own satisfaction that high-school boys, using an arithmetical formula, could construct a poem on the same subject presumably no worse than Poe's. (26)

What the professor failed to see is that even though his opinion that "The Bells" is a mechanical, "head-made" poem be true, no boy, unless he be dowered with the gifts of a Poe, could have created it or anything like it. Mrs. Shew may have suggested the subject, she may even have written (as she claimed) the first line or two, but it takes more than a subject to produce a poem. Moreover, there is ample evidence to justify the belief that the idea of using bells as a subject was in Poe's mind long before Mrs. Shew felt inspired. There is Woodberry's suggestion that a passage in Chateaubriand's *Génie du Christianisme*, published in 1836, supplied the spark. There is Poe's own statement to his friend F. W. Thomas that Dickens's *Chimes* furnished the "final inspiration." And, then there is the possibility that the many poems on bells which appeared in the periodicals of the day may have started him off. (27) A poet's mind is a dark, mysterious reservoir. It took John Livingston Lowes years of research to trace the ideas that gave rise to a few of Coleridge's poems, and it is still doubtful if *The Road to Xanadu*, in which Mr.

Lowes so brilliantly set down his findings, exhausts all the clues.

But whatever ideas may have inspired "The Bells," or whatever ideas it may have acquired during composition and successive revisions, the poem shows remarkable craftsmanship. If sound be its outstanding characteristic it is certainly more than sound imitative of other sound. Undoubtedly it was written — like all of Poe's poems — to be read aloud. His ear was extraordinarily sensitive and it heard every word he wrote, both prose and verse. Verse, however, was more important, because, by his own confession, poetry with him was not a purpose but a passion. (28) His criticism of the poetry of other writers may sometimes have been excessively minute, almost petty, but his sensitive response to rhythm, to the melodious line and the musical phrase cannot be questioned. For him music was a prime quality in poetry; he believed this to such an extent that he deplored the very necessity which obliges the poet to use words at all; and he appreciated verse only as "an inferior or less capable Music." (29) Since, however, the necessity does exist, he arrived at the more dignified and face-saving definition of the poetry of words as the rhythmical creation of beauty.

The word "rhythmical" was the core of his definition. It is not surprising therefore to find that metrics should have been so vital and constant a subject for his study and speculation. Early in his career — in December, 1835 — he boasted to Nathaniel Beverley Tucker that he had made prosody, in all the languages which he had studied, "a particular subject of inquiry." (30) Iambs, trochees, dactyls, anapests, spondees, long vowels and short vowels, alliteration and assonance, and medial and

11

terminal rhymes were, for him, more than devices for adornment, more than mere frills; they were means by which the poet approaches as closely as possible to music. He envied the old bards who perfected their verses by reciting them or singing them as songs. (31) And although, as I have already noted in this book, such "modern" young men as Basil Gildersleeve and John Esten Cooke were unfavorably impressed by his emphasis of rhythm in public readings of his poems, the rhythm is there and is undoubtedly a major reason for the innumerable musical settings to the poems that have been created by composers great and small, including Rachmaninoff, MacDowell, Lazare Saminsky, Sir Arthur Sullivan, Joseph Holbrooke, and John Philip Sousa.[3]

While men like Gildersleeve and Cooke failed to appreciate Poe's stressing of the rhythm of a poem in his own reading, Poe on the other hand found the slighting or, worse, the ignoring of rhythm in the reading of others equally objectionable. He complained to Miss Susan Archer that he had never heard "The Raven" delivered correctly, even by the best readers. (34) Very likely he would have approved of Vachel Lindsay's rendition of the poem. The author of "The Chinese

---

[3] The late Miss May Garretson Evans discovered 219 musical settings to poems by Poe. The five top-ranking poems, judging by the number of settings they have inspired, are: "Annabel Lee" — 32; "Eldorado" — 28; "The Bells" — 22; "The Raven" — 18; "To Helen" — 15. (32)

Poe's influence on composers of music has also come from another source than his poems and stories. His theory of deliberate and calculated procedure in the creation of a poem has affected at least one world-famous modern composer: "As a matter of fact, as regards musical technique, my teacher has certainly been Edgar Allan Poe. To me the finest treatise on composition, certainly the one that has influenced me the most, is Poe's essay on the genesis of a poem." — Maurice Ravel. (33)

Nightingale," "The Congo," and "The Kallyope Yell" was in certain respects a kindred spirit of Poe's, a troubadour for whom words had musical meaning. Furthermore, he liked verse "where every line may be two-thirds spoken and one-third sung, the entire rendering, musical and elocutionary, depending upon the improvising power and sure instinct of the performer." (35) Lindsay, like Poe, was richly endowed with the gifts he demanded of "performers" of poetry. I was once fortunate to hear him recite not only "The Raven" but "The Bells" and "Annabel Lee" as well, and I remember thinking at the time that the poems had suddenly acquired melodic qualities which my own mute reading had utterly failed to apprehend. A superb tintinnabulator himself, Lindsay found in Poe's bells, for instance, variations of tone and modulations of meaning which made Rachmaninoff's effort to translate the poem into pure music explicable. Here was an eloquent and clear demonstration of the rightness of Poe's ear in increasing — in revision — the number of "bells" from four to seven. And here, also, one began to understand what so shrewd a dramatist as George Bernard Shaw had meant by his assertion that "The Raven," "The Bells," and "Annabel Lee" were as fascinating at the thousandth repetition as at the first. (36)

Vachel Lindsay knew how to read Poe's poems because they were both bards in the ancient tradition by which verse was transmitted orally. We who have become accustomed to reading only with our eyes miss much of the sensuous beauty which resides in the sound of words, just as Poe, were he alive today, would miss the visual appeal of the typographical subtleties in much of modern poetry. Very likely he would consider the spatial pyrotechnics of e. e. cummings — the broken lines, the jagged patterns, the erratic use of small and capital letters, and the telescoping of words — mere "tricks." Not that Poe was completely unaware of the value of visual appeal in printed verse. He was too good a magazinist for that. Half a century ago Professor Fruit called attention to Poe's revision of "Lenore." (37) The first version, published in 1831 as "A Paean," employed a short lyrical measure completely unsuited to the idea of a slow dirge. A revised version, the "Lenore" of 1843, began with the following stanza:

> Ah, broken is the golden bowl!
>   The spirit flown forever!
> Let the bell toll! — A saintly soul
>   *Glides down* the Stygian river!
>   *And* let the burial rite be read —
>   The funeral song be sung —
> A dirge for the *most lovely* dead
>   That ever died so young!
>   And, Guy De Vere,
>   Hast *thou* no tear?
>   Weep now or nevermore!
>   See, on yon drear
>   And rigid bier,
>   Low lies thy love Lenore!

Two years later this stanza became:

> Ah, broken is the golden bowl! — the spirit flown!
> Let the bell toll! — a saintly soul floats on the Stygian
>   river: —
> And, Guy De Vere, hast *thou* no tear? — weep now or
>   never more!
> See! on yon drear and rigid bier low lies thy love,
>   Lenore!
> Come, let the burial rite be read — the funeral song be
>   sung! —

An anthem for the queenliest dead that ever died so
    young —
A dirge for her the doubly dead in that she died so
    young. (38)

"Here," Professor Fruit remarked, "one can test what
effect the form of the verse upon the page as presented
to the eye has upon the reading." The revision shows
that by 1845 Poe had learned from his journalistic
experience that the spatial appearance of a poem added
to its appeal. The substitution of a flowing, dignified
line, suited to the solemnity of the theme, for a choppy,
irregular line indicates the measure of Poe's technical
growth. But Poe's basic appeal to the ear remains, for
it is significant that the revised stanza has no run-on
lines at all and that the pauses at the end of each line
are heavily punctuated.

One is therefore still justified in saying that, were
Poe alive today, he might fail to perceive the value in
Cummings's typographical arrangements. But he would
hardly fail to recognize Cummings's excellent lyrical ear.
For Poe was above all a lyrist in the ancient sense of
oral tradition. If his poems, for some of us, fail to come
alive it is because we have lost the art of uttering poetry.
A recent scholar has remarked that "The Bells" must
be read mainly in sounds and tempos and that the poem
is therefore modern. In the next breath, however, he
asks: "But where is such reading learned?" (39)

Certainly "The Bells" does not make of Poe a jingle
man. If it — and "The Raven" as well — appears to be
neither profound nor "significant" philosophically or
sociologically, it is significant artistically. The poem has
structure and tension and builds up, incrementally, to a
crashing climax which is psychologically sound. For Poe

was not alone in hearing the merry bells of winter sports or the happy bells of love finally replaced by the tolling, tolling, tolling bells of death; all of us have had intimations of mortality; and all of us sometimes

> In the silence of the night,
> . . . . . shiver with affright
> At the melancholy menace. . . .

In the end, all the bells have merged in the tolling menace; the cycles are completed; sound has, imperceptibly, become substance. And Poe's poetic devices, including the repetitions and refrains, far from being merely adventitious, are now seen as part of the substance.[4]

4

Other, and major, parts are structure, imagery, and a strangely suggestive symbolism which has made him — in the clever phrase of Karl Shapiro — "the Lenin of the Symbolists." (41)

No better example of lucidity of structure is needed than "The Conqueror Worm." The poem has five stanzas which correspond roughly to the five acts of a play. (42) The dramatic line is unmistakable. The first three stanzas contain the exposition — the where, when, and who — and prepare us for the climactic entry, in the next stanza, of the villain, the Conqueror Worm, or, as Poe ironically calls him, the "hero." The closing

[4] Four years before the publication of "The Bells" Poe wrote a review of Elizabeth Barrett's *The Drama of Exile*. One sentence in it read: "The thoughts . . . belong to the highest order of poetry, but they could not have been wrought into effective expression, without the instrumentality of those repetitions — those unusual phrases — in a word, those *quaintnesses*, which it has been too long the fashion to censure, indiscriminately, under the one general head of 'affectation.'" (40)

stanza contains the dénouement with choruses, as in
Greek tragedy, lamenting the conquest of Man, and the
Doctor, as in medieval morality, summarizing the significance of the play. The appropriateness of this structure is obvious, since the basic theme of the poem is the
very old one that man's life is like a play which is over
when Death has conquered.[5]

The imagery of the poem is at once vivid and tan-
talizingly indefinite:

> Lo! 't is a gala night
>   Within the lonesome latter years!
> An angel throng, bewinged, bedight
>   In veils, and drowned in tears,
> Sit in a theatre, to see
>   A play of hopes and fears,
> While the orchestra breathes fitfully
>   The music of the spheres.
>
> Mimes, in the form of God on high,
>   Mutter and mumble low,
> And hither and thither fly —
>   Mere puppets they, who come and go
> At bidding of vast formless things
>   That shift the scenery to and fro,
> Flapping from out their Condor wings
>   Invisible Wo!

Presumably this is a play within a play. We see the
angel throng, the winged scene-shifters, the mumbling
mimes; but we see no features, no outlines of forms, no
colors of dress or scenery; nor do we hear a single word.
The concrete orchestra breathes abstract music; the
"vast" stage hands flap synesthetically. The vividness

---

[5] Poe found the symbol useful again in his short story, "The Premature Burial": "the unseen but palpable presence of the Conqueror
Worm."

is muted, Strindbergean (as in *To Damascus* and *A Dream Play*), stylized. And the mood, in spite of the "gala" night, is hushed, full of low, liquid alliterations, expectant like the breathlessness in a theatre just before the curtain goes up on a serious dramatic presentation.

The indefiniteness of Poe's imagery was as deliberate as his structure and verbal music. Again and again his prose writings reiterate that indefiniteness is an essential element of good poetry and good music. "Give to music," he argued, "any undue *decision* — imbue it with any very *determinate* tone — and you deprive it . . . of its . . . intrinsic and essential character. You dispel its dream-like luxury: — you dissolve the atmosphere of the mystic in which its whole nature is bound up. . . . It then becomes a tangible and easily appreciable thing — a conception of the earth, earthy." (43) He praised Tennyson for "deliberately proposing to himself" — in such pieces as the "Lady of Shalott" — a "suggestive indefiniteness" in order to produce an effect of "vague definiteness." (44) For similar reasons he praised George Pope Morris as "our" best writer of songs. (45) That Poe's theory may not have been completely original with him does not alter the fact that he made it his own, that it suited his temperament and his genius, and that he illustrated it in his own practice with poems of power and beauty.

It is significant that in the first version of "The Conqueror Worm" he had written "A Mystic throng" instead of "An angel throng" (line 3) and "vast shadowy things" instead of "vast formless things" (line 13). (46) These adjectives which first sprang to his mind are more descriptive of his conceptions than the latter, less literal substitutions. In a style which in our

century has come to be known as "expressionistic" —
especially as applied to drama — Poe peopled his stage
with veiled, shadowy figures, with troops of Echoes and
"evil things, in robes of sorrow" ("The Haunted
Palace"), with ill angels and ghouls ("Dream-Land"),
and with dim "nothings which were real" ("Tamerlane"). Even his protagonists or featured characters
remain indistinct, like the gallant knight seeking Eldorado. All we know of him is that he started out "gaily
bedight"; and all we know of the one person he encountered on his way is that he was a pilgrim Shadow.

The bright flash of "gaily" with which "Eldorado"
opens is, like "gala" in the opening line of "The Conqueror Worm," a characteristic color-note, a sort of pre-
ludal flourish which lightens and at the same time
intensifies the somberness soon to follow. Metaphorical
lines such as

> Banners yellow, glorious, golden,
> On its roof did float and flow
> > ("The Haunted Palace"),

in spite of their vividness of color, actually serve similar
purposes: they are suggestive and preparative rather
than descriptive. They also, of course, exist in and for
themselves. For while the specific purposes of poetic
imagery, structural and tonal, are only a matter of inference, its effect at any given point is immediately
apparent. "Who shall say," inquires an investigator of
Poe's use of color words, "whether a poet uses a given
color in his poem because of metrical exigencies, because
of the euphony of its name, because of personal liking
for the color, or because descriptive accuracy demands
it?" (47)

Any or all of these reasons may have influenced Poe's choice of color and image, but, in his case, there is an additional reason that must be mentioned: it is the demands of his symbolic pattern. Many of his poems — and they are among the best — are allegories, although they hardly ever imply the simple preachment usually associated with this type of poem. Their themes — as in "The Conqueror Worm," "The Haunted Palace," and "Eldorado" — are simple enough, but the poems themselves, as artistic creations, are subtly intricate. They suggest levels of meaning which no paraphrase, no mere statement of theme or "message" can convey. To translate a Poe poem into prose is to destroy it. Structure, cadence, and image merge into an atmosphere, a climate of idea and sensation which transcends the various elements that compose the poem. This is as true of his subjective lyrics — "To Helen," "Annabel Lee," "Ulalume" — as of his more objective allegories. Whether "Annabel Lee" is an elegy on the death of Virginia or on the lost love of Elmira (48); whether the "bleak December" of "The Raven" is an allusion to the death-month of Poe's mother and the "sere October" of "Ulalume" is a prophetical naming of his own death-month (49); whether the imagery of "The Conqueror Worm" ("full as it is of theatre memories, — mimes, puppets, shifting scenery, funereal curtains, phantom forms —") reflects Poe's childhood memories of the burning of the Richmond Theatre in which his mother had played just before her death (50); whether in "Eldorado" Poe writes "of the search for the golden land as the quest of human happiness" (51) or of his vision of death (52) — these are conjectures and problems which hardly affect either the content or the form

of the poems.[6] We should do better to hark back to a
critic of Poe's own day who, a few months after the
poet's death, published a brief article with the happy
title "Mere Music." In it he recognized that American
literature had "at last" produced Poe, "who writes
poems that move us deeply, but in which the meaning
is only hinted at, and even that sometimes so obscurely
that it is impossible to find out an unbroken connexion;
but there is always an evident design, and an extremely
artistic construction." (54) These are qualities that
should suffice.

In our own day, Edward Shanks has found the reading of "Ulalume" a peculiar and exciting experience,
although he has been unable to discover, afterwards,
that it has also been an intellectual experience. This,
however, as far as he is concerned, does not matter. The
value of the poem to him is in the sensation of "spiritual
disturbance deepening to dismay and terror" which it
generates in the reader. Nor is he concerned with the
possibility that the poem might be autobiographical.
"'Ulalume,'" he says, "is as much and as little autobiographical as a nocturne by Chopin." (55) This is
not the view held by professional exegesists. Professor
Pattee, for instance, builds up a reasonable explanation
of the meaning of the poem. "Ulalume" is "a sob
from the depths of blank despair"; it is an expression of
Poe's sorrow over his failure to obtain the love of Mrs.
Shew, at a time when he was lonely and desperate. (56)
This may be perfectly true.[7] Just as Edwin Markham's

---

[6] Poe himself indicated, succinctly and forcefully, the irrelevance and
futility of such critical considerations: "Every work of art," he wrote in
a review of Mrs. Elizabeth Oakes Smith's poems, "should contain
within itself all that is required for its own comprehension." (53)

[7] Although there is considerable evidence tending to prove that the

guess that the poem is "a deep drama of temptation and memory" may be true. (59) Yet no poem can be said to possess virtue only because it originated in grief or joy, no matter how genuine or — to echo Wordsworth — powerful the feeling. Mr. Pattee believes that "Ulalume" is a "spontaneous" poem; in this he is wrong. Willis was closer to the truth when he called it "a curiosity in philologic flavor," a "skilful exercise of rarity and niceness of language." It is of course more than that; but it is hardly an artless, spontaneous effusion. Its pattern is too complex and its effect too successful to have been achieved by inspiration only. Whatever its meaning — and perhaps, like all good poetry, it has a multiplicity of meanings — its craftsmanship, faulty as it is in spots, is indisputable. Lafcadio Hearn once suggested that the poem contains elements of madness, but he was discerning enough to suggest also that the madness was *intentional*. (60) At any rate, in "Ulalume" we have once again proof that Poe — and he alone — had the skill to combine darkly colorful and rhythmical words, extravagant and terror-striking images, and haunting repetends into a type of poetry from which we derive a special — if morbid — pleasure.

5

Edward Shanks's reference to Chopin in connection with Poe brings to mind the concluding paragraph of Professor Kent's introduction to Poe's poems:

Poe's genius is acknowledged and therefore neither its essence nor its phenomena can be fully explained; but this may be said

---

poem was written much earlier. (57) It is for this reason that Lauvrière offers the fanciful suggestion that the poem expresses Poe's despair " on the anticipated death of Virginia." (58)

—his is the genius not of mental power but of melody. He remains a Chopin, not even a Mendelssohn, much less a Beethoven, still less a Wagner. (61)

The acknowledgment of Poe's poetic genius has taken many forms. The Symbolists paid tribute to his poetry because of its closeness to " our sick souls " (62); perhaps they remembered and accepted his own famous statement that the terror of which he wrote was not of Germany but of the soul. (63) But, for that matter, even D. H. Lawrence, no great admirer of Poe's verse — he thought it mechanical, facile, secondary and meretricious — accepted its author as " an adventurer into vaults and cellars and horrible underground passages of the human soul." (64) A greater English poet than Lawrence, Thomas Hardy, declined to discuss Poe's soul but preferred to pay tribute to him for having been " the first to realize to the full the possibilities of the English language in thought and rhyme." (65) A combination of both appreciations, of Poe's services to the soul and to the English language, has been expressed by William Carlos Williams. "With Poe," he says, "words were figures; an old language truly, but one from which he carried over only the most elemental qualities to his new purpose; which was, to find a way to tell his soul." (66)

It is possible, however, that those who have undertaken to deflate Poe, or to enter reservations in their acceptance of him, have come almost as close to the truth as those who have whole-heartedly championed him. Parrington found him a poet, although one who lacked ideas.[8] The most violent deflator, Yvor Winters, finds

[8] In this connection another view is to the point: " It may be argued that his poems do not submit readily to analysis; yet ideas are there,

Poe obscure, uneven, without taste, and a bad stylist. Yet he is obliged to admit that "The City in the Sea" has admirable description and "an intense feeling of meaning withheld," that at least the physical material in "The Haunted Palace" has allegorical significance, and that "Ulalume" is "an excursion into the incoherence of dream-consciousness." (68) All of these comments are neither without relevance nor without validity.

What, it seems to me, both the accepters and rejecters, whole-hearted or partial, have overlooked is the special nature of Poe's poetry. Shaw, who deplores Poe's aloofness from the common people, his placing of grotesques, madmen, and gorillas "in his theatre," instead of ordinary peasants, citizens and soldiers, — Shaw nevertheless feels that Poe is great, and that he is great *because* of his aloofness, because "his kingdom is not of this world." (69) This becomes clearer and more pointed when one recalls the insistence of James Branch Cabell — a fellow-Virginian of Poe's — on the right of an artist to turn his back upon a world which does not suit him and to create another one, more to his liking. He credits Poe with having created his own private kingdom — a sort of Poictesme — "an impressive, a preternatural, and a laughterless kingdom." (70) Whether the kingdom Poe created in his poems was more to his liking is hard to say, but presumably he felt more at home in it. And one gains nothing by arguing with the vagaries of taste.

The special world of Poe's poems, the world from which he drew so much of his luxurious décor and strange images and sonorous phrases, was the theatre, a

nevertheless, for those who will take the trouble to seek them. His manner of presenting them may be made a subject of debate, but their presence in the poems is an indisputable fact." — Floyd Stovall in *Studies in English, The University of Texas Bulletin.* (67)

theatre which he partly remembered and partly created and in which he himself was the playwright, actor, *regisseur*, scene-designer, and, to a large extent, audience. Edmund Wilson has cautioned us that "the psychology of the pretender is always a factor to be reckoned with in Poe" and that, "though his mind was a first-rate one, there was in him a dash of the actor who delights in elaborating a part." (71) The elaboration of parts for himself to play and the imagining of a stage upon which to play them are perfectly clear. In all his poems there is the more or less remote glitter of stage ornamentation, the rising and falling rhythm of stage eloquence, and the startling impact of stage climaxes. Sometimes the illusion is so perfect that we get the glitter of precious stones, the eloquence of exquisite music, and the impact of genuine emotion. Sometimes, when the light wavers, the illusion fades and we perceive the glint of tinsel and hear inflated rhetoric and hollow words.

But poetry, too, has many mansions. In them many distinctive voices have spoken: those of Shakespeare, Donne, Pope, . . . and Poe.

CHAPTER V

A SKILFUL LITERARY ARTIST

"A skilful literary artist
has constructed a tale."

IF WITH POE the writing of poetry was a passion, the writing of short stories was definitely a purpose. He hungered for literary fame and he was convinced that poetry could achieve it; he also hungered for bread, and his tales sometimes procured it for him. In the end, they also helped him achieve fame. For it was his winning of the story prize with one of the *Tales of the Folio Club* that started him on his literary career. The poetry he had published until then had produced hardly more than a ripple. His "MS. Found in a Bottle," which he submitted in the contest sponsored by the *Baltimore Saturday Visiter*, brought him some much needed money, and, more important, introduced him to John Pendleton Kennedy through whom he secured his editorial position on the *Southern Literary Messenger*. His literary career was now really begun.

The exact number of stories which Poe wrote during his creative life is a matter of dispute. Perhaps when Professor Mabbott publishes his variorum edition we shall know the truth. In 1927 Killis Campbell stated categorically that "Poe published sixty-eight stories and sketches" (1) — excluding the two long narratives about Arthur Gordon Pym and Julius Rodman — and this was the number Professor Quinn included in his collection of Poe's *Complete Poems and Stories* published in 1946. (2) Very likely the actual number of such "tales" was well over seventy; but of these less than a third are known to the general reader, and only less than a dozen are of such wide fame as to warrant the inclusion of their author among the great story-tellers of the world. Yet there can be no question that it is by virtue of his contribution as a short story writer, no less than poet and critic, that Poe ranks as one of the great figures in literature. Certainly in the history of the American short story he occupies the honored position of pioneer, almost of founder; and just as certainly, unlike most literary pioneers, he is still being read. To cavil at the slightness of his best performance is to be unreasonable. One masterpiece enriches a whole generation, and Poe has left us more than one. If again, as is the case with his poetry, not all critics are willing to concede unreservedly that his best stories are masterpieces, it is because they are unwilling to concede that the narrative art can produce a variety of types, each possessing qualities and standards of excellence peculiar to its kind.

Poe's stories are very markedly of a certain type. They are — as he would have been the first to claim — unique. But they are not of a type to appeal to the modern reader or critic for whom fiction is either a criticism of life or a weapon in the struggle for a better form of society. Poe's abhorrence of the didactic, his dwelling in a story world of his own imagining, and his preoccupation with technique deprived him of any appeal for the naturalistically-minded, the sociologically-minded, or the salvation-minded. Thus Pattee complains that "Nowhere [in Poe's stories] is there realism. The characters are not alive; they move not at all our sympathies; we never see such people in real life. . . ." (3) Bernard Smith deplores Poe's "approaches to the ivory-tower philosophy" (4); and Brownell laments Poe's lack of "ideality" and religion. (5) These charges are not to the point. Poe's stories were not intended to be realistic,[1] to convey social significance, or to inspire ideality; nevertheless they exist, as a product of a particular kind of imagination and a no less particular kind of artistry.

2

By now every student of Poe or of the short story is familiar with his review of Hawthorne's *Twice-Told Tales* which he published in *Graham's Magazine* for May, 1842. In a preliminary review published a month earlier, Poe deplored the dearth of short tales of high merit in American writing, "skilful compositions" that "could bear examination as works of art." He inveighed against the existing superabundance of "twattle," of "cut-and-thrust blue-blazing melodramaticisms," and pointed to Hawthorne as one of the few men of indisputable genius engaged in tale-writing. He promised to do him honor. (7)

In the fulfillment of his promise Poe not only did honor to Hawthorne and his two volumes of stories but he also enunciated principles of composition which were destined to influence the development of the American short story. If the application of these principles has resulted too often in imparting to our story a formula

---

[1] Poe himself was clear and unequivocal on the subject of realism: "The defenders of this pitiable stuff uphold it on the ground of its truthfulness . . . this truthfulness is the one overwhelming defect. . . . In my view, if an artist must paint decayed cheeses, his merit will lie in their looking as little like decayed cheeses as possible." (6)

slickness, the blame cannot be laid upon Poe. Literary theories have a way of being misunderstood. We have but to think of the misinterpretation of Aristotle's exposition of Greek dramaturgic practices by the seventeenth century neo-classic critics; they accepted the rigidity of form, with its unities and proscription of the mixing of *genres*, as an immutable law of excellence rather than as an adaptation to the kind of stage for which they wrote. Poe's theory of the short story was also, in the main, an exposition of his own practices and a betrayal of his own limitations, but it has been accepted by many teachers and handbook writers as a body of rules underlying the writing of all short stories. Moreover, the course of development of American magazine fiction has favored Poe's theory. Our busy reader has found brevity and unity of effect — the two cardinal principles of Poe's theory — economical of his time and potent as a means of escape from practical preoccupations.

Everything that is significant in Poe's theory of the short story is contained in one comparatively short paragraph in his review of Hawthorne's tales:

A skilful literary artist has constructed a tale. If wise, he has not fashioned his thoughts to accommodate his incidents; but having conceived, with deliberate care, a certain unique or single *effect* to be wrought out, he then invents such incidents — he then combines such events as may best aid him in establishing this preconceived effect. If his very initial sentence tend not to the outbringing of this effect, then he has failed in his. first step. In the whole composition there should be no word written, of which the tendency, direct or indirect, is not to the one pre-established design. And by such means, with such care and skill, a picture is at length painted which leaves in the mind of him who contemplates it with a kindred art, a sense of the fullest satisfaction. The idea of the tale has been presented unblemished, because undisturbed; and this is an end unattainable by the novel. Undue brevity is just as exceptionable here as in the poem; but undue length is yet more to be avoided. (8)

The intention of the narrative artist is clear: it is to achieve a certain preconceived effect. We may object to this intention; we may prefer that the artist "express" himself, convey a message, point up the significance of his material, or present a slice of life; we may prefer that he begin with a theme, a plot, or a character rather than a preconceived effect; but once we are willing to accept the premise that the production of a "unique" effect is a legitimate function of art — at least of a certain species of art — we must also acknowledge the validity of Poe's theory.

And once we acknowledge its validity the artistry of the resulting narrative will depend upon the skill of the writer. "Skill" has come to have an unfortunate connotation for the modern critic. It is almost as objectionable as the word "mechanical." And yet without skill a story is lifeless; with it, it may not be the expression of genius, but it will at least possess craftsmanship. Poe's respect for craftsmanship was a healthy manifestation, at a time when few American story-tellers paid any attention to form, and his insistence that incidents — and everything else in the narrative — accommodate "thoughts" rather than the other way around was a valuable contribution to our developing short story.

For Poe then, the central problem was — as C. Alphonso Smith formulated it forty years ago (9) — "How may I produce the maximum of effect with the minimum of means?" What means he ultimately resorted to, and with what success, can be ascertained only by a careful reading and examination of the stories themselves. Here it is pertinent to call attention to the resemblance of the problem to the one which confronts every practitioner of an art, or rather a group of arts, generally considered different from that of fiction writing: the art or arts of the theatre. It is the production of effect in which every actor, director, stage designer, electrician, and costumer is engaged. And economy of means by which to produce this effect is a basic principle in the theatre. Everything on a stage, every word, movement, and gesture of the actor, every piece of decoration, furniture, or prop, must contribute to the creation of the preconceived effects in the minds of the actor and designer, and all these effects must blend into the final totality which the director has envisaged. Therefore every object, movement, word, and tone uttered — like every word and sentence in a story — must be purposeful and "tend to the outbringing" of the desired effect.

If the analogy does not at first glance seem to include Poe's principle of brevity, it nevertheless holds. For brevity, involving both a certain minimum and maximum duration, is imbedded in totality of effect. Every theatre man knows that the slightest digression or unnecessary prolongation of a scene or moment on the stage is weakening if not ruinous to a performance. And surely a play in the theatre fulfills Poe's requirement that a story must be read at one sitting. Theatre audiences know better than any reader, sitting in the privacy of his room, "the immense force derivable from totality." (10)[2]

Poe's ideas on the short story were undoubtedly

[2] So do playwrights. Some modern practitioners of the craft have insisted that their plays must not be broken up by intermissions. One example is Philip Barry who indicated in the stage directions for *Hotel Universe* that "The action of the play is continuous." And wisely, because the mood of his play is so tenuous that it might easily be dispelled by the mundane life of a theatre lobby.

derived, to a considerable extent at least, from his con-
templation of the processes underlying the creation of
poetry, and especially lyric poetry. Yet his knowledge of
dramatic practices and his native theatrical flair affected
all of his theories and practices. The means he employed
for bringing about the effects he preconceived for his
stories were largely theatrical. His plots, whatever their
nature or merits, were constructed with an eye to effectiveness as dramatic or melodramatic fables; his locales
were for the most part so many stage settings; his characters were, in his own frequently employed designation,
"dramatis personae"; his dialogue — weak as realistic
transcription of idiomatic speech — was emotionally intense and in its own peculiar way, if not actually stageworthy, at least "stagy"; and his devices for blending
visual and auditory elements into exciting climaxes were
deliberately theatrical. Whatever values one may find in
Poe's stories — psychological, symbolical, autobiographical — one can hardly appreciate the effectiveness of his
narratives without an awareness of their indebtedness to
the arts of the theatre.

3

For Poe, as for Aristotle, plot was the basic element
of a story. It was not theme, nor setting, nor characters,
nor style — important as these other elements might be —
but plot which contributed most to the achievement of
the author's intention. Other writers might regard plot
as "mere complexity of incident"; for him it was "*that
from which no component atom can be displaced without ruin to the whole.*" (11) Again and again he took
contemporary fictioneers to task for failure to construct
tight plots: John Neal, whom he otherwise praised as a

novelist of genius, was remiss in construction, always beginning well but soon digressing and hurrying his climaxes (12); even Dickens belonged to the class of author "totally deficient in constructiveness." (13) Conversely, he admired those novelists — like Godwin and Bulwer (the latter with occasional reservations) — who were good constructors of plot. Godwin's confession that he wrote *Caleb Williams* backwards impressed him, although he had doubts about recommending this mode of composition to writers with less idiosyncratic minds than Godwin's. Bulwer's *Pompeii* appealed to him as an instance of "an admirably managed plot." (14)

Especially in the short story — or what Poe called "the tale proper" — was "mere *construction* . . . imperatively demanded." For here "where there is no space for development of character or for great profusion and variety of incident" — as in the novel — defective plot could never escape observation. Yet apparently most American writers of tales, he observed, neglected this distinction, and began their stories without knowing how to end them; the results were generally disastrous: the endings of their stories appeared "to have forgotten their beginnings." (15) For himself, he had taken a hint from the Chinese, "who, in spite of building their houses downwards, have still sense enough *to begin their books at the end*." (16) In a note which he contributed to *The Opal* in 1845, and from which I have already quoted his rigorous definition of plot, he disapproved of authors "who sit down to write with *no* fixed design" but trusted to inspiration instead. "Pen," he went on, in the manner of a law-giver, "should never touch paper, until at least a well-digested *general* purpose be established."[3] This rule he apparently prescribed for all writing. As applied specifically to fiction, this would involve consideration and arrangement of the dénouement "before writing the first word" of the story, "and *no* word," he added, "should be then written which does not tend, or form a part of a sentence which tends to the development of the dénouement." (18)

Such, briefly, were Poe's ideas on plot construction. The embodying of these ideas in his stories was quite another matter. That is one reason why only a handful of them can be classed as masterpieces. "The Fall of the House of Usher," for one instance, shows clearly that before writing the first word he knew where he was going and what effect he intended to create. The narrator's careful and yet seemingly casual observation of the old building, with the crumbling condition of its individual stones and the fissure zig-zagging from the roof down the front wall, is obviously a "plant," preparation for the ultimate collapse of the building at the end of the story. Poe may, of course, have written his tale backwards, and having described the crumbling and disappearance of Usher's house he may have gone back to the opening paragraphs to insert the necessary preparatory observations in order to motivate the catastrophe at the end. In either case, the craftsmanship is so remarkable that it has justified students of the most popular *genre* in American writing to agree with Bliss Perry that it was Poe who "showed that the art of short-story writ-

[3] That this was evidently Poe's own practice is indicated by the testimony of Mrs. Clemm, who is quoted by Eugene L. Didier as saying: "He never sat down to write until he had completely arranged the plot, the characters, and even the language. His habit was to walk up and down while thinking out his work." (17)

ing, like that of the drama, is largely the art of preparation." (19)

There can be no doubt, for another instance, that in "The Cask of Amontillado," he plotted carefully and skilfully. The very opening sentence — "The thousand injuries of Fortunato I had borne as I best could, but when he ventured upon insult I vowed revenge" — gives us both the cause and outcome of the action planned. Moreover, it is an excellent exemplification of his own dictum that a good beginning must arrest attention and should contain, "at all risks — a few vivid sentences . . . by way of the electric bell to the telegraph." (20) The plausibility of every move is tightly, though unobtrusively, safeguarded. The victim must have no suspicion of the avenger's designs — "neither by word nor deed had I given Fortunato cause to doubt my good will"; he must be met casually — at a carnival; he must have a weak point — his pride in his connoisseurship in wine — through which he can be reached; allied to this weakness must come another, to induce him to follow Montressor — jealousy of a rival connoisseur; the carnival can also serve to explain why Montressor's home — a "palazzo" — is without attendants — their master had told them that he did not expect to return until morning; the trowel in the hands of the avenger — the first hint of the nature of the revenge — must not betray the design too soon: it is passed off jocularly as a masonic sign. In spite of the use of the first person, the story is told with objective directness and rigid economy unusual for Poe; in many ways — toughness of texture, barrenness of style, obliqueness, irony — it anticipates the narrative method of Hemingway, especially the Hemingway of "The Killers."

Large as is the contribution of the element of plot to the final effect produced by these Gothic stories, it is even larger in such a realistic fantasy as "A Tale of the Ragged Mountains." The label "realistic fantasy" is no doubt strange but it seems adequate to describe a type of fiction which makes vivid a dream and suggests the possibility that it represents the recapitulation of a previous existence.[4] There is nothing unrealistic in the story of a man, an invalid fed on morphine, who falls asleep and has a fantastic dream. Nor — in the light of recent psychology, especially that of Carl Jung with his theory of the racial unconscious — is there anything wildly inventive in the suggestion that the dream is a reliving of events that transpired in a different part of the world forty-seven years before. What is fantastic is the inference that the hero, presumably still a young man, had actually personally experienced the events perceived in the dream and that his present existence is a reincarnation.

These psychological overtones are not, however, for the moment, under consideration.[5] The skill with which Poe unfolds the story is. The illness of the hero; his taking of "very large" doses of morphine each morning; the indefiniteness of his age — he "seemed" young; the more definite advanced age of his doctor — "an old gentleman, perhaps seventy"; the doctor's interest in Mesmerism; the "magnetic relation" which existed between

---

[4] For an interpretation of this story as dealing with mesmerism rather than metempsychosis, see Sidney E. Lind, "Poe and Mesmerism," *Publications of the Modern Language Association*, December, 1947.

[5] Although it is worth noting that one excellent historian of the American short story as a form of literature credits Poe, as a psychological artist, with having anticipated and greatly surpassed James Joyce and Dorothy Richardson. (21)

the doctor and his patient; the doctor's experiences in India, not revealed until almost the very end; and, finally, the announcement in a Charlottesville newspaper of the death of the hero, Mr. Bedlo — with the seemingly inadvertent omission of the final e — and the narrator's conversation with the editor — these are all the touches of a master in the building up of a plot in which nothing is left unforshadowed, unmotivated, unprotected. The final stroke — the revelation that "Bedlo" is "Oldeb" (the hero of the exploits in the dream) conversed is a clear indication that it was Poe and not O. Henry who "invented" the twist at the end which has established itself as characteristic of so many modern American short stories. The ironic last sentence — "And the man tells me it is a typographical error" — is certainly more imaginative than O. Henry could have managed. It lifts the ending above mere trickery and sends us thoughtfully back to the story for investigation and speculation.

And yet Poe was not always, nor even often, so fortunate. His elaborate and subtle technique was at his service only intermittently. "The Premature Burial," for instance, has neither the beginning nor the ending which could withstand the test of Poe's own standards of structure.[6] The plot is a loose series of incidents related only to the general theme. The first three paragraphs would lead one to believe that he is reading a magazine article on the "terrific" experience of being buried alive. The "authenticated" instances which follow add but weakly to the atmosphere of fiction.

[6] Reviewing a novel by Bulwer, Poe recalled a short tale by the same author which he considered very bad because, among other structural faults, "it had, properly speaking, neither beginning nor end." — *Graham's Magazine*, June 1842.

The actual story does not begin until more than half the space allotted to this "tale" has been used up. Poe the critic had been right in calling most of Hawthorne's *Twice-Told Tales* essays rather than stories. Yet a little over two years later he himself published this short narrative which is hardly more than an essay containing a number of anecdotes illustrative of his subject.

Such lapses from his own theory of structure are numerous. His tendency toward lecturing, his overpowering need to exhibit his scientific interests and knowledge, like his tendency toward declamation, often led him astray. He wastes a thousand words on his introduction to "The Murders in the Rue Morgue" before telling us when and where he met Monsieur C. Auguste Dupin, the mental giant so like Poe himself in temperament as to be almost his double. All this preliminary material is not uninteresting in itself, but only as a dissertation on the analytical faculty. For the purposes of the story which is to follow it is extraneous and rather discouraging, a mere tuning-up unnecessarily prolonged. And even after the remarkable detective is introduced we are not permitted to plunge into the murder story for perhaps another thousand words, but must be told in great detail of Dupin's wonderful deductive powers. Brander Matthews was a little overenthusiastic in pronouncing "The Murders" a story of the "most marvelous skill . . . unsurpassed . . . unapproachable. . . ." (22)

In the third paragraph of "The Mystery of Marie Roget" Poe tells us that the depiction of the mental character of the Chevalier Dupin in "The Murders in the Rue Morgue" was his design. But his design undoubtedly also called for the construction of a story.

This he carried out even less economically in the later story. "The Mystery of Marie Roget" begins with a superfluous first paragraph which is a windy discourse on the Calculus of Probabilities. Surely Poe the theoretician of craftsmanship knew that the second paragraph with its striking opening sentence, "The extraordinary details which I am now called upon to make public . . ." was a logical and effective beginning, but Poe the exhibitor of great mental prowess could not forgo the opportunity to shine. Hence the story begins not with action, nor with a hint of action to come, but with generalizations on man's belief in the supernatural and coincidence, and on the application of mathematics — "the most rigidly exact in science" — to "the shadow and spirituality of the most intangible in speculation." The plot, to the extent to which it is at all developed, is buried in lengthy analyses of Dupin's mental dexterity. Even such an admirer of Poe's ingenuity as Howard Haycraft is obliged to admit that he finds "The Mystery of Marie Roget" interesting only as an essay, as "an able if tedious exercise in reasoning. As a story," he concludes, "it scarcely exists." (23) It is pertinent to add that Poe does not stop when his story has ended but returns to his speculations on the workings of the Calculus of Probabilities, as though his preconceived design were really that of an essayist rather than story-teller.

I hope that I have not conveyed the impression that I would rule out either the beginning or the ending of a short story with generalization. Both Kipling and O. Henry — to name but two widely accepted practitioners of the craft — often begin with the statement of a theme or a bit of philosophy; these statements, however, are generally very brief; besides, neither considered himself an expert on the technique of story-writing and therefore entitled to prescribe for others the laws for guiding a plot to perfection. Poe's violations of his own loudly-proclaimed principles of structure are important because they indicate that the psychological conflicts of the man frequently interfered with the efficient functioning of the creative artist and that if despite this interference, his stories remain memorable — and even a few of the structurally weak ones are not easily forgotten — it is because their power does not reside entirely in plot. This is equally true of his best stories — "The Fall of the House of Usher," "Ligeia" (Poe's own favorite), "The Purloined Letter" (certainly the most economically constructed of his detective stories), "The Tell-Tale Heart."

As a matter of fact, Poe's plots are in themselves not of first consequence, and offer no explanation for the effect of his stories. Most of them were derived from printed sources, mainly magazine and newspaper stories and articles, and were familiar to his readers.[7] Unlike his pedestalled Shakespeare he did not often subject the material he borrowed to any radical alteration, although it is not quite true, as Professor Napier Wilt claims, that he "did not take the trouble even to invent new situations." (26) It *is* true that his tales of terror exploited the same Gothic predicaments, coincidences, and melodramatic resolutions which he himself satirized unmercifully in such pieces as "Loss of Breath" and "How to Write a Blackwood Article." To be sure, his detective stories, or — to use the more inclusive term — tales of

---

[7] Two examples will suffice: "The Premature Burial" seems to have been suggested by a poem and an accompanying note published in the *Columbian Lady's and Gentleman's Magazine* for January, 1844, (24) and "The Man That Was Used Up" originated in the trial of a Captain Mann which was widely reported in the press during most of 1839, the year in which the story was published. (25)

ratiocination, are ingenious and were quite new in his day, but since Conan Doyle and "Ellery Queen" this type of fiction has acquired a breadth and variety which Poe's plots do not provide. His tales of imaginative science — "Hans Pfaall," "The Balloon Hoax," "Mesmeric Revelation," "Von Kempelen and His Discovery," — again a type of story in which he pioneered, are today more than matched in boldness of invention by the comparatively unknown writers appearing every month in the pseudo-science fiction magazines. His so-called "grotesques," mostly attempts, with varying success, at humor, burlesque, or satire, are inconsequential and may be dismissed from any serious consideration of his contribution to the art of the short story.

Decidedly, then, it is not the plots as such that can account for the effect of Poe's stories — when they are wholly or even partially successful. And yet plot cannot be dismissed lightly as a contributing factor. The mere selection of a particular plot by a writer, whatever its source, is in itself a disclosure of artistic inclination, temperament, bias, direction. The fact that Poe's range was a comparatively narrow one — most of his stories will be seen to revolve around crime or the terror of death — emphasizes the nature of his artistic bent. It is true that fashions in plot and mood may influence to some extent a writer depending upon his contributions to magazines for his daily bread. In the main, however, Poe's choice of material must be accepted as having been determined by the needs of his imagination. And these needs were perhaps more often artistic than psychological. In each plot he chose he saw possibilities for the kind of treatment, the unique craftsmanship, which his special talents could impose. The effect which we have come to denominate as "Poe-esque" — or what Kenneth Burke, referring specifically to the Poe story, calls "the one corrosive spell," (27) — is a result of many elements. Plot is but one of them.

4

Setting, or locale and, more important, the atmosphere derived from locale, is another. Action must of course take place somewhere; it must have a habitation; and the two interact and complement each other. The striking thing about Poe's settings is that while they appear impressively vivid they at the same time remain indefinite. He manages to depict enough of the background to set the mood, but his details are selected for suggestiveness and ornamentation rather than realistic fidelity. It might be interesting to inquire into the sources of his settings but it is likely to prove no more enlightening than to inquire into the sources of his plots. Even when we know that he drew upon his memories of specific places — as in "The Gold Bug," "William Wilson," "A Tale of the Ragged Mountains," and "Landor's Cottage" — the finished product obliterates any importance that might attach to the source. I feel about the sources of Poe's settings the way Professor Quinn feels about the sources of Poe's plots, and for the same reason: that it is "a critical stupidity" to speak of them at all, because "they are merely suggestions out of which a creative artist made something new." (28) In reality, with place as such Poe was not at all concerned; what it could be made to contribute to his story was all that mattered. And he saw to it that his settings — castle, hall, landscape — should contribute atmosphere, mood, character revelation, and, above all, decoration. The settings of Poe's stories — as Edward Shanks has observed — whether "good or bad, vivid or vague, were but so much dramatic *décor* for the action and the emotions. . . ." (29)

The opinions of Poe on matters theatrical — playwriting, acting, directing, staging, and lighting — are numerous and written down with supreme self-assurance. He not only criticized the plays of Mrs. Mowatt and Nathaniel Parker Willis; he almost rewrote them. He not only reviewed the productions he saw on Broadway during his brief tenure as dramatic critic; he indicated how they should and could have been directed. Unfortunately — or perhaps fortunately — he never was either a producer or an "angel." But he could and did take full charge of the productions he created as short stories. Here he could indulge his imagination and use his superb skill in achieving the most nicely calculated effects. Here he could mount his pieces as extravagantly or as austerely as he felt impelled to do. Here he could turn down the lights, tint them, splash color, throw eerie shadows in corners and on the backdrop, strew exotic rugs on floors and hang exotic tapestries on walls, arrange the furniture, and black out the whole thing with one lightning stroke. Here, in short, he could practice the craft of a master scenic designer.

Poe's taste in design was not always fastidious. Generally his mind envisaged the grandiose, the bizarre, the extravagantly sweeping. And yet the finished picture, in spite of many details, remains subdued and indefinite. Both in their imaginative sweep and in their indefiniteness, as in their essential impracticality, Poe's stage designs inevitably remind the student of the modern theatre of the strangely disturbing work of Gordon Craig. Lee Simonson, an eminently practical designer

13

himself, has clearly shown the impracticability of Craig's designs (30); yet Harold Helvenston is only stating a fact when he asserts that Craig "has exerted a great emotional influence." (31) Both of these things may be said with equal justice of Poe's sets for his fiction. In Poe's case, however, the impracticality of his sets does not much matter, since, highly theatrical as they are, they do not, after all, have to be assembled on a stage. The action of a Poe story takes place against a background so charged with emotional overtones that the background itself becomes part of the action; it is in fact, functionally, part of the story. The splendor which Poe loved found expression in the rich décor with which he mounted his tales. His scenery, as Hannay, his English editor, observed more than ninety years ago, "is everywhere magnificent." (32)

The magnificence was, of course, romantic. This rather protean adjective means, as used here, that in architecture, for instance, Poe's taste required not only size and nobility, but also the admixture of decay as a concomitant, and guarantee, of antiquity. Margaret Kane, in an excellent article on this subject, (33) has argued convincingly that "Poe's Gothic architecture derives, however remotely, from the conventional stage-setting for the terror school of eighteenth century English novelists." Another source — and probably a more creative one — was his own dim and therefore enlarged memories of the five years he had spent in England during his childhood. Still another possibility must not be excluded: the many books of travel and description, such as W. Howitt's *Visits to Remarkable Places*,[8] which were an expression of the romantic curiosity of the age.

[8] This book was reviewed by Poe in *Graham's Magazine*, March, 1841. (34)

But, again, neither the sources nor the extent of Poe's knowledge of architecture need detain us here. His imagination required a particular kind of setting, exterior or interior, and he proceeded to "invent" it. He blended impressions and details he had retained of places he had actually seen, come upon in books and articles he had read, and in pictures he had looked at.[9] With these he felt free to combine purely "original" elements which only his mind could conceive. Since strangeness was, for him, an indispensable quality of beauty, we may be sure that his story settings would not be without that quality, whether the inciting source had it or not. Ellison's idea (in "The Domain of Arnheim") of a landscape which should combine vastness and definitiveness, beauty, magnificence, and *strangeness* was, of course, also Poe's idea. The approach to Ellison's domain gave the visitor the feeling of being "enwrapt in an exquisite sense of the strange." The swan-like canoe which bore him toward the gigantic gate ("or rather door of burnished gold, elaborately carved and fretted, and reflecting the direct rays of the now fast-sinking sun with an effulgence that seems to wreath the whole surrounding forest in flames") was of ivory, "stained with Arabesque devices in vivid scarlet. . . . On its ermined floor [reposed] a single feathery paddle of satin-wood";

[9] Van Wyck Brooks speculates on the possibility that the house of Usher "might have been suggested by the ruinous old mouldering mansions in the Carolina woods." — *The World of Washington Irving*, p. 347. If this be true, Poe's assimilation of the original "suggestion" was complete; for the "house" has also the unmistakable air of the castles of Horace Walpole, Mrs. Radcliffe, and William Godwin. The same comment on Poe's absorption of whatever source or sources he used applies to Henry Seidel Canby's statements that the "crude original" of "Landor's Cottage" was a Currier & Ives print and that the rooms Poe described in "The Philosophy of Furniture" can be found in the steel engravings of the Annuals. (35)

but the canoe seemed to be self-propelled, creating by its gentle motion "soothing yet melancholy music." When he finally catches a glimpse of the castle, he sees "a mass of semi-Gothic, semi-Saracenic architecture, . . . glittering in the red sunlight with a hundred oriels, minarets, and pinnacles."

To the visitor to Arnheim this structure seems the "phantom handiwork, conjointly, of the Sylphs, of the Fairies, of the Genii, and of the Gnomes"; to the visitor into Poe's realm it is the work of an ambitious theatre designer who had been let loose to indulge his exuberant fancy and told that costs were of no consequence, since a fabulously wealthy "angel" named Ellison would take care of all the bills. The entire domain is obviously Kubla Khanish, Arabian Nightish, Beckfordian, Wagnerian, and Max Reinhardtish (at his lushest—and worst). The pendant piece to this vision, "Landor's Cottage," is infinitely less extravagant, shadowing as it does the outlines of both Poe's own cottage at Fordham and the more imposing Massachusetts home of Mrs. Richmond, the adored "Annie." But even into this idealized cottage Poe injects artificial décor which belongs more appropriately to a stage set.

Neither of these two brief works is a story in the true sense of the word. And it is in Poe's stories that his skill at constructing functional sets can be seen at its best. There are comparatively few exteriors, and these are mostly panoramic glimpses of approaches to castles, chateaux, mansions, and houses in which the action is scheduled to take place; they are, in fact, mere backdrops. Nevertheless the appropriateness of these exteriors is uncanny. The "lofty" Ducal Palace on the Canal in Venice, its black marble flagstones mirroring

the "small, bare and silvery feet" of the Marchesa
Aphrodite, is at once in splendid contrast to the solemn-
corniced prison of the Old Republic and complementary
to the plot of "The Assignation." Also in contrast to the
Ducal Palace is the Palazzo — "one of those huge struc-
tures of gloomy, yet fantastic pomp" — of the Marchesa's
lover. The melancholy house of Usher, the mansion of
gloom, with bleak walls, is a capital illustration of
Stevenson's famous saying that "Certain places speak
distinctly . . . certain old houses demand to be haunted
. . ."; and so is the deserted "time-eaten and grotesque
mansion" described in "The Murders in the Rue
Morgue." The large, rambling Elizabethan house, in a
misty-looking English village is an ideal setting for the
unfolding of the schizophrenic character of William
Wilson. The chateau in the Apennines, "one of those
piles of commingled gloom and grandeur," is a fitting
place in which to come upon the painting, and the story,
of "The Oval Portrait." The castellated abbey, an ex-
tensive and magnificent structure girdled by a strong and
lofty wall, is the inevitable rendezvous for the "Red
Death."

It is, however, in his interior scenes that Poe really
extends himself. The main action is usually enacted in
a remote tower or turret room or in a strange, high-
ceilinged room in a distant part of the building. Access
to these sequestered spots is by means of winding stair-
cases and mysterious passages. The room itself is seldom
normal in shape or dimension; it is vast, circular or
pentagonal, full of nooks and niches, and lighted only in
spots, so as to permit weird shadows to hide in corners
and tremble on walls and vaulted ceiling. In spite of the
vastness of the chamber, the action is generally con-

centrated in restricted sections, over a bed or an ottoman, a chair or a table, which is picked up by the flicker of a candle, the red glare of a torch or flambeau, or the dim waverings of a lamp, all in the manner of what we have come to call on the modern stage as "area lighting."

The furnishings are carefully selected and arranged for their atmospheric value. Margaret Kane is wrong in assuming that Poe "apparently had difficulty or was not interested in visualizing what was suitable for the peculiar character of his rooms, since the furniture is described only in very general terms." It is more likely that Poe's practice in this respect was deliberate. He knew the value of indefiniteness, or impressionistic suggestion, as against realistic photography. If the furniture in Usher's studio is described merely as "profuse, comfortless, antique and tattered," it is because Poe was striving to create the effect of antiquity and decay, neglect and dissolution. If in the seven bizarre apartments in "The Masque of the Red Death" we find an undistinguished "profusion of golden ornaments . . . scattered about" and in the turret-room in "Ligeia" a "few ottomans and golden candelabra, of Eastern figure," it is because the designer is again striving to catch the spectator's eye — not with the details of individual pieces of furniture, details which on a stage are usually missed anyway, but with spots of color and glitter, in contrast to the spectral dimness of the surrounding atmosphere.

In his essay on "The Philosophy of Furniture" Poe clearly reveals his taste in decoration. He disliked furniture arranged in straight lines or in curved lines "repeated into unpleasant uniformity." In general, he preferred little furniture to too much, a minimum of drapery — "the proper quantum" — to a profusion. Carpets and rugs were essential; and so were certain colors and patterns. "Indeed, whether on carpets or curtains, or tapestry, or ottoman coverings, all upholstery of this nature should be rigidly Arabesque." If he is not always consistent in his ideas or in his own practice in furnishing the rooms in his stories, we must allow for the difference in purpose. In his essay he was intent on attacking the bad taste of the American *parvenu* with whom costly clutter and flashiness passed for aristocratic elegance; in his stories his aim is to provide appropriate settings for Gothic characters and plots. The elegant simplicity and "repose" which he sought in his ideal room in real life could not possibly have served his purpose in furnishing the magnificent mansions and chateaux in which horrific deeds were to be performed.

Yet, undoubtedly, much of the taste he had acquired in the actual world he carried over into the imaginary world of his stories. He was fourteen years old when John Allan inherited a sizeable fortune and began buying costly furnishings, among them rich draperies and marble busts. "Here," says one of Poe's biographers, "might be found the germ for some tastes displayed in after years, — his minute descriptions of draperies and of furniture." (36) His use of draperies is especially interesting; it is constant and artistically subtle. They are as much a part of a Poe design as a dominating staircase has become a central part in a modern production of *Hamlet* since Leopold Jessner introduced his famous *Treppe*. They are far from being mere inert decoration; they are full of atmospheric color and even sound; they are dynamic. At the very outset of Poe's career as a story-teller, faded rich tapestry hangings "swing" gloomily on the walls in Metzengerstein castle. Two years later, in "The Assignation," rich draperies "in every part of the room" tremble to the vibration of low, melancholy music. Thereafter curtains, tapestries, hangings continue to participate in most of the stories Poe was to write. In "Shadow" black draperies shut out the moon, "the lurid stars, and the peopleless streets." In "Ligeia" the draperies are "gorgeous and fantastic"; the tapestry, of the richest cloth of gold, covers the floor, the ottomans, the ebony bed, and the window curtains; it is "spotted . . . with arabesque figures, about a foot in diameter, . . . in patterns of the most jetty black." Black, or "sable," are also the draperies the condemned man sees in "The Pit and the Pendulum." In "The Oval Portrait" the narrator's bed is enveloped in fringed curtains of black velvet. The draperies in the seven rooms of "The Masque of the Red Death" are of colors and shapes as fantastic — and perhaps symbolic — as the story itself. And one must not forget the "silken sad uncertain rustling of each purple curtain" in "The Raven" — which, of course, is also a story. Nor must we overlook the fact that when Poe needed no color, he had the artistic restraint to withhold it. Thus when in "The Black Cat" the curtains of the narrator's bed catch fire, they are mentioned simply as "curtains," without any hint as to their color or material. Poe knew how to use a "plot prop" without distracting the spectator's attention.

5

Color and lighting in Poe's stories are so important that they merit a section to themselves. Everyone knows that the primary purpose of light on the stage is visibility. An audience wants to see faces, gestures, and objects, and actors want to be seen. But the secondary purpose is no less important: it is to create a mood. The contribution of lighting to the final artistic and emotional effect produced by a play is immeasurably great. Such lighting, however, requires ingenuity, technical knowledge, taste, and imagination. The stage of Poe's stories offered him a remarkable opportunity for the employment of all these qualities, and he must have pondered deeply the psychology of color and light and the ways of blending them in such proportions and shadings as to produce the effects he desired. It is possible that sometimes the very architecture he adopted for a room — the shape and position of windows, for instance — was dictated by the opportunities it provided for ingenious lighting. At any rate, having adopted a type of architecture which suited his fancy he examined it carefully for appropriate lighting possibilities and, as with the architecture itself, let himself go.

Whatever one may think of the taste or fitness of the bridal chamber described in "Ligeia" one can hardly fail to be impressed by its theatrical effectiveness. Poe himself was aware that this time even *his* extravagance might be deemed excessive, for it is by way of subtle apology that he makes the narrator say: "I had become a bounden slave in the trammels of opium, and my labor and my orders had taken a coloring from my dreams." But whether with or without the aid of opium, the "set" he created is definitely a stage designer's dream:

The room lay in a high turret of the castellated abbey, was pentagonal in shape, and of capacious size. Occupying the whole southern face of the pentagon was the sole window — an immense sheet of unbroken glass from Venice — a single pane, and tinted of a leaden hue, so that the rays of either the sun or moon, passing through it, fell with a ghastly lustre on the objects within. . . . The ceiling, of gloomy-looking oak, was excessively lofty, vaulted, and elaborately fretted with the wildest and most grotesque specimens of a semi-Gothic, semi-Druidical device. From out the most central recess of this melancholy vaulting, depended, by a single chain of gold with long links, a huge censer of the same metal, Saracenic in pattern, and with many perforations so contrived that there writhed in and out of them, as if endued with a serpent vitality, a continual succession of particolored fires.

The last touch is worthy of David Belasco's famous electrician Louis Hartmann, creator of the spectral bridge of light for the production of "The Return of Peter Grimm." [10]

The immense window described here does not greatly differ from the two large windows, "reaching down to the floor," which Poe insisted on having in his ideal room ("The Philosophy of Furniture"). Except that their panes would have to be of crimson-tinted glass. And this is precisely the kind of glass we find in the room he pictures for us in "The Assignation." If in some stories he did not deem it feasible to incorporate this type of colored windowpane, he managed to supply the deficiency by means of artificial light from the wings. Thus "feeble gleams of encrimsoned light made their way through the trellised panes" into Usher's studio; there is the glare of ruddy light "thrown full by the flaming stables upon the windows of the apartment" in "Metzengerstein"; and since the windows in six of the

[10] Mr. Hartmann, too, had a "delicate" problem in lighting, since he was aware, he tells us, that three-fourths of the audience did not believe in supernatural manifestations. Mainly, like Poe, he sought to devise illumination which could keep any part of the scene in light or shadow. (37)

seven rooms so vividly described in "The Masque of the Red Death" are tinted the same colors as the rooms themselves, "in the corridors . . . there stood, opposite to each window, a heavy tripod, bearing a brazier of fire that projected its rays through the tinted glass and so glaringly illumined the room."

The purpose of such special lighting devices as the braziers of fire is, of course, to produce special effects. In this particular case Poe wished to induce "a multitude of gaudy and fantastic appearances." In other cases the intricate lighting devices are simply part of the scenic décor, like the large chandelier in the grand saloon in "Hop-Frog," which depended by a chain from the center of the sky-light and was lowered or elevated by means of a counterbalance. But, Poe adds, "in order not to look unsightly, this latter passed outside the cupola and over the roof." Both décor and the mechanics to achieve it are worked out in detail. In still other cases the type of lighting devised is determined by décor and function. Hence in "The Oval Portrait" we have a tall candelabrum with many candles; this can be moved from place to place so that the portrait hidden in the shadows can be made visible. In a story of less opulent color and mood, like "The Pit and the Pendulum," a different type of illumination was necessary. Here the unhappy prisoner's vision falls upon the seven tall candles on the table. Their effect is psychological: they expressionistically assume the shapes of white slender angels, then change into spectres with heads of flame, before becoming once again mere candles throwing a dim light on an alien room. In a more completely psychological story like "The Tell-Tale Heart," lighting becomes closely integrated with plot, a means of forwarding it; the creation of mood, important as it always is with Poe, is here subordinated to the demands of the action. The murderer enters the room of his sleeping victim carrying a lantern. He opens the tin fastening, "a very, very little crevice," and permits "a single dim ray, like the thread of a spider," to fall upon the face of the hated victim.

But whether for purposes of plot or pure decoration, or for the intensification of a mood or effect, Poe's lighting designs are carefully planned and executed; materials, shape, size, color, quantity and quality of light — all is calculated, arranged, and blended into the scene and the story-line. The modern mechanisms by which illusion is created on the stage were unknown to him, but he did supremely well with the excellent mechanism he possessed — his imagination. His lights flamed, glared, writhed, sputtered, frightened, brooded, and moved, or — like the seven iron lamps in his grim prose poem "Shadow" — they only burned "pallid and motionless."

And they never burned without regard to the shadows they cast or the general color scheme they illuminated. Color is definitely part of Poe's wizardry. After a first superficial reading of a few of his stories, especially those in the category which he called the grotesque and arabesque, one somehow carries away an impression of profusion and opulence of color. Yet upon a closer acquaintance one finds that impression greatly altered. The stories are indeed colorful, and the colors are rich and striking, but they are generally confined to a few artistically significant spots. They attract the eye by their vividness, strangeness, and exoticism, and keep it away from the rest of the scene, where all is mysterious darkness.

As a matter of fact, black is the prevailing color in Poe. There is as yet no concordance of Poe's prose, but a study made by Wilson O. Clough of color words appearing in fifty-four of his stories yielded the grand total of 240 for "black," "dark," "ebony," and "sable," as against 152 for "red," "crimson," and "scarlet" and eighty-eight for "gold" and "yellow." (38) It is true that next to black Poe used such color words as "white," "pale," "pallid," "gray," and "silver," but these usually describe faces and clothing of characters and natural objects. Mr. Clough's conclusion is worth repeating: his three statistical tables reveal the preponderance of white and gray and confirm "the customary color associations with Poe's work as those of pallid figures against a black background, across which are shot occasional streamers of crimson and red." (39)

6

The pallid figures are another element in the uniqueness of a Poe story. Their lack of physical vividness is, in his special art, a source of strength rather than weakness. They are not memorable fictive characters in themselves, but they exist as an inseparable part of the strange milieu which Poe has imagined for them. If he deprecated Bulwer's "actors" because they impressed him, like Spenser's knights, as "mere stalking horses for particular vices and virtues," (40) shall we likewise condemn his own "actors" because they impress us as so many talking abstractions for particular moods and sensations?

Poe's characters may lack body as realistic transcriptions, but in the light of his own intention they are artistic creations nevertheless. In a marginal note he

once differentiated between two kinds of original characters in literature: those which present qualities known
in real life but never before depicted and those which
present qualities either unknown or known only hypothetically and "so skilfully adapted to the circumstances
which surround them that our sense of fitness is not
offended." The second kind, Poe felt, belongs to a
species of originality which "appertains to the loftier
regions of the Ideal." (41)

This is not very clear. Poe's concepts of originality
and Ideality are vague and contradictory, and what he
deemed effective characters in literature can only be
judged from his stories, especially those which, like
"Ligeia," he considered successful. As a practicing reviewer he had ample opportunity to express his views on
every phase of fiction, but he often wrote hastily and the
views of the moment were later modified or rejected
entirely. What conclusions, for instance, could we draw
from his definition of the novel as "a picture of real
life"? "The plot," he adds, "may be involved, but it
must not transcend probability. The agencies introduced must belong to real life." (42) How much
"real" life is there in his own short stories? How much
of their action does *not* transcend probability? And to
what extent are his characters "real" people?

The answer is not an easy one. There is a sort of
abstract reality about the best of Poe's actors which
serves his artistic purposes well. Poe seemingly did not
go around studying people, jotting down details of appearance, behavior, and expression for later use. Edmund Clarence Stedman was undoubtedly right in
concluding that character "did not seize" upon Poe's
interest, "except when marked by traits which he felt to

be his own." (43) He was in nearly everything he wrote his own protagonist: he describes himself, reveals himself, proudly exhibits his own mental and emotional acuteness, his aristocratic and aesthetic sensibilities, his ideal steadfastness and actual vulnerability, and his pale, feverish dreams and fancies.[11] Woodberry believed that Poe's hero first came upon the stage in "Berenice" (1835), but there is much to suggest that he appeared even earlier; in fact, at the very beginning of Poe's story-writing career. His first published tale, "Metzengerstein" (1832), contains a hero who in many ways — orphaned youth, nobility, impetuosity, courage, propensity toward meditation, and strange obsessive attachment — anticipates all the protagonists of the stories which Poe was to write during his entire career.

Two years later, in "The Assignation," we get another "ill-fated and mysterious" young man. But this time we have detailed physical description: the hero is below medium in height; his figure is slender and symmetrical; his mouth and chin would grace a deity; his eyes are "singular, wild, full, liquid," with shadows that vary from pure hazel to intense and brilliant jet; his hair is black and curly; his forehead is of unusual breadth; and his features are classically regular. Equally detailed is the description of the young man's mental and temperamental eccentricities: his eery laughter; his antic erudition; his knowledge and love of art; his habit of "intense continual thought"; his nervousness to the point of trepidation; his poetic creativeness, expressing

[11] " His presence pervades such tales as ' The Pit and the Pendulum,' ' The Cask of Amontillado ' or ' The Tell-Tale Heart ' no less densely than it pervades his ' William Wilson,' his ' Masque of the Red Death,' his ' Ligeia ' and ' The Haunted Palace.' " — Walter De La Mare, " A Revenant."

itself in the beautiful lines which Poe was later to publish separately under the title, "To One in Paradise"; and, finally, his death — a purposeful journey to the land of dreams. There can be no question that this hero is largely an embroidered projection of Poe himself.

Yet Woodberry's suggestion is true to the extent that in "Berenice" the self-delineation is bolder and clearer. The narrating "hero" avows that he loitered away his boyhood in books and dissipated his youth in reverie and that the realities of the world affected him only as visions. Berenice is his cousin with whom he grew up in his "paternal halls." It is, of course, the same cousin who reappears six years later in "Eleonora." In the earlier story the hero suffers from a strange malady, but Poe still hesitates to call it madness; he prefers to call it a monomania, a morbid irritability of the *attentive* faculties. In the later story he is bold enough to announce unequivocally, "I am mad." Thus the pattern of the Poe hero grows, becomes enlarged, assumes definite form.

The fullest portrait was achieved before "Eleonora." It is that of Roderick Usher (1839). Essentially we have the same hero from "Berenice," only he has grown a little older and much sicker. Poe's descriptive vocabulary has in the meantime — while still retaining many of the old adjectives — grown richer. Usher has

a cadaverousness of complexion; an eye large, liquid, and luminous beyond comparison; lips somewhat thin and very pallid, but of a surpassingly beautiful curve; a nose of delicate Hebrew model, but with a breadth of nostril unusual in similar formations; a finely moulded chin, speaking, in its want of prominence, of a want of moral energy; hair of a more than web-like softness and tenuity; these features, with an inordinate expansion above the regions of the temple, . . . altogether a countenance not easily to be forgotten . . . .

He also suffers from "habitual trepidancy — an excessive nervous agitation" and is given to action alternately vivacious and sullen. His voice varies from a tremulous indecision to "that species of energetic concision — that abrupt, weighty, unhurried, and hollow-sounding enunciation — that leaden, self-balanced and perfectly modulated guttural utterance, which may be observed in the lost drunkard, or the irreclaimable eater of opium, during the periods of his most intense excitement."

The language strives to be exact and vivid, but, for Poe's own day, it had the added significance derived from the then popular "science" of phrenology. Poe, who was interested in all science, had dipped into the numerous phrenological treatises with which the literary market was flooded and had appropriated many of its concepts and much of its vocabulary. (44) The writings of Gall, Combe, and Spurzheim were known to him; craniology with its division of the human head into areas in which the various faculties — Ideality, Causality, Constructiveness, Imagination, etc. — were supposed to reside impressed Poe. Individual temperament, aptitudes, and susceptibilities could be deduced from the shape, size and expression of features: forehead, eyes, nose, lips. Yet this special meaning which Poe apparently gave to his words must not blind us to their poetic coloring, descriptive aptness, suggestiveness, evocativeness of sensations, and power to help the story move.

If in "The Imp of the Perverse" Poe undertakes, as he announces in the first sentence, to add one more faculty, impulse, or propensity to the classifications of the phrenologists, he nevertheless manages to tell us, in

14

the latter part, an interesting murder story. The murderer is physically almost non-existent but psychologically he emerges strikingly self-revealed. The impulse to confession, whether phrenologically or psychologically sound, achieves the purpose of a brilliant dénouement.

The range of Poe's characters is narrow. Even where, as in "Hop-Frog," the hero is a crippled dwarfish court jester he still remains essentially the same suffering, ingenious, imaginative, sardonic protagonist of a macabre action. "We want characters," cries the king, "*characters*, man — something novel — out of the way. We are wearied with this everlasting sameness." But neither the jester nor Poe was capable of supplying variety; a man contemplating himself, spinning his creations out of himself, can only multiply his own likeness; masks can add lines, age, frozen grins, but they remain masks.

This narrowness of range is even more evident in Poe's women characters. The typical woman character in most of his stories is young, beautiful, noble, good, and wraith-like. Nearly always she suffers from a strange malady and comes to a sad end. If, like Berenice, she begins her story life "overflowing with energy," she soon becomes ravaged by disease, so that even her beauty is marred. More usually, however, Poe is too skilful a story-teller to try to encompass more than the last act in the life of his character.[12] As in "The Fall of the House

[12] The resemblance of the typical Poe story to a Greek tragedy is at times striking. The unities are approximated fairly closely. The cast of characters is generally kept down to a minimum. Except for the final dramatic moments, most of the "fable" is not enacted but reported by a participant, a ubiquitous eye-witness or — as in the case of the poisoning of the Marchesa di Mentoni — by a messenger. Much of the swiftness and power of the best of Poe's stories derive from this "Greek" concentration.

of Usher," everything but the climax and the dénouement has already happened before the rise of the curtain. The disease which has baffled Lady Madeline's
physicians completes its course the very evening of the
narrator's arrival. Antecedent action is introduced here
and there with a few dexterous strokes worthy of Henrik
Ibsen. Or, if it is the whole action — as in "The Oval
Portrait" — it is confined to one final paragraph, a quotation from a quaint and curious volume of forgotten lore.

The sad end of Poe's heroines is, as in all tragedy,
death. Those who have speculated on the psychological
reason for his obsession with the death of a beautiful
woman as a dominant theme in his tales and poems may
be right in ascribing it to his early impressions of the
death of his mother and, eleven years later, of Mrs.
Stanard. They may be right, also, in adding, as a major
factor, the long dying of Virginia. And, indeed, his
heroines — the Berenices, Morellas, Ligeias, Eleonoras
— bear many resemblances to the three women — perhaps even a fourth should be added: Mrs. Frances
Allan — who died young, bequeathing to him a sense of
desolation, impotent rebellion, and the haunting mystery
of vanished loveliness. Yet Poe was always the conscious
artist and his choice of this theme was ideally suited to
his creative patterns. It is significant that, although we
speak of his "heroines," actually Poe never wrote a story
in which a woman is the central character; all stories
revolve around a man, a romantic hero, and the woman
is presented only insofar as she impinges upon his consciousness and helps to solve his problem, his dilemma,
or to inspire his philosophy, release his eloquence, create
his mood.

The Marchesa Aphrodite, possessor of superhuman

beauty, also bears in her countenance "that fitful stain of melancholy which will ever be found inseparable from the perfection of the beautiful." It is the same stain which is imbedded in the lustre of Morella's eyes and is related to the "strangeness" without which Ligeia's beauty would perhaps not have been so exquisite. Ligeia is indeed the fullest development of Poe's ideal woman. She is tall, slender, yet majestic, with lovely but irregular features, with a lofty and pale forehead, a skin rivalling the purest ivory, glossy, raven-black, luxuriant hair, a delicate nose, a sweet mouth with a short upper lip and a soft, voluptuous under lip, startlingly brilliant teeth, a radiant smile, and large black eyes under long jetty lashes. Her voice, like that of Morella — and like the reputed voice of their creator — is low, placid, distinct, musically eloquent, and magically modulated. Her movements are incomprehensibly light and elastic. And her erudition, again like that of her creator, is prodigious.

And yet who is this woman? Is she more than one of the tribe whom Bliss Perry once so aptly characterized as "Ghostly, low-voiced women, tall, emaciated by mortal illness, but with more than mortal beauty in their eyes"? (45) She and her sisters existed only in Poe's imagination and they now exist in his stories and poems. For variety they may differ in minor features or little ways: the tresses may be fair instead of dark, or intellectuality may be wanting, as in Eleonora. But essentially they are alike, all modelled on one image. The exceptions are singularly few and insignificant. Aside from dying and thus fulfilling their appointed role in the plot and in the thoughts of the hero, they have little substantiality or individuality. Often, like Poe's male characters, they too are projections of Poe himself, as he was or imagined himself to be. The fanciful suggestion of Joseph Wood Krutch that Poe could not describe real women because he could not love in a " normal " way must be discarded for lack of proof.[13] It is more likely that Poe created his lost Lenores because they suited his artistic purposes. Why not believe him that he did find the death of a beautiful woman a disturbing and poetic theme? Moreover, for this theme he had memories of several models; and as these " real " women receded in time they acquired in his memory the necessary vagueness, indefiniteness, opaqueness, ethereality which his creative temper required.

It is not necessary to go into the more " normal " characters Poe describes in his tales of ratiocination and his so-called humorous sketches. I have already remarked on the resemblances between Mr. Poe and the brainy M. Dupin.[14] The Dr. Watson in these stories is merely a point of view. A character like Madame Lalande, in " The Spectacles," is too unbelievable to deserve serious comment. In short, only the " arabesque " actors and actresses are drawn with any distinction, and even to them the adverse judgment pronounced half a century ago by Lewis E. Gates applies: " Complex human characters, characters that are approximately true to the whole range of human motive and interest, Poe never gives us. He conceives of characters merely as means

[13] There is more validity in Roy P. Basler's hint of a confession of erotic love in Poe's description in the first paragraph of " Ligeia." (46) I believe this hint, if followed up by a study of the other stories, and the poems as well, would yield interesting results.

[14] Poe's confession to Philip Pendleton Cooke (" You are right about the hair-splitting of my French friend: — that is all done for effect.") does not contradict this resemblance; it rather confirms it. (47)

for securing his artificial effects on the nerves of his readers." (48) All this is quite true and has been repeated by many scholars and critics. But it is not the whole truth.

7

If, then, it is not plot, nor setting, nor characters, nor dialogue [15] which makes a Poe short story, other qualities must be sought for. The elements already discussed suggest the answer. Each taken separately remains part of a figure and has little meaning until joined with the other parts, for it has been *designed* to blend into a larger whole. Poe did not write stories of character, of plot, or of place: all the usual designations break down in his case. He wrote stories which attempted to transcribe the totality of a mood or impression or feeling and to create within the reader the same totality of mood, impression, or feeling. Poe's great achievement was the creation and mastery of a method for capturing and evoking in others his special type of imaginative experience.

This achievement was possible for him because he was, first and foremost, a story-teller. Along with his acquired literary and critical sophistication he possessed the gift of the primitive bard who was always aware of his audience, of himself as the center of attention, and of the tale he was to unfold in such a way as to hold his auditors spell-bound. The primitive bard was, of course, a poet, and so was Poe. It is significant that so many of his poems tell stories and that so many of his

[15] Dialogue has been treated in Chapter II. I have seen no reason for adding anything on this topic in connection with Poe's short stories. The weaknesses of the playwright are perhaps more glaring but they are essentially the same as the weaknesses of the story-teller.

stories can be classified as poems. Stedman regarded
"'Ligeia,' 'Usher,' 'Shadow,' 'Arnheim,' and the like"
as prose poems. (49) The opening of "The Raven"
is clearly in the bardic tradition of story-telling:

> Once upon a midnight dreary, while I pondered,
>   weak and weary,
> Over many a quaint and curious volume of for-
>   gotten lore —
> While I nodded, nearly napping, suddenly there
>   came a tapping,
> As of some one gently rapping, rapping at my
>   chamber door.

Four lines, one periodic sentence, telling when, where,
who, and beginning the action. An even better example
is the opening of "Annabel Lee": Once upon a time,
in a kingdom by the sea, there lived. . . . A story has
been promised, has begun. We, the auditors, settle
down to listen.

And what we hear is believable only because it is told
in a voice which bears the tints of conviction. The *tone*
is right. The tale itself may be strange, unearthly, full
of darkness and terror, but the teller is believable: he
has unmistakably been there himself; he has seen, heard,
smelled, felt, experienced the things of which he tells.
The tale may be unreal but the tone of verisimilitude
cannot be denied. Most of his stories — all the memorable ones, at any rate — are told in the first person; they
are strikingly like recitations, like dramatic monologues:

Of my country and of my people I have little to say. Ill
usage and length of years have driven me from the one, and
estranged me from the other.[16] ("MS. Found in a Bottle")

---

[16] It is interesting to note the similarity of this opening, and a few
of the others, to the beginnings found in many Old English story-poems
like "The Seafarer."

With a feeling of deep yet most singular affection I regarded my friend Morella. Thrown by accident into her society many years ago, my soul, from our first meeting, burned with fires it had never before known. . . .   ("Morella")

I cannot, for my soul, remember how, when, or even where, I first became acquainted with the Lady Ligeia.   ("Ligeia")

During the whole of a dull, dark, and soundless day in the autumn of the year, when the clouds hung oppressively low in the heavens, I had been passing alone, on horseback, through a singularly dreary tract of country; and at length found myself, as the shades of the evening drew on, within view of the melancholy House of Usher . . . . a sense of insufferable gloom pervaded my spirit.   ("The Fall of the House of Usher")

I am come of a race noted for vigor of fancy and ardor of passion. Men have called me mad. . . .   ("Eleonora")

For the most wild, yet most homely narrative which I am about to pen [tell], I neither expect nor solicit belief. Mad indeed would I be to expect it, in a case where my very senses reject their own evidence. Yet, mad am I not — and very surely do I not dream.   ("The Black Cat")

Not only is a tone of reality, something analogous to what we have learned to denominate as "reportage," struck in these first sentences, but also a distinctive melody. Poe's prose has subtle rhythms; it has the quality which he himself often praised in others, the quality of *repose.* Yet when smoothly flowing sentence is added to sentence and paragraph to paragraph, the undercurrent of emotion comes through with a terrific impact. Poe's melody is a compound of many elements: structure — variety of sentence length and order; color — darks and shades with flashes of light; distinctive adjectives and adverbs — "singular," "soundless," "dreary," "oppressively"; alliteration and assonance — "during . . . dull, dark . . . day," "low," "alone"; and unobtrusive repetition and oblique emphasis of crucial words and phrases. The final effect is certainly unique.

But the effect is achieved not alone by means of a distinctive prose. Everything — plot, characters and their names, setting and atmosphere, "props" and sounds — blends into this prose. If a character such as Usher is to possess a favorite book it must be the *Mad Trist* by Sir Launcelot Canning. The invention is made real by the narrator's casual assumption that his auditors are, of course, familiar with the volume: "I had arrived at that well-known portion of the story where Ethelred. . . ." This casual assumption of familiarity with a famous book is repeated in the next sentence: "Here, it will be remembered, the words of the narrative run thus." This is both ingenious and disarming. Similarly, if Ligeia is to compose a poem it must be "The Conqueror Worm," no less. Her shriek upon hearing the recitation of these verses is one that we can share: "O God! O Divine Father! — shall these things be undeviatingly so? — shall this Conqueror be not once conquered?" A futile and therefore stupid exclamation but one which mortal man, in his spasms of rebellion, has indulged in from time immemorial.

The moments when Poe's audience participates most fully in the action are carefully prepared for. The timing of an event or apparition is superbly calculated. It is precisely when the narrator arrives at the passage in the mythical volume "where Ethelred . . . proceeds to make an entrance by force" that the terrifying climax occurs. The passage, couched in a cleverly simulated archaic diction and style, begins:

And Ethelred, who was by nature of a doughty heart, . . . waited no longer to hold parley with the hermit, who, in sooth, was of an obstinate and maliceful turn, but, feeling the rain upon his shoulders, and fearing the rising of the tempest, uplifted his mace outright, and, with blows, made quickly room in the plankings of the door for his gauntleted hand; and now pulling therewith sturdily, he so cracked, and ripped, and tore all asunder, that the noise of the dry and hollow-sounding wood alarummed and reverberated throughout the forest.

It is precisely then that the narrator's ears become aware of "the very cracking and ripping sound which Sir Launcelot had so particularly described" echoed somewhere in a remote part of the mansion. Poe knows, however, with the instinct of a good showman as well as a good bard, that the time has not yet come to bring on the climax. This is but the first ominous sound of preparation; it must be repeated, varied, magnified until it, too, becomes a character in the action, the fearful Unknown, Fate.[17] For the present it is best to cast doubts upon its actuality by such parenthetical remarks as "(although I at once concluded that my excited fancy had deceived me)" and by describing the harmonizing storm which rages outside the mansion.

The narrator proceeds with the tale of Ethelred until he comes, in the very next paragraph, to the slaying of a prodigious fiery dragon. And now the harsh, horrid shriek with which the dragon dies is echoed by a "harsh, protracted, and most unusual screaming or grating sound" somewhere in the house. This time both the narrator and his auditors are certain that the sound is real. And once more the story of the doughty knight is resumed. Ethelred approaches the wall of the castle in

[17] Compare with Eugene O'Neill's use of the beating tom-toms in *Emperor Jones*. A careful reading of the script will reveal that O'Neill wishes the sound to increase, diminish, recede or come closer at appropriate moments in the thought-monologue of the fleeing "Emperor."

order to fetch the brazen shield when that object falls down "at his feet upon the silver floor, with a mighty great and terrible ringing sound." Immediately there is "a distinct, hollow, metallic, and clangorous, yet apparently muffled reverberation." The narrator leaps to his feet. The climax of his tale is approaching; it is to be enacted: the preparation has been completed. He turns to Roderick Usher. Does *he* hear the morbid assault of sounds? The answer comes in a "low, hurried, and gibbering murmur." Yes; how could he not hear it? These are the sounds of his sister trying to free herself from her coffin: she is still alive. She *has* freed herself! Even now her footsteps can be heard approaching. The "heavy and horrible beating of her heart" penetrates the door. Usher, too, springs to his feet. "I tell you," he shrieks, "that she now stands without the door." And the two men stand with their backs to the audience, as it were, watching with horrible fascination the "huge antique panels" slowly throwing back "their ponderous and ebony jaws" and disclosing the "lofty and enshrouded figure of the Lady Madeline of Usher."

Melodrama? Grand Guignol stuff? Perhaps. But how vividly and completely realized, and how superbly staged! No wonder John Macy found himself reluctantly admitting that "Even if [Poe's] tales of horror no longer give us the creeps, they will always give to any one who cares about writing, that shiver of pleasure which comes when we watch a dexterous craftsman at work." (50)

Powerfully as "The Fall of the House of Usher" illustrates Poe's use of sound effects, the device merits further attention. His ear was remarkably sensitive and his skill in manipulating a variety of sounds — variety in tone, quality, volume, range — at moments when their effect would be most telling was uncanny. Seldom, if ever, are his sounds mere additions to the plot, adventitious theatrical enrichment; usually, they are so well integrated with the plot that they are, or seem to be, an inseparable part of it, a dramatic means of unfolding it. The ironic jingling of bells which marks the end of "The Cask of Amontillado" is as perfect a curtain as could be devised. It is the inevitable touch which conveys the whole spirit of the piece. Just as the whole point of "The Devil in the Belfry" depends upon the behavior of the bells in the steeple. This story is, however, one of the Poe's lighter performances, and any effect he intended to create is hardly impressive.

For the full force of Poe's use of sound we must return to his psychological stories of guilt and terror. The monologuist in "The Tell-Tale Heart" is so acute of hearing that he claims having heard all things in heaven and earth — and many things in hell. With this figurative emphasis as preparation, we are willing to believe that he managed to open his victim's door eight midnights in succession without causing the hinges to creak; that on the last night he heard the old man's "slight" groan of mortal terror and the "low, dull, quick" beating of his heart, which soon increased to a "hellish tattoo" and filled the silence of the room until the murderer began to fear the sound would be heard by a neighbor; that after he had dismembered the body and washed off all blood stains he heard a bell strike the hour of four and, at the same moment, a knocking at the street door; and that he finally betrayed himself to the three police officers because he was certain that they too must hear the steady *"low, dull, quick sound —*

much such a sound as a watch makes when enveloped in cotton" — the incessant beating of the dead man's heart.

Only slightly less firmly integrated with the plot, and more theatrically effective, is the gigantic ebony clock in the black chamber in "The Masque of the Red Death." Any stage director would be immeasurably grateful for such clear, specific, and stimulating directions as the following passage contains:

Its pendulum swung to and fro with a dull, heavy, monotonous clang; and when the minute-hand made the circuit of the face, and the hour was to be stricken, there came from the brazen lungs of the clock a sound which was clear and loud and deep and exceedingly musical, but of so peculiar a note and emphasis that, at each lapse of an hour, the musicians of the orchestra were constrained to pause, momentarily . . . to hearken to the sound; and thus the waltzers perforce ceased their evolutions; and, while the chimes of the clock yet rang, it was observed that the giddiest grew pale, and the more aged and sedate passed their hands over their brows as if in confused reverie or meditation. But when the echoes had fully ceased, a light laughter at once pervaded the assembly; the musicians looked at each other and smiled as if at their own nervousness and folly, and made whispering vows, each to the other, that the next chiming of the clock should produce in them no similar emotion; and then, after the lapse of sixty minutes . . . , there came yet another chiming of the clock, and then were the same disconcert and tremulousness and meditation as before.

Poe knew well the electrifying effect of sudden silence in the midst of revelry, revelry staged as escape from intolerable fear. His silences are as eloquent as those of Chekhov, except that the emotional lava with which Poe's silences are charged is different. "For a moment, all is still, and all is silent save the voice of the clock. The dreams are stiff-frozen as they stand." And the voice, too, reaches a climax, at midnight, when it rings out twelve strokes, and the revellers become aware of the presence of an uninvited masque in their midst, a masque hiding the face of Death.

One of the means by which Poe achieves his effects is contrast. His silences are eloquent because they alternate with sound. His lighting is spectacular and mood-creating because it is arranged in little islands, focuses, surrounded by shadows. His colors are intense because they are glowing spots in the midst of darkness or no-color. The gentleness of the narrator in "The Black Cat" — his tenderness of heart, his love of animals — is in violent contrast with the sudden eruption of his latent sadism. That this use of contrast is deliberate cannot be doubted. Poe plays upon our senses, and he does it so effectively because he knew so well the dramatic value of sudden interruption, cessation, or diversion of sound or light; as well as he knew the value of pause and modulation in his own voice when he "entertained," debated, lectured, recited, or "conversed."

He was himself the source, the reservoir, and the object of his sensuous effects. The almost preternatural keenness of one sense or another avowed by his heroes was characteristic of Poe himself. He revelled in the rich scenery and splendid properties he imagined. He delighted in the touch of silk, velvet, brocade, and damask. He was thrilled, soothed, and saddened by music.[18] And the vividness with which he transcribes

[18] And since his stories — excellent theatre as they are — were cast in the *form* of fiction, he did not need to forgo the advantages to be derived from transcribing olfactory sensations. "I believe," he wrote in one of his *Marginalia*, "that odors have an altogether peculiar force, in affecting us through association; a force differing *essentially* from that of objects addressing the touch, the taste, the sight, or the hearing." (51) He was a good enough "associationist" to record: "The senses were oppressed by mingled and conflicting perfumes, reeking up from strange convolute

his sensory experiences contributes powerfully to the response his stories evoke. It is one of the elements with which he weaves the artistic and emotional pattern he envisages as the finished story.

In the end, we must come back to the art of pattern-weaving as Poe's strongest point. His plots may be melo-dramatic, his characters may lack roundness and their dialogue may be monotonic, his décor, lighting, timing, and other devices may be theatrical, but they blend per-fectly into a style which is absorbing, individual, unique. His was indeed the sort of mind that Gordon Craig wished for in the theatre: "a single directing mind that can give a production artistic unity." (52) It is not any single part that is outstanding or even distinguished but the synchronization or — better still — the orchestration. His stories are frequently dramatic productions in which Poe displays his craftsmanship as bard, playwright, stage-designer, electrician, actor, elocutionist, and, above all, director. This display has at times worried his critics, such as Edward J. O'Brien who felt that Poe would have been stronger had he more successfully concealed his elaborately calculated artifice. (53) Had Poe been able to read this opinion he would have agreed with it. "It is the curse of a certain order of mind," he once wrote, "that it can never rest satisfied with the consciousness of its ability to do a thing. Still less is it content with doing it. It must both know and show how it was done." (54)

And yet even this weakness has proved, in the century that has elapsed since his death, a source of strength to others. Craftsmen everywhere have derived added joy

censers . . ." ("The Assignation"). Or: "the tar or paint with which it [the oblong box] was lettered . . . emitted a strong, disagreeable, and . . . a peculiarly disgusting odor."

in reading Poe's stories from catching a glimpse at times of his superb methodology. There have always been "poets' poets" and "writers' writers"; Poe has been one of the few exceptional creative artists who have been able to impart joy to other writers and to hold the general reader as well. Philip Rahv, in his introduction to a recently published collection of *The Short Novels of Tolstoy* (55) speaks with respect of "the conception of writing as of something calculated and constructed — a conception first formulated explicitly by Edgar Allan Poe." But Poe did more than formulate a conception; he embodied it in stories which testify to the artistic validity of the conception. "Art," said Henry James with quiet enthusiasm, after he had seen Ibsen's *Hedda Gabler*, "is a legerdemain." James and Poe were poles apart as men and writers, but each proved, in his own way, that artistic discipline is a living principle.

8

To leave this study of Poe's short stories with the impression that all the values they contain are his method and his masterly use of it would amount to a blanket approval of the criticism that has been levelled against him for being a literary craftsman and nothing else. The substance of most of this criticism is, I believe, fairly expressed in the following passage by Lewis E. Gates:

Whether the effect that Poe aims at is a shiver of surprise at the sudden ingenious resolution of a riddle, or a shudder of horror at the collapse of a haunted house, his methods of work are substantially the same, and the stuff from which he weaves his tale is equally unreal and remote from what ordinary life has to offer; it is all the product of an infinitely inventive intellect that devises and plans and adroitly arranges with an un-

flinching purpose to attain an effect. The better poetry, the
more feigning; and Poe is an excellent poet in these prose-
poems. He can invent with endless ingenuity and plausibility,
play-passions, play-moods, play-sensations, play-ideas, and play-
complications of incident. He is an adept in fitting these mock
images of life deftly together, in subtly arranging these simu-
lacra of real feeling and real thought so that they shall have
complete congruity, shall have the glamour and the momentary
plausibility of truth, and shall rally together at the right
moment in a perfect acclaim of music. (56)

Since much of this is true, it would be folly to attempt a
defense of Poe. Besides, Poe has spoken for himself;
we but need to recall his statement in the "Poetic
Principle" that "there neither exists nor *can* exist any
work more thoroughly dignified — more supremely
noble" — than a "poem written solely for the poem's
sake." (57) I feel certain that Poe would enter no
objection to our substituting "story" for "poem." If he
chose to write stories solely for the stories' sake, there is
little point in implying that his "infinitely inventive
intellect," his adroitness in planning and devising, his
"endless ingenuity" — in other words, the marked qualities which prove his talent for his chosen task — were
somehow against him.

It has been my aim in these pages to emphasize the
kinship of Poe's art with the arts of the theatre. That
kinship impresses me as lending strength to his work,
and accounts for much of its effectiveness. The best
tales of Poe are masterpieces of theatrical contrivance,
but it would be critical blindness not to note that they
contain other levels of significance. The theatre itself,
tight little world of make-believe that it is, in which
everything is planned and arranged and nicely balanced,
operates on more than one level. It always makes room

15

for the display of the incalculable and indefinable human personality. Poe's stories, like the world of the theatre, bear this animating spirit; they are permeated with this subtle infusion.

In providing him with opportunities for displaying himself, these carefully contrived fictions managed to reflect many facets of a complex personality. Here along with his showmanship, his histrionic skill and gusto, are also serious betrayals of thoughts, reflections, desires, aspirations, and objective observation. One cannot quarrel with Professor Floyd Stovall's words that "Poe was absorbed in himself, in analyzing his mind and soul and in worshiping them with incense and exotic offerings," (58) but one can add that in staining the pages of his books with his moods and passions Poe also managed to give to the world a picture of his mind. And it is, indeed, an "incisive and curious mind," full of vagaries and strange fancies, but also full of sensitive perceptions.

A more recent critic than Gates objects to Poe's theory of "a certain single or unique effect" because it seems "to define, if anything, an impossibly simple and crude story." (59) As if the production of a single effect necessarily demands the exclusion of other values! Because Poe employed his disciplined artistry in imparting to his tales unity of tone and impression, does it follow that he had left behind him his keen intellect and his complex tangled personality, so that the materials with which he worked are bare of any implications, any significance for the student of ideas, character, or life in general? Ludwig Lewisohn credits him with at least moments of insight and praises him for defining originality in literature as the ability to bring out "the half-formed, the reluctant, or the unexpressed fancies of mankind." (60) That definition was easy for Poe and he probably enjoyed writing it, for it makes his own literary pages appear to be full of originality. And, in truth, besides managing to construct a number of absorbingly readable and stageworthy short fictions, he also managed to imbue them with psychological overtones which have stimulated the speculations of numerous professional and lay psychologists.

Poe's contribution to our understanding of the mind, especially in its less "normal" manifestations, is not easy to estimate. In recent years it has been his misfortune to attract the attention of many psychoanalysts. He seems to be an ideal subject upon whom they can hang their theories. Undoubtedly much of what they have written about him and his work has an air of plausibility, but it is safe to say nevertheless that most of their deductions and inductions are pure fantasy. Just as lack of evidence did not stop Mr. Krutch from ascribing sexual impotence to Poe, so lack of evidence has not deterred psychoanalytically-minded interpreters of his work from drawing inferences that, at least to the uninitiated, seem absurd.

Thus in an article entitled, "A Psycho-Analytical Study of Edgar Allan Poe," (61) Lorine Pruette indulges in a whole series of speculations regarding the hidden meaning of his stories.[19] Some of Miss Pruette's observations appear to be merely too positive and too sweeping but otherwise unobjectionable. Such, for example, is her comment that Poe's women

are never human; they are not flesh and blood, loving, hating or coming late to appointments — they are simply beautiful lay

---

[19] The article is, of course, equally concerned with his poems, his critical writings, his life, and his unconscious.

figures around which to hang wreaths of poetical sentiments. His emotional interest lay in himself, rather than in outer objects; he wished to be loved, rather than to love.

What, however, can be said for her elaborate reading of sex symbolism into Poe's use of color and lights? There are no "ifs," "perhapses," "maybe's" in Miss Pruette's vocabulary. She notes that in "Ligeia" there are three colors: gold, black, and red, and concludes that they symbolize death and sex. She notes the intricate lighting fixture Poe designed for his heroine's chamber; it, too — or rather "the serpent-like flames" it creates — represents sex. Her summary of sex symbols includes

red lights, crimson-tinted glass, scarlet panes, the ruddy reflection from burning buildings, the fiery colored horse, fiery colored clouds, blood-red metal, intense light of rubies, the red poppies, wine red as blood, rain that changed to blood, the fiery wall of the horizon, red clouds, the red eye of the sun, the crimson moon.

Miss Pruette is, of course, not the only worker in this colorful vineyard. On this very subject of the possible signification of Poe's use of color, Clement Wood, a poet gone psychoanalyst, picks one of Poe's flowers and writes learnedly of it:

To the Greeks, asphodel was the pale plant of the dead; in its corrupted form "dafodill," it was golden; it was never ruby-red but in Poe: and red was the color of lust, of the scarlet woman, of the flames of hell that punished sinful lovers. . . . (62)

For Miss Pruette, the seventh chamber, in "The Masque of the Red Death," with its black draperies and scarlet panes, is a supreme example of the sex motif which, consciously or unconsciously, underlies much if not all of Poe's work. And the tired criminal in "The

Tell-Tale Heart" wishing for the sweet rest of the grave is, with the authority of Jung and Silberer, really wishing to creep back into the mother's womb. Mr. Wood goes even beyond Miss Pruette in attributing to Poe an unconscious obsessive longing for his mother. "The sea imagery," he informs us, "like the 'Descent into the Maelstrom,' remotely hints at the mother; even in a mere adventure fantasy, Poe has himself drawn three times into the hideous womb of mother earth. . . ." (63)

All this — and the numerous speculations of sadism and masochism and the death wish in Poe's work — is not, however, as reprehensible as Miss Pruette's acceptance of "rumors which still go the round of the clubs in Baltimore" that Poe was "definitely" syphilitic and her building upon them a pyramid of analysis of Poe's characteristics. It is in deploring the manner in which he has often been used to "prove" all sorts of theories that one is tempted to join his doting female biographers and exclaim "Poor Poe!"

The truth is that Poe's stories have a tremendous amount of symbolic and psychological significance. But his symbols were those of a poet whose native idiom was figurative language, whose mind habitually thought in rich imagery, at once luxurious, indefinite, and romantic. And his psychology was the inevitable reflection of a sharp intellect giving full artistic (and therefore subject to interpretation and misinterpretation) expression of his own observations, impulses, and contradictions. That his field of observation and exploration was largely limited to himself has deprived his work of range and variety but has subtilized and intensified the subjective segment of inner human experience upon which his mind focused.

There is more justice and understanding in the comments of a man like Dostoievsky, a literary artist and
natural-born psychologist himself, who early perceived
the real nature of Poe's contribution to our understanding of psychological phenomena. Poe, for Dostoievsky,
was not really fantastic at all, in the sense in which
Hoffmann — who in certain minor ways influenced Poe
(64) — was, but capricious and audacious.

He chooses . . . the most extravagant reality, places his hero
in a most extraordinary outward or psychological situation, and,
then, describes the inner state of that person with marvellous
acumen and amazing realism. Moreover, there exists one characteristic that is singularly peculiar to Poe and which dis-
tinguishes him from every other writer, and that is the vigor of
his imagination. (65)

Dostoievsky does not make the mistake of abstracting
Poe's psychology from his work. Separated, it ceases to
exist. Its reality depends upon its being imbedded in
an imaginative setting. Even his "marvellous acumen
and amazing realism" are qualities of his descriptive
powers and are, presumably, generated or called to life
in the process of creation. Aesthetic and psychological
values in Poe do not exist independently. Stedman
realized this when he called Poe an artist bent on psychological effect. (66)

We definitely can read a Poe story on more than one
level, since it is certain that every artist creates on more
than one level. Art like life carries many layers of meaning. A recent critic, George Snell, sees in "Ligeia" an
allegory "for belief in the impossibility of finding a substitute for a first love, when that love is obsessive." As
an expression of the unconscious, Mr. Snell believes, the
story anticipates Freud by nearly a century. (67) He
sees in the "MS. Found in a Bottle" a parable of man's

passage through life and in "William Wilson" and "The Fall of the House of Usher" two studies of the schizophrenic mind. All these readings are tributes to the richness of Poe. He yields meanings to those who seek them.

It is, however, doubtful that Poe had any consciousness of planting allegories or psychological riddles. He was drawn to certain paradoxes and "perversities" in human behavior and thought they might eventuate in effective fictions. If the result, as in "The Tell-Tale Heart" and in "The Black Cat," was also an impressive revelation of the burden of a guilty conscience, it was merely incidental. Nothing was more distasteful to Poe than a didactic or "teaching" story. If in many stories he anticipated Freud or Jung or Lombroso,[20] that too was incidental. Robert Louis Stevenson considered "The Imp of the Perverse" an important contribution to morbid psychology. (68) So undoubtedly it was — and is. But for a true understanding of Poe it is well for us to remember that his stories were by intention and hope meant to be works of art.

There cannot be the slightest doubt that "The Masque of the Red Death" describes the terror man has of impending death and that in his method of description Poe employed imaginative symbolism in word and object and incident. Yet M. H. Bobrova, the Russian scholar who in 1937, in a doctoral dissertation, (69) worked out in detail the resemblance of this story to a play has added a great deal to our comprehension and enjoyment of this remarkable work and of Poe's artistic intention. Miss Bobrova divides the play into a prologue (enacted in front of the curtain) and a number of scenes

---

[20] See his suggestion, in "Eleonora," that madness and genius are related.

leading up to a climax in the confrontation between the
Prince and Death. If we bear in mind that Poe himself
called his story "The Masque of the Red Death" and
that he was familiar with Elizabethan and post-Elizabethan masques, both the elaborate pageantry — unusual
even for Poe — and the dramatic power of the piece
become explicable as an artistic creation. Other levels
of meaning — the unconscious betrayal of fear, possible
hidden sex motifs, etc., — are of secondary importance.

Poe used psychological situations and symbolism to
gain aesthetic effects. He worked in certain colors because they represented for him certain subjective associations and helped him to achieve certain desired effects.
What color could have served him better than black for
conjuring an atmosphere of dread and gloom, than purple or gold for representing opulence and magnificence,
than scarlet and crimson for intensifying the illusion of
bloody catastrophe? [21] The colors of the seven chambers
in the "Masque" suggest to Professor Blair the allegorical signification of the seven ages of man who progresses "from the blue of the dawn of life to the black
of its night." (71) Did Poe mean to imply this signification? It would be interesting to know, but since we
cannot — unless some new Poe material is discovered —
we must accept the story as we accept a piece of music:
in spite of program notes which would limit the meaning
of what we hear, we generally let ourselves go and create
our own meaning. But to make us let go and become
creative the music must be good.

[21] And what could have suited his imagination better, for such a story
as " The Thousand-and-Second Tale of Scheherazade," than the invention of a blue rat, a sky-blue cow and a pink horse with green wings?
The only inference Van Wyck Brooks wisely draws from these creations
is that Poe anticipated certain modern painters. (70)

CHAPTER VI

THE ANGEL ISRAFEL

" None sing so wildly well
As the angel Israfel . . . ."

THE NUMBER of writers who have attempted to
exploit Poe as a fictional and dramatic character
has been legion. Perhaps "exploit" is too strong and
ungracious a word; perhaps in many cases the authors
have been misled by their admiration of the poet or by
their sympathy with his tragic life into believing that
they could build around him a memorable novel or play.
Their efforts have been fruitless. Not one piece of
literature of any importance — except half a dozen fine
lyrics — has been the result. Somehow this most tantalizing of romantic figures in literary history has proved
singularly uninteresting as the hero in a novel or on the
stage.

It may be argued that so far no first-rate novelist or
dramatist has undertaken the task. This is a fact, but it
proves only that first-rate novelists and dramatists know
better than to expend their creative energy on unpromis-
ing material. On the other hand, merely competent
novelists and playwrights have done very well with
Shelley, Byron, George Sand, Zola, Oscar Wilde, the
Brontë sisters, the Brownings, and even the recluse
Emily Dickinson. The lives of these writers provide
material which can be shaped into plots; the characters

217

of these writers can be recreated into living personalities. Poe's life, in spite of its hectic succession of incidents or events, remains static and his character emerges as pallid as that of one of his own heroes.

There is meaning in the fact that while his life and personality dramatize but poorly or not at all, his work when enlarged and reshaped into a novel, a play, a radio script, or a motion picture scenario often has both strength and beauty. Plays especially, when based on Poe's life, have been unrewarding; when based on his short stories and poems, they have been generally successful. This interesting phenomenon, it seems to me, is an important part of the "mystery" that is Poe. It points to a significant relationship between his literary work and his personality and helps to define the nature and meaning of both.

No complete chronological list of novels and short stories in which Edgar Allan Poe figures either as protagonist or subsidiary character has ever been compiled. Most of the early attempts at fictionized biography of him have died, and — judging by the few that survive — mercifully. What was wrong with them can be surmised from a perusal of Mary Newton Stanard's *The Dreamer*, first published in 1909 and reissued in 1925.

This novel evidently had a fairly popular reception, for its author tells us in a foreword to the reissue that "Home papers praised it, favorable press notices from all parts of the country flowed in, people bought and read it and sent it off in various directions as birthday and Christmas presents." Apparently, interest in Poe was as great in the earlier decades of our century as it is today. Readers, however, got only what the author claimed her work was meant to offer: "a romantic rendering" of

Poe's life-story. To the serious student the book could offer little that he did not already know and much that contradicted what he knew. For even in 1909 scholars knew that Elizabeth Arnold Poe had not "lately lost a dearly loved and loving husband," that it was highly questionable that Eliza White, "for all her beauty and charm, and many suitors," had remained a spinster because she had remained in love with the poet, and that it was more than questionable that "The Raven" was written in Philadelphia, where Poe read it to Mr. Graham's office force.

To the general reader, the novel offered what he — or more likely she — expected: a sentimental story about a handsome unhappy genius who composed great poems and stories and who, despite poverty, ill health, and many temptations, remained constant to his only love, the pathetic little Virginia, the "lost Lenore." According to Mrs. Stanard there were always two Poes: Edgar Goodfellow, an outgiving, lovable chap, and Edgar the Dreamer, who lived in an invisible world of mystery. All of the troubles that came upon the handsome hero arose from the clash of these two personalities: Edgar Goodfellow would have got along nicely in the world, but Edgar the Dreamer would not let him. Of course, there were also jealousy, envy, and villainy — in the person of the wicked Doctor Griswold — which the genius had to contend with. Long before Mrs. Stanard's novel it had been known that Rufus Wilmot Griswold was not a very scrupulous antagonist, and Professor Quinn's recent researches have confirmed this knowledge; but there is still not the slightest shred of evidence to justify Mrs. Stanard in portraying him as the villain who did not "permit" the publication of "The Raven"

in *Graham's Magazine.* Of this particular wickedness
he was not, and could not have been, guilty.

We must remember, however, that — in spite of the
author's claim that she made an attempt to conform her
story "to the latest discoveries regarding Poe's life" —
she was writing fiction. And it is as fiction that we must
judge her performance. A few sentences selected almost
at random are sufficient to indicate the literary tone of
Mrs. Stanard's novel. Nat Howard, a boy at school who
offensively reminds fourteen-year old Edgar that his
mother had been a "common actress," receives a lengthy
reply, part of which reads:

Yes! she was an actress! And I'm proud of it as surely as she is
an angel in Heaven! And I'm proud that my father — the son
of a proud family — had the spirit, for her sweet sake, to fly in
the face of convention, to count family, fortune and all well
lost, to become her husband, and to adopt her profession; to
learn of her, in order that he might be always at her side to
protect her and to live in the light of her presence. If I had
choice of all the surnames and of all the lineage in the world,
I would still choose the name of Poe, and to be the son of David
and Elizabeth Poe, players!

We are told that during Poe's residence in Philadelphia
he walked along the street and "passers-by whispered
to one another, 'There goes Mr. Poe. Did you notice
his eyes? They say he has the most expressive eyes in
Philadelphia.'" Or we get this description of Virginia
dying: "in the bed-chamber upstairs, under the shelving
walls of the low Dutch roof, The Dreamer's hearts-ease
blossom lay broken and wan upon the white bed . . . .
At the foot of the bed sat a silver-haired woman with
saint-like face uplifted in resignation and admiration."
Fortunately we are spared the soft music of the age of
sound pictures.

What novelists and "biographers" like Mrs. Stanard represent is the tribe of ladies whom Arthur Hopkins had in mind when he referred to Poe's posthumous sweethearts. In his own day Poe attracted the adoring attention of many literary ladies; he accepted their sympathy, their lyrics to Israfel, their celebration of his magnetic eyes and magic voice,[1] until their jealousy of one another involved him in irksome situations and he was provoked to calling them "pestilential." But, whether contemporary or posthumous, they helped to spread the legend of the ill-starred genius who battled manfully — albeit at times weakly, and therefore all the more deserving of sympathy — for wife and mother-in-law and Art and the Ideal. When they came to write his life-story they approached him with pleasant trepidation and hearts full of sentiment. They have all been more or less like the lady whose lengthy account of a visit with Poe has recently come to light. (2) "I silently recalled 'The Raven,'" the lady records, "by way of sobering my spirits to a proper degree of seriousness, being about to enter the presence of a grave and melancholy poet, as I imagined Poe to be."

He has been approached "soberly" ever since. Even disciplined writers like Dorothy Dow and Laura Benét — neither of whom can be remotely connected with the tribe — have entered his presence with a proper degree

[1] The following episode — told by a lady who one day, in 1847, accompanied Poe and a group of admirers on a walk along the banks of the Bronx — characterizes the antics of the tribe and Israfel's acceptance of them: "In one of the pauses of this pleasant talk, one of the ladies placed on the head of the poet an oak-leaf wreath; and as he stood beneath the tree, half in the shade, the sun's rays glancing through the dark-green leaves, and lighting up his broad white forehead, with a pleasant gratified smile on his face, my memory recalls a charming picture of the poet. . . ." (1)

of seriousness. Miss Dow's *Dark Glory* (1931) maintains the tone of her title; she manages to portray an always grave and melancholy poet, but her hero remains without light; and her novel remains shapeless. Miss Benét's more modest offering, *Young Edgar Allan Poe* (1941), is by all odds the best of the many Poe biographies which avowedly contain legendary material and imaginary conversation. Clearly intended as a boy's book, this "story of a great American artist" emphasizes the earlier years of Poe's life and tries valiantly to be both reasonably truthful and entertaining. In the end, it is no more successful than Miss Dow's *Dark Glory*.

Neither of the two estimable authors is to blame. The material they chose lacks excitement. Miss Dow finds it easier to convince her readers of her subject's darkness than of his glory. And Miss Benét, breaking off her narrative with Poe's more successful and relatively happy years in Philadelphia, finds herself obliged to look into the future when "the somber genius," having early sealed a compact with a Shadow, or Fate, would continue to write "without the aid of riches or lasting peace of spirit," hearing, as his reward, "the harsh croaking of a raven over his head."

Those novelists who have made use of Poe as a minor character have fared much better. Anya Seton, whose *Dragonwyck* was a popular seller in 1943-1944 and served as the basis of a moving picture a short time later, was not troubled by the problem of fidelity to the known facts of Poe's life. Her hero, a Dutch patroon named Nicholas Van Ryn, and his wife Miranda accompany Mrs. Ellet on a visit to Poe at Fordham. It is a hot day in the summer of 1846. Nicholas brings with him a bottle of brandy and the poet proceeds to get himself unpleasantly drunk, in spite of the fact that Virginia's physician — the famous Dr. Francis — happens to be with him at the time. However, he is still able to read and he regales his guests with a rendition of "Ulalume," accentuating each syllable with delicacy and rounding each word to the fullest melody. "From his actor parents," Miss Seton informs us, "he had inherited the talent of communicating emotion to an audience." (3) The novelist encounters no difficulty in "explaining" Poe's having written an elegy on the death of his wife many months before she died: it "foreshadowed" the event, we are told, "and the recurring defeat of his own soul."

Still more fortunate have been the fictioneers who have used Poe's work rather than Poe to complicate or embellish their plots. Certainly a most readable murder yarn was invented by Amelia Reynolds Long in *Death Looks Down* (1944). Her novel is divided into a prologue, five books, and an epilogue, and each of these divisions is headed by a title borrowed from Poe: "Ulalume," "The Cask of Amontillado," "The Mystery of Marie Roget," "The Murders in the Rue Morgue," "Metzengerstein," "The Fall of the House of Usher," and "Eureka." The various chapters in each division are headed by quotations taken from those works of Poe which have supplied their titles for the major divisions; thus under Book One, The Cask of Amontillado, Chapter I is headed by the phrase, "Into the inmost recesses of the catacombs," and under Book Five, The Fall of the House of Usher, Chapter III is headed by the phrase, ". . . within view of the melancholy House of Usher."

The author is an apt student of Poe. Her plot is as

ingenious as the pattern in which she has cast it. The story is located in Philadelphia, with the action originating in the library of a university named after that city. The characters are mainly the students of Professor Patrick Rourke who is conducting a seminar in the life and works of Edgar Allan Poe. The plot begins when a member of the seminar finds in an old *Graham's Magazine* a handwritten copy of "Ulalume." The university buys it from him for $10,000, but a wealthy private collector is willing to pay $15,000 for it. As the story progresses no less than four murders are committed and almost everybody is suspected of being the perpetrator of these bloody deeds. In the end, the murderer is discovered in a manner as theatrical as Poe himself might have staged it[2] and as full of ratiocination as M. Dupin might have enjoyed exhibiting.

3

If it seem remarkable that Poe's life and character should fictionize so indifferently, it is even more remarkable that they should dramatize so much less than indifferently. Almost anyone would guess that this fascinating personality would translate well on the stage and that the tragic story of his life would supply a surefire plot with plenty of complication, tension, romantic interest, and emotional appeal. In the course of a century many writers — and some of them men and women of considerable creative talent — have thus guessed, and lost. Only a few years ago Sophie Kerr hazarded the opinion that "Poe with a dark moustache and longish

[2] The sensational close of this mystery thriller is, in fact, not unlike that of Poe's "Thou Art the Man." The quality of the writing — mood, style, tone — is of course different.

locks — Poe would have been a natural for films." (4)
Since Miss Kerr has been eminently successful in meeting the requirements of our large-circulation magazines
one is tempted to credit her with shrewd judgment of
public taste, yet Miss Kerr was mistaken in her opinion.
Poe has proved far from "a natural" either for films or
for the stage.

It is not conceivable that we shall ever know all the
plays that have been written around Poe's life. Until
comparatively recent years it was not the practice of
playwrights to publish their work, and even now only
a small number of the plays produced in any season
find their way into print. The bulk of all scripts written
remains, of course, unproduced and unprinted. The
frequency with which one meets references to plays —
long or short — on the life of Poe indicates that he has
been used, again and again, as a subject in drama. If
those that have survived, in published or manuscript
form, can in any way be accepted as representative exhibits, then one is forced to shake his head with regret
at this vain expenditure of effort.

Poe began to serve as a model for a character in a play
as early as 1827, when he was not quite eighteen years
old. In August and September of that year Lambert
A. Wilmer serialized in the Baltimore *North American*
a poetic drama in three acts entitled *Merlin*. (5) What
little plot it contained revolved around two young lovers,
Elmira and Alphonso, who had been separated by a
cruel father (hers) and who were reunited by the be-
nign magic of Merlin. One recognizes in this "complication" the early love story of Edgar Poe and Elmira
Royster. Professor Mabbott's conjecture that Wilmer
obtained the details of the story from Poe's brother,

16

William Henry Leonard Poe, is highly plausible. (6)
Henry had been in correspondence with Edgar, had met
Elmira in Richmond, and had read Edgar's poetic rendering of his unhappy experience in *Tamerlane*. (7)
His brother's romantic episode had impressed him
strongly enough to stimulate his own creative imagination. The same periodical which published Wilmer's
play on the subject, also published, a few months later,
"The Pirate," a short story in which the plot is obviously
based on the Edgar-Elmira incident. (8)

Although Poe, the brilliant young critic of the
Southern Literary Messenger, found portions of *Merlin*
"full of the truest poetic fire," (9) it is, as a whole,
undistinguished as poetry and downright impossible as
drama. The four major characters are as misty as the
numerous sprites and furies that drift in and out as
messengers, terpsichoreans, and singers. More important, young Alphonso reveals himself as a whining, self-
pitying puppet of fate; he lacks even a modicum of the
dignity which might qualify him for a hero undergoing
what has come to be known as romantic agony. Wilmer's play marks the beginning of Poe's long career as
an imaginary being — and it was not an auspicious beginning.

Ever since, the approach to Poe as a possible protagonist in drama has been solemn and lugubrious. To
come closer to our own age, there was *Edgar Allan Poe,
or The Raven*, a five-act prose opus by George Hazelton, Jr., which opened, appropriately enough, in Baltimore on October 11, 1895. The leading part was
interpreted by no less an actor than Creston Clarke,
grandson of Junius Brutus Booth and nephew of the
great Edwin Booth. Yet since Mr. Hazelton undertook

his task — as he informed an interviewer — because he had been attracted by "the sadly romantic career of the most interesting figure in American literature," (10) his play turned out to be only an unimpressive melodrama about "a person with a wild, sombre, morbid imagination, a pale intellectual face, and an expression almost habitually sad." (11) Having been an actor himself [3] — before taking up the practice of law — Mr. Hazelton foresaw the unrelieved gloom of his play and proceeded to supply comic relief by creating a few farcical characters and scenes. His intentions were undoubtedly praiseworthy but his achievement was severely condemned by the Baltimore dramatic critics of the day. The *Sun* reviewer resented the "boorish people whose coarse wit was entirely out of keeping with the innate refinement of Poe and whose presence upon the stage amounted to positive irreverence when they interrupted the poet as he was kneeling beside the grave of his dead wife." And the *American* reviewer found the scenes "intended to lighten up the sombre story" in atrocious taste; they had the effect of "desecration." (13) Evidently Mr. Hazelton had chosen the wrong moments in which to indulge his humor. Evidently, also, the Baltimore reviewers — and no doubt the Washington and Richmond reviewers as well (for the play was featured in all three cities) — wished to take their Poe straight. Levity, in their opinion, did not become Israfel.

The action of *Edgar Allan Poe* is a weird mixture of fact and fancy. The first act takes place in the Allan home in Richmond just after Edgar's return from the University of Virginia. According to Mr. Hazelton, Edgar was even then wildly in love with his cousin

[3] He had played with Edwin Booth in *Hamlet*. (12)

Virginia Clemm, but the course of his love was blocked by Roscoe Pelham, A. M., Mr. Allan's secretary; and it was this villainous individual, himself in love with Virginia, who disclosed Edgar's gambling debts to Mr. Allan. The second act shifts the action to the Poe cottage at Fordham. Mr. Pelham arrives while Poe is out selling or trying to sell some of his manuscripts and seizes the opportunity to force his love upon Virginia. She fights him off until Poe returns; but she does not tell her husband of Pelham's love making, for fear that the impetuous poet might challenge the villain to a duel and be killed. However, the excitement of her encounter has exhausted her and she dies in Edgar's arms. The third act — . But perhaps the synopses of the two acts are enough to indicate the nature of Mr. Hazelton's inventiveness. Eight years later Mr. Hazelton published a revised version of the play under the title *The Raven; A Play in Four Acts and a Tableau,* and six years still later he rewrote the whole thing in the form of a lengthy novel, *The Raven; The Love Story of Edgar Allan Poe.*

It is interesting to note that although playwrights like Mr. Hazelton usually profess to have made a detailed "study" of Poe's life they nevertheless feel free to violate all the known facts. This is more than indulgence in so-called poetic license; this is, in the case of a subject like Poe, a psychological phenomenon. Mr. Hazelton, for instance, felt no need to account for the presence of Virginia in Richmond at the time of Edgar's return from Charlottesville, nor for Mrs. Whitman's presence at Fordham and in Baltimore. But what is perhaps more significant still is that a playwright who was, not so many years later, to turn out such a workmanlike dramaturgic product as *Yellow Jacket* (in collaboration with

Benrimo, to be sure) could permit himself to write the kind of dialogue ascribed to Poe. In one love scene young Edgar is insistent that Virginia give him another kiss. When she playfully refuses he is made to say:

Refuse me a kiss, one kiss, a paltry kiss? A niggard of a kiss? Why the zephyrs, playing in your glossy curls, rob you of them every day you live, as they lovingly pass by, and you never say them " nay "; the sunbeams wrest them from your lips to feed the daisies with; they are silvered by the moonbeams on a summer's night; the joyous song bursting into bloom between these love-lips breathe millions of kisses into life. Why, worse than the hoarder of the mountain's gold, or the gray-beard, tottering to a lonely grave, clutching, as some drowning man, the jewels of a selfish life, is the miser of a kiss.

This apparently was meant to be " poetry," the every-day language a poet would use.

The same type of language appears in Olive Tilford Dargan's *The Poet*, another five-act drama on the life of Poe. (14) Here again fact and fantasy unite to produce a story which is not quite either. Mrs. Dargan creates a Helen whose beauty haunts the poet from the first moment he meets her, at her father's home in New York, to the last moment of his life when he is thrown out of a barroom in Baltimore, presumably to die in the gutter. In between he marries Virginia, suffers poverty, yields to his weakness for drink, and talks, talks, talks. The glamor in which he walks is such that Helen, when she first meets him, tells her mother, Mrs. Truelord, "We know angels at first sight, mamma," and Helen's aunt, who is herself smitten with the angel, exclaims, "Why, you couldn't hand him a cup of tea without feeling the planet quake!" But it is Poe's own talk which is most memorable — in a way which Mrs.

Dargan, who in more recent years, under the name of "Fielding Burke," was to write such bravely realistic novels as *Call Home the Heart* and *A Stone Came Rolling* — did not anticipate. Poe proposes to Virginia in these words: "Virginia, you who have the face of a houri, the form of a sylph, and the heart of an angel, will you be my wife?" In a later act, when Mrs. Clemm reprimands her son-in-law for having walked in the snow without a coat, he replies: "Could I take the least warmth from yon shivering angel?" One wonders what happens to otherwise talented writers when they undertake to deal with Poe.

Charity forbids prolonging the list of bad plays which have been written as a result of the mistaken notion that Poe is a "natural" for drama. A mere catalogue of all the Ravens alone, not to mention the Lenores (mostly one-acters and radio scripts), would make a sizeable book. Three of the most recent exhibits deserve to conclude this record because of the ambition that inspired them and the ability that went into their creation. A mere mention is enough for a fourth one, the *Edgar Allan Poe* by B. Iden Payne and Thomas Wood Stevens — two experienced theatre men — which had its world premiere, for five performances, at the University of South Carolina in 1933. (15)

Without question the most ambitious play on the life of Poe ever written and produced has been Sophie Treadwell's *Plumes in the Dust*. Miss Treadwell is a gifted playwright, as her *Machinal* once proved; Arthur Hopkins is a justly famous producer; and no one would dispute Henry Hull's histrionic flair and experience. Yet with a combination such as this it was clear at the opening performance of *Plumes in the Dust*, on Novem-

ber 2, 1936, in Baltimore, that the play was doomed.
In summarizing the failure of the Broadway production,
less than two weeks later, Brooks Atkinson wrote in the
New York *Times* (16): "If it were possible to translate
the life of Edgar Allan Poe into a drama, Sophie Treadwell, Henry Hull and Arthur Hopkins could do it."
They did not do it because "it is impossible to write of
Poe on the stage without turning him into an actor."
The main facts of his life were chronicled with respect
but they did not add up to an exciting drama. Mr.
Atkinson was right in his belief that if Poe "had not
been a writer of genius the queer, insane squalor of his
life would not be a matter of much importance." He
was wrong in implying that because Poe had been a
writer of genius a play merely recounting the squalor of
his life would be a matter of much importance. It takes
more than squalor to make up a dramatic life. What had
evidently fetched Miss Treadwell and Mr. Hopkins to
Poe was what they tried to make the public see, in a
program note: "the climatic [sic!] turns, the infinite
drama which pursued him all his days." (17) The
"infinite drama" proved monotonous and inert.

The second exhibit of interest is *Edgar Poe* by Valentin Bulgakov, written in Russian in Prague in 1938 and
published in the same language in Tientsin, China, in
1940. This dramatist was evidently not so well informed
as Miss Treadwell about the facts of Poe's biography —
or he chose to ignore them — but he was wise enough to
confine himself to the last seven years of his protagonist's
life, so that his play does not thin out into a mere
chronicle piece, and he was skilful enough to endow
him with some humor and a sense of the joy of life.
Wrong as Mr. Bulgakov was about many things that

actually happened, his play is rather unique in that it attempts to present a Poe with more than one tone in his voice. Yet, its merits notwithstanding, this drama, too, falls far short of artistic achievement.

The third and final exhibit is *Edgar Allan Poe*, a screenplay by Samuel Hoffenstein and Tom Reed, released in 1942 as *The Loves of Edgar Allan Poe*. With all the research talent available to Hollywood, the truth, it would seem, need not have suffered as it did. Poe had no such weighty problem as having to choose between accepting an editorial offer from Mr. Graham of Philadelphia or Mr. White of Richmond; Griswold was never editor of the *Broadway Journal* and therefore Poe never had to undergo the humiliation of begging him to accept the "Raven" for that publication; and Elmira Royster Shelton never visited the Poes at Fordham cottage. . . . If these and numerous other departures from the facts were meant to be concessions to popular appeal, they proved inadequate. The picture was one of the weakest Twentieth Century-Fox ever released and was received coolly. In our gallery of exhibits it merits an extra pause only because here for the first time almost *all* of Poe's life — from the day of his mother's death to the moment of his own — was dramatized by two clever professional continuity writers, but the result was, once more, far from edifying. Even for a movie hero, Poe sounded too theatrical to be convincing, and his life unreeled as a string of squalid setbacks without color, heroism, or the breath of romance.

4

By way of contrast, I must return to the observation made at the beginning of this survey of Poe's fate in the theatre: that his literary creations have had a livelier fate. Almost as soon as his short stories appeared in print they were translated on the stage and were received with pleasurable excitement. An actor, Robert B. Kegerries played one hundred times in his own adaptation of "The Tell-Tale Heart" in Boston, New York, Philadelphia, "and elsewhere." (18) Another actor-playwright, Silas S. Steele, chose for his benefit night, August 8, 1843, at a Philadelphia theatre, his own dramatization of "The Gold Bug." (19) In France, the famous André Antoine thrilled his rather select patrons, in 1889, with a one-acter by Ernest Laumann, *Le Coeur révélateur*, adapted from Baudelaire's translation of "The Tell-Tale Heart." (20) "The Cask of Amontillado," "The Fall of the House of Usher," "The Premature Burial," "The Purloined Letter," "The Assignation," "Hop-Frog," "Thou Art the Man," "Three Sundays in a Week," . . . in fact, most of Poe's stories and not a few of his poems have been dramatized numerous times; they have been performed on the professional stages in the Americas, Europe, and Asia; they have played to acclaim in vaudeville, in art theatres, in little theatres; they have been turned into Grand Guignol thrillers, into psychological dramas, into grand operas, and into ballets;[4] they have been broadcast over all the radio networks; they have been filmed; and now they are being televised.

Any examination of this vast amount of drama which Poe's imaginative work has inspired discloses at once

---

[4] Claude Debussy transformed "The Fall of the House of Usher" and "The Devil in the Belfry" into operas and Lazare Saminsky made an opera-ballet out of "The Masque of the Red Death." (21) These are but two of many composers who have seen possibilities in Poe's tales and poems.

its superiority over the similarly vast amount of dramatic effort which his life has inspired. "The Raven," a motion picture released by the Universal Pictures Corporation in 1935, had an effective scenario by David Boehm (22) and featured Boris Karloff in the leading role; based on Poe's poem rather than on his life, it was, as drama, infinitely more rewarding to watch than the more ambitious offering of the Messrs. Hoffenstein and Reed. "The Fall of the House of Usher" served, a few decades ago, as a basis for a highly imaginative experiment in Expressionism on the screen; this European film is still shown in various museums over the country as an epoch-making chapter in the development of cinema as an art form. The same story has served countless playwrights and radio script writers. (23) Two dramatizations of "The Tell-Tale Heart" are in the catalogues of publishing houses (24) supplying plays to the thousands of non-professional acting groups which constitute a sort of people's theatre in the United States today. And one publishing-agency circulates widely thirteen radio scripts each based on a Poe short story. (25) These are all successful dramatic offerings, capable of attracting and holding mass audiences.

5

A century of evidence supports the conclusion that Poe the man — artist, lover, husband, dreamer — does not dramatize; Poe's work does. Perhaps Mr. Brooks Atkinson said it all: placed on the stage Poe turns actor. And the actor has little or nothing to offer an audience — except as actor. It is when he enters into other lives, speaks with their voices, walks with their measured steps, and suffers with their intensity of emotion that he acquires stature and creates empathy. As a private citizen, off the boards, his figure is slight, his voice is low, and there is no halo over his head; he may or may not be interesting, but only as a human being; and the standards of "interestingness" which we apply to persons whom we meet on our side of the proscenium arch are harder to meet, especially for men like Poe.

The life that Poe infused into his poems, stories, and critical essays is the only life that has color and romance and logic and reality. . . . The showmanship that went into his work — whether superb artistic discipline or, as sometimes happened, mere surface effects intended to attract the attention of an audience engrossed with "elocutionists, travelers from the Holy Land and the freaks in Barnum's Museum" (26) — this showmanship is the stamp of his personality, his gait and voice and signature. All that Poe had to give to the world is in the collected edition of his works. It is in "The Raven" and "Ulalume," in "The Fall of the House of Usher" and "Ligeia," in "The Philosophy of Composition" and "The Poetic Principle." It is this work which drained his life and contains all the drama that was in him. Perhaps it left nothing in the man, and perhaps it left much but the richness of his work prevents us from seeing it; his work obtrudes itself and confuses the fictioneers and playwrights.

It is noteworthy that every dramatist who has used him as a character has made him read his poems: they are so much more effective than his own dialogue. Invariably the tone of his work is used to set the tone of his own speech, as if it were habitual for a person of his creative nature to express himself in the imagery of his creations. Lowell may have been right to some extent when he introduced him, in *The Fable for Critics*, as one "Who talks like a book of iambs and pentameters," but for a playwright to assume that his hero always speaks in maundering poetic phrases is to create a cartoon, an unconscious take-off of a mad poet. Surely there must have been times, hours, moments, when even Israfel did not sing for the angels, when his lute was silent, and when he spoke quietly and temperately, in an idiom that mortals may recognize as their own. Poe the critic may have believed that the poet was above passion and that poetry had nothing to do with the heart, (27) but Poe the boy and man had a heart and what he did and said had much to do with it. Yet in the plays which we have examined he appears cold, aloof, and wrapped in an insubstantial haze. Very likely he was cautious in public, on his guard, posturing and exhibiting his superiority, rejecting beforehand any possible condescension toward the players' offspring, any possible unbending toward the frustrated Virginia gentleman, but it is safe to suppose that he had his moments of privacy, when caution was no longer needed and he could afford to be relaxed, simple and natural and ordinary.

George Bernard Shaw is said to believe that what compels a man to go on the stage is a species of egoism which springs either from terrible vanity or fierce shyness. Perhaps Poe's egoism comprehended both drives. He felt "happier" behind the illusory fourth wall, as it were, strong and famous and learned and clever. When he performed the world was at his feet, for he knew that he performed uncommonly well. It is regrettable that no novelist or playwright has so far been able to surprise him when he was not performing, when he was neither elocuting nor being bitter, tragic, or unhappy. And no one, a French critic has remarked, was more methodically unhappy than Poe. (28) That his unhappiness was a form of enjoyment, part of his dark exultation, is a plausible interpretation of its character. Walt Whitman caught this meaning in his memorable imagistic summary of Poe:

In a dream I once had, I saw a vessel on the sea, at midnight, in a storm. It was no great full-rigged ship, nor majestic steamer, steering firmly through the gale, but seemed one of those superb little schooner yachts I had often seen lying anchored, rocking so jauntily, in the waters around New York, or up Long Island Sound; now flying uncontrolled with torn sails and broken spars through the wild sleet and winds and waves of the night. On deck was a slender, slight, beautiful figure, a dim man, apparently enjoying all the terror, the murk, and the dislocation of which he was the centre and the victim. That figure of my lurid dream might stand for Edgar Poe, his spirit, his fortunes and his poems. (29)

We have no choice but to leave him standing there, a beautiful figure and a dim man. He has eluded those who would find great tragedy, nobility, or romance in his private life. We have not been content with crediting him with a normal share of all three but have insisted on exaggerating that share to extravagant proportions. The world in which he acted so effectively has chosen to create a man whom it could attack, defend, admire, pity, exalt, and employ as a symbol of romantic attachment. A whole literature has been created around him which, though mostly mythical, we have no choice but to accept. Poe was no more the martyr crucified by an insensitive philistinism — as Baudelaire and Hanns Heinz Ewers imagined — than he was the unfortunate genius whose frailties needed the forgiveness of a wise mother — as the good lady novelists and playwrights have imagined. But with myth-makers sober facts have no value. The corrective scholarship of a man like Professor Taylor — (that "Poe could laugh not only at the Transcendentalists, but at himself as well"; that he was "a gaily irreverent wit who delighted in tossing darts of mockery among the heavy moralizers of his age"; and that he was always "ready to entertain his public with a roystering farce as well as a Gothic thriller") (30) — can have no influence upon them. Legend has it that Poe sometimes smiled but that he *never* laughed. The kind of laughter this refers to is not, of course, the kind Mr. Taylor has in mind, yet the picture of Poe that objective scholarship yields would greatly modify the picture of the legendary Poe. The world's imagination, however, must be respected, for, as Brownell remarked long ago, "It is the people's imagination that has made him what popularly he seems — something quite other than reality." (31)

And perhaps — since we cannot dismiss him — there is much that can be said for the legendary Poe. It is an enormous tribute to any man to acknowledge that he has passed into the realm of myth. It is given to but few individuals to impress the world so powerfully that its imagination is stimulated to creative activity. Poe has inspired a vast literature of fable and fancy, with himself as hero. How much of the inspiration was generated by the poor orphan, the disinherited gentleman, the good swimmer and poor drinker, the lover and husband of the delicate Virginia Clemm, and how much by the literary histrio no one can tell. It is certain, however, that the largest part of Poe which has survived in the people's imagination is a composite of Politian and Usher and

Dupin and Tamerlane and Israfel and the proud magazinist whose pen was mighty and fearless.

It matters little that the "real" Poe will probably
never be known. A college-mate of his once wrote that
"no one could say he knew him." (32) And now that
all his extant letters have been published — three hundred and thirty-three of them (33) — the task of knowing him will become even harder. For Poe, like the
myth-making world, was a lusty romancer, and it is only
by accepting his romancing about himself as part of the
truth that we can form any picture of him at all. And
in this picture the sad, tragic personality is not completely obliterated, but neither is the apparent enjoyment which Whitman perceived. Perhaps Poe really
believed, at times, that he was the grandson of Benedict
Arnold, (34) or that he had been arrested in far-off St.
Petersburg: this was his way of riding in triumph
through Persepolis. There is no "perhaps" about his
having frequented Miss Lynch's salon in Waverly Place,
in New York, where he read "The Raven,"

repeating the lines very quietly, his uncanny, weird eyes staring
forth from below the broad high forehead, so that even Greeley
was spellbound and Mrs. Osgood wept. He was the observed
of all observers, the lion of the coterie, the bewitching Bohe-
mian among the more respectable littérateurs. (35)

That, too, was a way of riding in triumph through
Persepolis.

But the best, and no doubt most enjoyable, way was
by losing himself in a world of his own creation. This
is also the most enduring way, for it is the way of the
artist, the type of artist that Poe was. We shall be wise
to remember one of his cherished beliefs: that the work
of the artist is more important than the artist himself.

The popular imagination is not to blame for confusing the man with his work: it cannot be expected to differentiate between the intense subjectivity of the one and the rigid, almost mathematical objectivity of the other. Poe had the faculty of subjecting himself, as well as anything else that served his creative needs, to the discipline of his artistry. In this he was, of course, no different from other creative spirits. Who can tell where Melville disappears in Ahab or Dostoievsky in Raskolnikov? If Usher begins as Poe he ends up as an inhabitant of a world that has its own contours and climate, a world far different from the one which Edgar Allan Poe of the biographies knew. If Eleonora begins as a relative of Poe she ends up as a dweller in that same world which was the unique creation of Poe.

In the end, it is only as a creator that Poe endures and is real. All else is of minor importance. Whoever and whatever he was his other self, the creator, managed to tame, subdue, transform, and merge into the world he evolved. We may feel somewhat baffled and uncertain by his creation because it approaches the insubstantiality of pure form, but it exists: strange and weird, fitfully lighted, and peopled with dim figures that move fantastically and speak a haunting, cadenced language. It is a world almost wholly conjured up by the wizardry of his art; and if the wizardry is not entirely free from mere artifice, it is wizardry nevertheless, and can no more be exorcised than an obsessive dream. And it is the black-cloaked wizard, standing gracefully in the center of his world, who does not laugh, but the pleased smile on his pale face is unmistakable.

BIBLIOGRAPHY

The fullest published bibliography on Poe is in the third volume of *Literary History of the United States*, edited by Robert E. Spiller, Willard Thorp, Thomas H. Johnson, and Henry Seidel Canby (New York, 1948). A still fuller one, as yet unpublished, is in the Bibliography of American Literature at the University of Pennsylvania. The following bibliography is highly selective and is printed here in the hope that readers will find it convenient for reference. I have, of course, indicated in the footnotes the texts and sources used in the preparation of this study.

Allen, Hervey, *Israfel: The Life and Times of Edgar Allan Poe*, New York, 1926, 2 vols.

——, and Mabbott, Thomas Ollive, *Poe's Brother. The Poems of William Henry Leonard Poe*, New York, 1926.

Alterton, Margaret, *Origins of Poe's Critical Theory*, Iowa City, 1925.

——, and Craig, Hardin, *Edgar Allan Poe: Representative Selections, with Introduction, Bibliography, and Notes*, New York, 1935.

Arndt, Karl J., "Poe's *Politian* and Goethe's *Mignon*," *Modern Language Notes*, XLIX (February, 1934), 101-104.

Astrov, Vladimir, "Dostoievsky on Edgar Allan Poe," *American Literature*, XIV (March, 1942), 70-74.

Atkinson, Brooks, "On the Life of Poe," *New York Times*, November 15, 1936.

Bailey, J. O., "Sources for Poe's *Arthur Gordon Pym*, 'Hans Pfaall,' and Other Pieces," *Publications of the Modern Language Association*, LVII (June, 1942), 513-535.

Baldwin, Summerfield, "The Aesthetic Theory of Edgar Poe," *Sewanee Review*, XXVI (April, 1918), 210-221.

Bandy, W. T., "A Source of Poe's 'The Premature Burial,'" *American Literature*, XIX (May, 1947), 167-168.

241

Basler, Roy P., "The Interpretation of 'Ligeia,'" *College English*, V (April, 1944), 363-372.

———, "Byronism in 'To One in Paradise,'" *American Literature*, IX (May, 1937), 232-236.

Benét, Laura, *Young Edgar Allan Poe*, New York, 1941.

Blair, Walter, "Poe's Conception of Incident and Tone in the Tale," *Modern Philology*, XLI (May, 1944), 226-240.

Bobrova, M. H., *O Prozë Edgara Poe*, Publication of the Irkutsk State Pedagogical Institute, 1937. (In Russian)

Bond, Frederick Drew, "The Problem of Poe," *The Open Court*, XXXVII (April, 1923), 216-223.

Bondurant, Agnes M., *Poe's Richmond*, Richmond, 1942.

Booth, Bradford A., "The Identity of Annabel Lee," *College English*, VII (October, 1945), 17-19.

———, and Jones, Claude, *A Concordance of the Poetical Works of Edgar Allan Poe*, Baltimore, 1941.

Boynton, Percy H., "Poe and Journalism," *English Journal*, XXI (May, 1932), 345-352.

Brigham, Clarence S., *Edgar Allan Poe's Contributions to Alexander's Weekly Messenger*, Worcester, Massachusetts, 1943.

Brooks, Van Wyck, *The World of Washington Irving*, Philadelphia, 1944. (Chapter XV, "Poe in the South," and Chapter XIX, "Poe in the North")

Brownell, W. C., "Poe," in *American Prose Masters*, New York, 1909; The Modern Students' Library, 1923, pp. 172-223.

Bruce, Philip Alexander, "Background of Poe's University Life," *South Atlantic Quarterly*, X (July, 1911), 212-226.

———, "Edgar Allan Poe and Mrs. Whitman," *South Atlantic Quarterly*, XII (April, 1913), 129-140.

Bulgakov, Valentin, *Edgar Poe: Drama in Five Acts and Seven Scenes*, Tientsin, China, 1940. (In Russian)

Cabell, Branch, "To Edgar Allan Poe, Esq.," in *Ladies and Gentlemen*, New York, 1934, pp. 243-262.

Campbell, Killis, *The Mind of Poe, and Other Studies*, Cambridge, 1933.

Campbell, Killis, " Poe," in *Cambridge History of American Literature*, New York, 1918, II, 55-69.

———, " The Poe Canon," *Publications of the Modern Language Association*, XXVII (1912), 325-353.

———, " Poe's Indebtedness to Byron," *The Nation*, LXXXVIII (March 11, 1909), 248-249.

———, " Poe's Reading," *University of Texas Studies in English*, V (October, 1925), 166-196.

———, " Poe's Reading: *Addenda* and *Corrigenda*," *University of Texas Studies in English*, VII (November, 1927), 175-180.

———, " The Relation of Poe to His Times," *Studies in Philology*, XX (July, 1923), 293-301.

———, ed., *The Poems of Edgar Allan Poe*, Boston, 1917.

———, ed., *Poe's Short Stories*, New York, 1927.

Cambiaire, Célestin P., *The Influence of Edgar Allan Poe in France*, New York, 1927.

Canby, Henry Seidel, "Edgar Allan Poe," in *Classic Americans*, New York, 1931.

Cherry, Fannye N., " The Sources of Poe's ' Three Sundays in a Week,'" *American Literature*, II (November, 1930), 232-235.

Clark, David L., "The Sources of Poe's ' The Pit and the Pendulum,'" *Modern Language Notes*, XLIV (June, 1929), 349-356.

Clough, Wilson O., " The Use of Color Words by Edgar Allan Poe," *Publications of the Modern Language Association*, XLV (June, 1930), 598-613.

Coad, Oral S., " The Meaning of Poe's ' Eldorado,'" *Modern Language Notes*, LIX (January, 1944), 59-61.

Cobb, Palmer, *The Influence of E. T. A. Hoffmann on the Tales of Edgar Allan Poe*, Chapel Hill, North Carolina, 1908.

———, "Edgar Allan Poe and Friedrich Spielhagen: Their Theory of the Short Story," *Modern Language Notes*, XXV (March, 1910), 67-72.

Coburn, Frederick W., " Poe as Seen by the Brother of ' Annie,'" *The New England Quarterly*, XVI (September, 1943), 468-476.

Colum, Padraic, ed., *Edgar Allan Poe's Tales of Mystery and Imagination*, London and New York, 1908.

Cooke, Alice L., "The Popular Conception of Edgar Allan Poe from 1850 to 1890," *University of Texas Studies in English*, XXII (1942), 22-46.

Cooke, John Esten, *Poe as a Literary Critic*, edited by N. Bryllion Fagin, Baltimore, 1946.

Cowley, Malcolm, "Aidgarpo," *New Republic*, CXIII (November 5, 1945), 607-610.

Cox, John L., "Poe as Critic," *English Journal*, College Edition, XXI (November, 1932), 757-763.

Dargan, Olive Tilford, *The Poet*, in *Semiramis and Other Plays*, New York, 1909.

De La Mare, Walter, "A Revenant," in *The Wind Blows Over*, New York, 1936.

De Mille, George E., "Poe," in *Literary Criticism in America*, New York, 1931.

Didier, Eugene L., *The Life and Poems of Edgar Allan Poe*, New York, 1876; revised edition, New York, 1882.

————, *The Poe Cult and Other Papers*, New York, 1909.

Dow, Dorothy, *Dark Glory*, New York, 1931.

"A Dreamer of Things Impossible," *The Academy*, LXI (September, 1901), 263-264.

Du Bois, Arthur E., "The Jazz Bells of Poe," *College English*, II (December, 1944), 240-244.

Dudley, Fred A., "Tintinnabulation: And a Source of Poe's 'The Bells,'" *American Literature*, IV (November, 1932), 296-300.

"Edgar Allan Poe," in *Literary History of the United States*, New York, 1948, I, 321-342, and III, 689-696.

Englekirk, J. E., *Edgar Allan Poe in Hispanic Literature*, New York, 1934.

Evans, May Garretson, *Music and Edgar Allan Poe*, Baltimore, 1939.

————, "Poe in Amity Street," *Maryland Historical Magazine*, XXXVI (December, 1941), 363-380.

Ewers, Hanns Heinz, *Edgar Allan Poe*, New York, 1917.

Fitzgerald, Bishop O. P., "The Night I Saw and Heard Edgar Allan Poe," in *Fifty Years*, Nashville and Dallas, 1903.

Foerster, Norman, *American Criticism: A Study in Literary Theory from Poe to the Present*, Boston and New York, 1928.

Françon, Marcel, "Poe et Baudelaire," *Publications of the Modern Language Association*, LX (September, 1945), 841-859.

French, John C., "Hewitt, John H.," in *The Dictionary of American Biography*, New York, 1932, VIII, 606-607.

——, "Poe and the *Baltimore Saturday Visiter*," *Modern Language Notes*, XXXIII (May, 1918), 257-267.

——, ed., *Poe in Foreign Lands and Tongues*, Baltimore, 1941.

——, "Poe's Literary Baltimore," *Maryland Historical Magazine*, XXXII (June, 1937), 101-112.

Fruit, John Phelps, *The Mind and Art of Poe's Poetry*, New York, 1899.

Gambrill, J. Montgomery, ed., *Selections from Poe*, Boston, 1907.

Gates, Lewis E., "Edgar Allan Poe," in *Studies and Appreciations*, New York, 1900.

Gates, William Bryan, "Poe's *Politian* Again," *Modern Language Notes*, XLIX (December, 1934), 561.

Gibson, T. W., "Poe at West Point," *Harper's*, XXXV (November, 1867), 754-756.

Gilder, Jeannette L., "Poe not as Black as He Was Painted," *Critic*, XLII (1903), 499-503.

Gill, William F., *The Life of Edgar Allan Poe*, New York, Philadelphia, and Boston, 1877; London, 1878.

Greenlaw, Edwin, "Poe in the Light of Literary History," *The Johns Hopkins Alumni Magazine*, XVIII (June, 1930), 273-290.

Gregory, Horace, "Within the Private View: A Note on Rereading the Poetry of Edgar Allan Poe," *Partisan Review*, May-June, 1943.

Griswold, Rufus Wilmot, ed., *The Works of the Late Edgar Allan Poe. With a Memoir by Rufus Wilmot Griswold and Notices of his Life and Genius by N. P. Willis and J. R. Lowell*, New York, 1850-1856, 4 vols.

Gruener, Gustav, "Notes on the Influence of Hoffmann upon

Edgar Allan Poe," *Publications of the Modern Language Association*, XIX (1904), 1-25.

———, " Poe's Knowledge of German," *Modern Philology*, II (June, 1904), 125-140.

Gwathmey, Edward M., " Kennedy the Patron of Poe," in *John Pendleton Kennedy*, New York, 1931.

Hannay, James, ed., *The Poetical Works of Edgar Allan Poe of America. With a Notice of his Life and Genius.* Second Edition. London, 1856.

Harrison, James A., ed., *The Complete Works of Edgar Allan Poe.* Virginia Edition. New York, 1902, 17 vols.

———, ed., *Last Letters of Edgar Allan Poe to Sarah Helen Whitman*, New York, 1909.

Hart, Richard H., " The Supernatural in Edgar Allan Poe," mimeographed copy of address delivered before the Edgar Allan Poe Society of Baltimore, January 19, 1936; in the Enoch Pratt Free Library, Baltimore.

Haycraft, Howard, *Murder for Pleasure: The Life and Times of the Detective Story*, New York and London, 1941.

Hazelton, George C., *The Raven; a Play in Four Acts and a Tableau*, New York, 1903.

———, *The Raven; the Love Story of Edgar Allan Poe*, New York, 1909.

Hearn, Lafcadio, " Poe's Verse," in *Interpretations of Literature*, New York, 1926, II, 150-166.

Heartman, Charles F., and Canny, James R., *A Bibliography of First Printings of the Writings of Edgar Allan Poe*, Hattiesburg, Mississippi, 1943.

———, and Rede, Kenneth, *A Census of First Editions and Source Materials by Edgar Allan Poe in American Collections*, Metuchen, New Jersey, 1932, 2 vols.

Hewitt, John H., *Shadows on the Wall; or, Glimpses of the Past*, Baltimore, 1877, pp. 40-43 and 154-159.

Hoffenstein, Samuel, and Reed, Tom, *Edgar Allan Poe*, mimeographed copy of " screenplay " (1942) in the Enoch Pratt Free Library, Baltimore.

Hosford, Frank H., " A Booth Plays Poe," *Detroit Free Press*, November, 24, 1895.

Hughes, William L., ed., *Contes inédits d'Edgar Poe traduits de l'anglais*, Paris, 1862.

Hull, William Doyle, II, *A Canon of the Critical Works of Edgar Allan Poe, with a Study of Poe as Editor and Reviewer*, University of Virginia doctoral dissertation (unpublished).

Hungerford, Edward, " Poe and Phrenology," *American Literature*, II (September, 1930), 209-231.

Hutcherson, Dudley, " Poe's Reputation in England and America, 1850-1900," *American Literature*, XIV (November, 1942), 211-233.

Ingram, John H., *The Works of Edgar Allan Poe*, Edinburgh, 1874-1875, 4 vols.

———, *Edgar Allan Poe: His Life, Letters, and Opinions*, London, 1880, 2 vols.

———, " Poe's *Politian*," *The Southern Magazine*, X (November, 1875), 588-594.

Jackson, David K., *Poe and the Southern Literary Messenger*, Richmond, 1934.

Jones, P. M., " Poe, Baudelaire, and Mallarmé: A Problem in Literary Judgment," *Modern Language Review*, XXXIX (July, 1944), 236-246.

Kane, Margaret, " Edgar Allan Poe and Architecture," *Sewanee Review*, XL (January-March, 1932), 149-160.

Kent, Charles W., and Patton, John S., eds., *The Book of the Poe Centenary*, Charlottesville, Virginia, 1909.

Kirkley, Donald, " Edgar Allan Poe's Play, Politian, Given at Goucher," *The Baltimore Sun*, February 19, 1933.

Krutch, Joseph Wood, *Edgar Allan Poe: A Study in Genius*, New York, 1926.

———, " Edgar Allan Poe, Sick Genius in Harsh World," New York *Herald Tribune Weekly Book Review*, December 19, 1948.

———, " A Baleful and Self-Consuming Meteor," *The New York Times Book Review*, August 6, 1944.

Laverty, Carroll D., " Poe in 1847," *American Literature*, XX (May, 1948), 163-168.

Lauvrière, Émile, *Edgar Poe: Sa Vie et Son Oeuvre*, Paris, 1904, 2 vols.

Lauvrière, Émile, *The Strange Life and the Strange Loves of Edgar Allan Poe*, Philadelphia, 1935.

Lawrence, D. H., *Studies in Classical American Literature*, New York, 1930, pp. 93-120.

Le Breton, Maurice, "Edgar Poë et Macaulay," *Revue Anglo-Américaine*, XIII (October, 1935), 38-42.

Leigh, Oliver, *Edgar Allan Poe, the Man: the Master: the Martyr*, Chicago, 1906.

Lemonnier, Léon, *Edgar Poe et les Poètes Français*, Paris, 1932.

————, *Edgar Poe et la Critique Française de 1845 à 1875*, Paris, 1928.

————, "L'influence d'Edgar Poe sur les conteurs Français symbolistes et decadents," *Revue de littérature comparée*, XIII (Paris, 1933), 102-133.

————, "Edgar Poe et le Théâtre de Mystère et de Terreur," *Grande Revue*, CXXX (1929), 379-396.

Lewisohn, Ludwig, *Expression in America*, New York, 1932, pp. 153-168.

Lind, Sidney E., "Poe and Mesmerism," *Publications of the Modern Language Association*, LXII (December, 1947), 1077-1094.

Long, Amelia Reynolds, *Death Looks Down*, Chicago and New York, 1945.

Mabbott, Thomas Ollive, ed., *Politian: An Unfinished Tragedy*, Richmond, Virginia, 1923.

————, ed., *Merlin, Baltimore, 1827, Together with Recollections of Edgar A. Poe by Lambert A. Wilmer*, New York, 1941.

————, "The First Book Publication of Poe's 'Raven,'" *Bulletin of the New York Public Library*, XLVII (August, 1943), 581-584.

————, "The Sources of Poe's 'Eldorado,'" *Modern Language Notes*, LX (June, 1945), 312-314.

————, "The Text of Poe's Play *Politian*," *Notes and Queries*, CLXXXIX (July 14, 1945), 14.

Macy, John, "Biographies of Poe," in *The Critical Game*, New York, 1922.

————, "Poe," in *The Spirit of American Literature*, New York, 1913.

Magidoff, Robert, "American Literature in Russia," *Saturday Review of Literature*, November 2, 1946.

Marchand, Ernest, "Poe as Social Critic," *American Literature*, VI (March, 1934), 28-43.

Mathews, Frances Aymar, "Writing of the Raven," *Bachelor of Arts*, III (August-September, 1896), 328-337.

Matthews, Brander, *The Philosophy of the Short Story*, New York, 1901.

Mauclair, Camille, *Le Génie d'Edgar Poe; la légende et la vérité—la méthode—la pensée—l'influence en France*, Paris, 1925.

McLuhan, Herbert Marshall, "Edgar Poe's Tradition," *Sewanee Review*, LII (January-March, 1944), 24-33.

Melton, Wightman F., "Poe's Mechanical Poem," *Texas Review*, III (January, 1918), 133-138.

Mencken, H. L., "The Mystery of Poe," *Nation*, CXXII (March 17, 1926), 289-290.

Miller, Arthur M., "The Influence of Edgar A. Poe on Ambrose Bierce," *American Literature*, IV (May, 1932), 130-150.

Moore, George, ed., *An Anthology of Pure Poetry*, New York, 1924.

More, Paul Elmer, "A Note on Poe's Method," *Studies in Philology*, XX (July, 1923), 302-309.

Mowatt, Anna Cora, *Autobiography of an Actress; or Eight Years on the Stage*, Boston, 1859.

Muse Anthology of Modern Poetry, Poe Memorial Edition, New York, 1938.

Nolan, J. Bennett, *Israfel in Berkshire: Edgar Allan Poe's Visit to Reading, March, 1844. Published for the Bicentennial of Reading, Penna., 1748*, 1948.

O'Brien, Edward J., *The Advance of the American Short Story*, New York, 1923.

Ostrom, John Ward, ed., *The Letters of Edgar Allan Poe*, Cambridge, Massachusetts, 1948, 2 vols.

———, ed., *Check List of Letters to and from Poe*, Charlottesville, Virginia, 1941.

Parrington, Vernon Louis, "Edgar Allan Poe," in *The Romantic Revolution in America, 1800-1860*, New York, 1927.

Parry, Albert, " The Lone One," in *Garrets and Pretenders: A History of Bohemianism*, New York, 1933.

Pattee, Fred Lewis, *The Development of the American Short Story*, New York, 1923.

———, " Poe's ' Ulalume,' " in *Side-Lights on American Literature*, New York, 1922.

Paul, Howard, " Recollections of Edgar Allen [sic] Poe," *Munsey's Magazine*, VII (August, 1892), 554-558.

Peck, G. W., " Mere Music," *The Literary World*, L (March 9, 1850), 225-226.

Perry, Bliss, ed., *Little Masterpieces: Edgar Allan Poe*, New York, 1905.

Phillips, Mary E., *Edgar Allan Poe: The Man*, Philadelphia, 1926, 2 vols.

Poe, Edgar Allan, " Does the Drama of the Day Deserve Support? " *The New York Evening Mirror*, January 9, 1845.

———, " Marginalia," *The United States Magazine and Democratic Review*, XIX (July, 1846), 30-32.

———, Review of *The Classical Family Library* Numbers XV, XVI, and XVII. Euripides. . . . *Southern Literary Messenger*, I (September, 1835), 779-780.

" Poe a Bricklayer in 1834? " *American Notes and Queries*, III (June, 1943), 36.

Politian Papers at the Enoch Pratt Free Library, Baltimore.

Pope-Hennessy, Una, *Edgar Allan Poe, 1809-1849: A Critical Biography*, London, 1934.

Prescott, Frederick C., ed., *Selections from the Critical Writings of Edgar Allan Poe*, New York, 1909.

Pritchard, John Paul, *Return to the Fountains*, Durham, N. C., 1942, pp. 26-43.

Pruette, Lorine, " A Psycho-Analytical Study of Edgar Allan Poe," *The American Journal of Psychology*, XXXI (October, 1920), 370-402.

Quinn, Arthur Hobson, *Edgar Allan Poe: A Critical Biography*, New York, 1941.

———, and Hart, Richard H., eds., *Edgar Allan Poe Letters and Documents in the Enoch Pratt Free Library*, New York, 1941.

Quinn, Arthur Hobson, and O'Neill, Edward H., eds., *The Complete Poems and Stories of Edgar Allan Poe, with Selections from His Critical Writings*, New York, 1946, 2 vols.

Ransome, Arthur, *Edgar Allan Poe: A Critical Study*, New York, 1910.

Rede, Kenneth, "Poe Notes: From an Investigator's Notebook," *American Literature*, V (March, 1933), 49-54.

Rede, Willys, "Edgar A. Poe: Citizen of Baltimore," *The Baltimore Sun*, January 17, 1932.

Robertson, John W., *A Bibliography of the Writings of Edgar A. Poe*, San Francisco, 1934, 2 vols.

———, *Edgar A. Poe*, New York, 1923.

Rourke, Constance, *American Humor*, New York, 1931, pp. 179-186.

"The Satanic Streak in Poe's Genius," *Current Literature*, XLVIII (January, 1910), 93-96.

Schick, Joseph H., "The Original of 'The Cask of Amontillado,'" *American Literature*, VI (March, 1934), 18-21.

———, "Poe and Jefferson," *Virginia Magazine of History and Biography*, LIV (October, 1946), 316-320.

Schulte, A. P., "The Portraits and Daguerreotypes of Edgar Allan Poe," in *Facts about Poe*, ed. by James Southall Wilson, [Charlottesville, Va.], 1926.

Seton, Anya, *Dragonwyck*, Philadelphia, 1946.

Shanks, Edward, *Edgar Allan Poe*, New York, 1937.

Shaw, Bernard, *Pen Portraits and Reviews*, in *The Collected Works of Bernard Shaw*, New York, 1932, Vol. XXIX, pp. 231-238.

Shockley, Martin Staples, "American Plays in the Richmond Theatre, 1819-1838," *Studies in Philology*, XXXVII (January, 1940), 100-119.

Smith, Bernard, *Forces in American Criticism; A Study in the History of American Thought*, New York, 1939, pp. 185-202.

Snell, George, "First of the New Critics," *Quarterly Review of Literature*, II (1946), 333-340.

———, "Poe: The Terror of the Soul," in *The Shapers of American Fiction*, New York, 1947.

Spannuth, Jacob E., and Mabbott, Thomas Ollive, eds., *Doings of Gotham, in a Series of Letters by Edgar Allan Poe* . . . , Pottsville, Pennsylvania, 1929.

Stanard, Mary Newton, ed., *Edgar Allan Poe Letters Till Now Unpublished, in the Valentine Museum, Richmond, Virginia*, Philadelphia, 1925.

———, *The Dreamer, A Romantic Rendering of the Life-Story of Edgar Allan Poe*, Philadelphia and London, 1925.

Stedman, Edmund Clarence, and Woodberry, George Edward, eds., *The Poems of Edgar Allan Poe*, New York, 1922.

———, *The Works of Edgar Allan Poe*, Chicago, 1894-1895; New York, 1914, 10 vols.

Stevenson, Robert Louis, "The Works of Edgar Allan Poe," in *The Works of Robert Louis Stevenson*, vol. V, New York, 1925.

Stoddard, Richard Henry, ed., *The Works of Edgar Allan Poe*, New York, 1884, 6 vols.

———, "Mrs. Botta and Her Friends," *Independent*, XLVI (February, 1894), 145.

Stovall, Floyd, "Poe's Debt to Coleridge," *University of Texas Studies in English*, X (1930), 70-127.

———, "Poe as a Poet of Ideas," *University of Texas Studies in English*, XI (1931), 56-62.

———, "An Interpretation of Poe's 'Al Aaraaf,'" *University of Texas Studies in English*, IX (1929), 106-133.

———, "The Women of Poe's Poems and Tales," *University of Texas Studies in English*, V (1925), 197-209.

Taylor, Walter Fuller, "Israfel in Motley," *Sewanee Review*, XLII (July-September, 1934), 330-340.

Trompeo, Pietro Paolo, "Poe a Roma," *La Nuova Europa*, 15 Aprile 1945.

Tucker, Beverly Randolph, *The Lost Lenore: A One Act Play*, Richmond, Virginia, 1929.

Tyler, Alice M., "Poe's Footsteps around Richmond," *The Times-Dispatch* (Richmond), January 17, 1909.

Van Cleef, Augustus, "Poe's Mary," *Harper's New Monthly Magazine*, LXXVIII (March, 1889), 634-640.

Varner, Cornelia, " Notes on Poe's Use of Contemporary Materials in Certain of His Stories," *The Journal of English and Germanic Philology*, XXXII (January, 1933), 77-80.

Wächter, P., *Edgar Allan Poe und die deutsche Romantik*, Leipzig, 1911.

Walcott, Charles Child, " The Logic of Poe," *College English*, II (February, 1941), 438-444.

Weiss, Susan Archer, *The Home Life of Poe*, New York, 1907.

———, " Last Days of Edgar A. Poe," *Scribner's Monthly*, XV (March, 1878), 707-716.

Wells, Henry W., " Discoveries in Imagination," in *The American Way of Poetry*, New York, 1943.

Werner, W. L., " Poe's Theories and Practice in Poetic Technique," *American Literature*, II (May, 1930), 157-165.

Whitman, Sarah Helen, *Edgar Poe and His Critics*, New York, 1860.

Whitman, Walt, " Edgar Poe's Significance," *The Critic*, II (June 3, 1882).

Whitty, James H., " Poeana," *The Step Ladder*, XIII (October, 1927), 225-243.

———, ed., *The Complete Poems of Edgar Allan Poe*, Boston, 1911; revised ed., Boston and New York, 1917.

Williams, Stanley T., " New Letters about Poe," *Yale Review*, XIV (July, 1925), 755-773.

Williams, William Carlos, " Edgar Allan Poe," in *In the American Grain*, Norfolk, Connecticut, 1925.

Wilson, Edmund, *Axel's Castle*, New York, 1936, pp. 13-19.

———, *The Shock of Recognition*, Garden City, N. Y., 1943, pp. 1-20 and 79-184.

———, " Poe as a Literary Critic," *Nation*, October 31, 1942.

Wilson, James Southall, " Poe's Philosophy of Composition," *North American Review*, CCXXIII (December/February, 1926-27), 675-684.

———, " The Devil Was in It," *American Mercury*, XXIV (October, 1931), 215-220.

———, " The Young Man Poe," *Virginia Quarterly Review* (April, 1926), 238-253.

Wilt, Napier, " Poe's Attitude toward His Tales: A New Document," *Modern Philology*, XXV (August, 1927), 101-105.

Winter, William, *Life and Art of Edwin Booth*, New York, 1893.

———, *Old Friends*, New York, 1909.

Winters, Yvor, " Edgar Allan Poe: A Crisis in the History of American Obscurantism," *American Literature*, VIII (January, 1937); also in *Maule's Curse*, Norfolk, Connecticut, 1938.

Woestyn, H. R., ed., " Politien, Une Tragédie Inédite d'Edgar Poe," *Revue de France*, LIV (Paris, 1925), 5-46.

Woodberry, George E., " Selections from the Correspondence of Edgar Allan Poe," *Century Magazine*, XLVIII (1894), 572-583; 725-737; 854-866.

———, *Edgar Allan Poe*, Boston, 1885 (American Men of Letters).

———, *The Life of Edgar Allan Poe, Personal and Literary, with His Chief Correspondence with Men of Letters*, Boston, 1909, 2 vols.

NOTES

CHAPTER I

(1) Killis Campbell in *Cambridge History of American Literature*, II, 55.

(2) Susan Archer Weiss, *The Home Life of Poe*, p. 117.

(3) John H. Hewitt, *Shadows on the Wall*, p. 155.

(4) Susan Archer Talley Weiss, "Last Days of Edgar A. Poe," *Scribner's*, XV (March, 1878), 711.

(5) Mrs. Clarke of Richmond; reported by Mrs. Weiss in *Home Life*, p. 160.

(6) "Exordium," *Graham's Magazine*, January, 1842. See *The Complete Works of Edgar Allan Poe*, Virginia Edition, edited by James A. Harrison, New York, 1902, XI, 2, hereinafter referred to as *Works*.

(7) John Macy, *The Spirit of American Literature*, p. 126.

(8) Eugene L. Didier, *The Poe Cult*, p. 8.

(9) Letter from White to Nathaniel Beverley Tucker, dated December 27, 1836. Quoted by Quinn, *Edgar Allan Poe*, p. 259.

(10) Weiss, *Home Life*, p. 223.

(11) Joseph Wood Krutch, *Edgar Allan Poe*, pp. 51-62.

(12) Quinn, *Poe*, p. 768.

(13) *Ibid.*, p. 219.

(14) See Frederick W. Coburn, "Poe as Seen by the Brother of 'Annie,'" *New England Quarterly*, XVI (September, 1943), p. 471.

(15) Quinn, *op. cit.*, 479-498. Some authorities, however, believe that Mrs. Clemm, perturbed by her "Eddie's" infatuation with Mrs. Osgood, confidingly showed the letter to Mrs. Ellet.

(16) *Ibid.*, p. 592.

(17) George E. Woodberry, *Life of Edgar Allan Poe*, I, 185.

(18) See Augustus Van Cleef, "Poe's Mary," *Harper's New Monthly Magazine*, LXXVIII (March, 1899), 634-640.

(19) Mary E. Phillips, *Edgar Allan Poe the Man*, I, 421-423.

(20) Quinn, *op. cit.*, p. 594.

(21) *Poe* (American Men of Letters Edition), p. 322.

(22) Weiss, *Home Life*, p. 171.

(23) *Op. cit.*, p. 578.

(24) *Works*, I, 314.

(25) *Op. cit.*, II, 1089.

(26) *Poe* (AML ed.), p. 26.

(27) Richard Henry Stoddard, "Mrs. Botta and Her Friends," *Independent*, XLVI (February 1, 1894), 145.

(28) *Romanticism and the Modern Ego*, Boston, 1943, p. 109.

(29) *The Shock of Recognition*, p. 84.

(30) Quinn, *op. cit.*, 83.

(31) Didier, *The Life and Poems of Edgar Allan Poe*, p. 31.

(32) Bailey Millard, "Precocity and Genius," *The Bookman*, XLII (November, 1915), 342.

(33) See *American Notes & Queries*, III (June, 1943), 36; also Quinn, *Poe*, p. 118, and Weiss, *Home Life*, p. 63.

(34) Letter to F. W. Thomas, dated February 14, 1849. In Griswold Collection, Boston Public Library. Also quoted, in its entirety, by Quinn, pp. 601-603, and by Ostrom, *Letters*, II, 426-428.

(35) *Complete Poems*, Whitty ed., p. 184.

(36) This comment is part of a letter, dated January 26, 1830, written by Neilson Poe. A Ms. copy of this letter (in the handwriting of Amelia F. Poe) is in the Enoch Pratt Free Library in Baltimore.

(37) *Poe* (AML ed.), p. 61.

(38) John Paul Pritchard, *Return to the Fountains*, p. 43.

(39) Fred Lewis Pattee, *The Development of the American Short Story*, p. 134.

(40) Frederick W. Coburn, *op. cit.*, p. 475.

(41) While the point is not very important, scholarly differences deserve recording; seven miles, says Harrison (*Works*, I, 25); six miles, says Quinn (*Poe*, p. 84).

(42) Edward Shanks, *Edgar Allan Poe*, p. 29.

(43) *French Poets and Novelists*, London, 1878, p. 76.

(44) *Edgar Allan Poe*, p. 51.

(45) See *The Book of the Poe Centenary*, edited by Kent and Patton, p. 192.

(46) "Poe not as Black as He Was Painted," *Critic*, XLII, 499.

(47) *Edgar Allan Poe Letters Till Now Unpublished, in the Valentine Museum*, Richmond, Virginia, p. 63.

(48) *Ibid.*, 77.

(49) *Ibid.*, 88.

(50) *Ibid.*, 267.

(51) *Ibid.*, 279-280.

(52) *Ibid.*, 291.

(53) Quinn, *op. cit.*, 190; see also Valentine Letters, p. 287.

(54) Quinn, pp. 589-592. From a copy made by Mrs. Richmond, in the Library of the University of Virginia.

(55) *Edgar A. Poe, a Psychopathic Study*, p. 92.

(56) John H. Ingram, *Edgar Allan Poe, His Life, Letters, and Opinions*, I, 216.

(57) *Works*, I, 180-181.

(58) "The Mystery of Poe," *Nation*, CXXII (March 17, 1926), 289.

(59) *Works*, I, 160. The letter was first published in the Baltimore *American*, April, 1881.

(60) Weiss, 'Last Days of Edgar A. Poe," *Scribner's Monthly*, XV (March, 1878), 712.

(61) Bishop O. P. Fitzgerald, "The Night I Saw and Heard Edgar Allan Poe," in *Fifty Years*, p. 192.

(62) *Autobiography of an Actress*, pp. 139, 445.

(63) *Works*, XII, 185-186; originally published in the *Broadway Journal*, July 19, 1845.

(64) Albert Parry, *Garrets and Pretenders*, p. 5.

(65) Weiss, *Home Life*, p. 34.

(66) *Op. cit.*, p. 138.

(67) *Poe*, p. 85.

(68) Woodberry, *Life of Poe*, I, 18-19.

(69) *Works*, I, 14.

(70) *Ibid.*, I, 24.

(71) Woodberry, I, 1.

(72) Weiss, *Home Life*, pp. 25-26. Other references to this episode are Harrison, *Works*, I, 28-29; Phillips, I, 201-202; Quinn, 87; and "Poe's Footsteps around Richmond," by Alice M. Tyler, in *The Times-Dispatch*, January 17, 1909.

(73) Ms. in the Valentine Collection in Richmond.

(74) Quinn, pp. 118-119.

(75) Una Pope-Hennessy, *Edgar Allan Poe*, pp. 30-31. For another description of Poe parading in the uniform of the Junior Morgan Riflemen, see Harrison, *Works*, I, 25-26.

(76) *Works*, I, 196.

(77) Weiss, *Home Life*, p. 21.

(78) *Works*, I, 25.

(79) The source is Col. Ellis, but see Phillips, I, 209.

(80) T. W. Gibson, "Poe at West Point," *Harper's*, XXXV (November, 1867), 754-756.

(81) *Works*, I, 198.

(82) The whole of this review is reprinted by Dr. Robertson in his *Poe*. The passage appears on p. 244.

(83) James Southall Wilson, "The Young Man Poe," *Virginia Quarterly Review*, II (April, 1926), 239.

(84) Phillips, II, 926-927. Woodberry (II, 422-423) gives the name as "Perley." Both accounts are based on Gabriel Harrison's articles. It seems that Mr. Harrison confused the name between one article (published in 1875) and another (published in 1899).

(85) *Selections from Poe*, p. xxi.

(86) *Op. cit.*, p. 314.

(87) Letter dated September 18, 1849, in *Edgar Allan Poe Letters and Documents in the Enoch Pratt Library*, edited by A. H. Quinn and R. H. Hart, p. 25.

(88) Hervey Allen, *Israfel*, II, 855.

(89) *Ibid.*, I, 98.

(90) Quinn, *Poe*, p. 274.

(91) Phillips, I, 351.

(92) Quinn, p. 197.

(93) Ms. of a long article in the William H. Koester Collection in Baltimore. The article apparently was published in an unnamed "paper" in June, 1885.

(94) *Dictionary of American Biography*, VIII, 606-607. See also *Maryland Historical Magazine*, XXXII (June, 1937), 105-107.

(95) Willys Rede, "Edgar A. Poe: Citizen of Baltimore," *Baltimore Sun*, January 17, 1932.

(96) Émile Lauvrière, *The Strange Life and the Strange Loves of Edgar Allan Poe*, pp. 187, 316, 400; Phillips, II, 1183.

(97) *Poe*, p. 276.

(98) *Israfel*, II, 455.

(99) Una Pope-Hennessy, *op. cit.*, p. 199.

(100) Horace W. Smith, *Life and Correspondence of Reverend William Smith*, Philadelphia, 1879-1880, II, 529. (See Quinn, p. 344).

(101) Allen, *Israfel*, II, 574. See also Killis Campbell, *Mind of Poe*, pp. 11-12, and Woodberry, II, 421.

(102) Phillips, II, 1102.

(103) Pope-Hennessy, *op. cit.*, p. 244.

(104) Phillips, II, 1003, and Allen II, 639; both biographers base their accounts on articles by Alexander Taylor Crane published in newspapers (New York *Times Review*, Nov. 27, 1909; *Sunday World-Herald*, Omaha, Nebraska, July 19, 1902).

(105) Phillips, II, 772.

(106) *Dictionary of American Biography*, VIII, 339-340.

(107) See letter from "Gabriel" to Mrs. Clemm, dated December 27, 1865, in *Poe Letters and Documents* (Quinn and Hart), p. 73.

(108) Thomas Ollive Mabbott, "The First Book Publication of Poe's 'Raven,'" *Bulletin of the New York Public Library*, XLVII (August, 1943), 583.

(109) *Old Friends*, p. 35.

(110) See sketch in *DAB*, III, 95-96, by Walter Pritchard Eaton.

(111) See sketch in *DAB*, XX, 512-513, by Nelson F. Adkins.

(112) See sketch in *DAB*, XIII, 207-209, by Roy W. Sellars.

(113) Pope-Hennessy, *op. cit.*, p. 244. For the appearances of Mr. and Mrs. David Poe at the Park Theatre see Quinn, pp. 719-722.

(114) *Works*, I, 301.

(115) Quinn, pp. 611-612.

(116) David M. Robinson, *Sappho and Her Influence,* Boston, 1924, p. 218.

(117) "The Wizard in the Street," (1911), in *Selected Poems,* New York, 1931.

(118) *The Poe Cult,* pp. 241-242.

(119) Pope-Hennessy, p. 264.

(120) Julius Bab, *Das Theater der Gegenwart,* Leipzig, 1928, p. 130.

(121) Testimony of Mrs. Sarah Heywood Trumbull ("Annie's" sister) in William F. Gill, *The Life of Edgar Allan Poe,* p. 210. See also Phillips, II, 1292, and *Works* (Harrison), I, 303.

(122) *The Works of the Late Edgar Allan Poe with a Memoir,* I, liv.

(123) Phillips, II, 1126.

(124) Pope-Hennessy, p. 266.

(125) Phillips, II, 954-955.

(126) Sarah Helen Whitman, *Edgar Poe and his Critics,* pp. 41-42.

(127) Phillips, II, 1310.

(128) See Spannuth and Mabbott, eds., *Doings of Gotham,* p. 101.

(129) *Works,* I, 60.

(130) George Tucker, a fellow-student; quoted by Harrison in *Works,* I, 42.

(131) Letter of Mary I. Dixon, dated September 11, 1872, in "Poeana," at the New York City Authors' Club. See Phillips, I, 120, and II, 1623.

(132) *Works,* I, 108-109.

(133) *Ibid.,* I, 222-223.

(134) Anonymous letter addressed to Mrs. Whitman, dated January 7, 1846. See Didier, *Life and Poems,* p. 13.

(135) *Munsey's Magazine,* VII, 557.

(136) Didier, *The Poe Cult,* p. 62.

(137) *Weekly Mirror,* March 12, 1845. Quoted in Phillips, II, 950-951.

(138) W. T. Scott, "New England's Newspaper World," *Saturday Review of Literature,* May 22, 1943, p. 20.

(139) Phillips, II, 1055.

(140) *Ibid.*, II, 1350.

(141) Weiss, "Last Days of Edgar A. Poe," *Scribner's*, XV, 713.

(142) *Fifty Years*, p. 196.

(143) *Works*, I, 316.

(144) For a complete transcript of the *Examiner* article see Whitty's Memoir in his edition of *The Complete Poems of Edgar Allan Poe*, pp. lxxiv-lxxvi.

(145) See report by Mrs. Clarke in Weiss, *Home Life*, p. 163.

(146) *Poe as a Literary Critic*. Ms. in the Koester Collection, Baltimore. Published by the Johns Hopkins Press, 1946.

(147) *Broadway Journal*, I (March 29, 1845), 205.

(148) William Fearing Gill, *The Life of Edgar Allan Poe*, p. 210.

(149) Karl Mantzius, *A History of Theatrical Art*, London, 1921, vol. VI, p. 288.

(150) *Sat. Rev. of Lit.*, April 3, 1937.

(151) "Edgar Poe's Significance," *The Critic*, II (June 3, 1882), 147.

(152) "The Satanic Streak in Poe's Genius," *Current Literature*, XLVIII, 93.

(153) James S. Wilson, *Virginia Quarterly Review*, II, 238.

(154) *Home Life*, p. 132.

(155) *Works*, I, 316.

(156) *Ibid.*, I, 132.

(157) See Samuel Longfellow, *Life of Longfellow*, Boston and New York, 1891, vol. II, p. 150.

(158) Many scholars have attempted to explore his social and political ideas and ideals. Two of the best studies are: Killis Campbell, "The Relation of Poe to His Times," *Studies in Philology*, XX (July, 1923), 293-301, and Ernest Marchand, "Poe as Social Critic," *American Literature*, VI (March, 1934), 28-43.

(159) Vernon Louis Parrington, *The Romantic Revolution in America, 1800-1860*, p. 59.

(160) Phillips, II, 1130.

(161) *Op. cit.*, p. 59.

(162) Letter from Margaret Fuller to Elizabeth Barrett Browning, December 6, 1849; in the Abernethy Library of American Literature at Middleberry College. See *American Literature*, IX (March, 1937), 70-71.

(163) *American Prose Masters* (Modern Student's Library), p. 215.

(164) Testimony of F. W. Thomas, in Whitty's Memoir (*Complete Poems*), p. xxi.

(165) Didier, *The Poe Cult*, p. 192.

(166) William Winter, *Life and Art of Edwin Booth*, p. 281.

CHAPTER II

(1) Letter from Kennedy to Poe, dated September 19, 1835, in the Griswold Manuscripts, Boston Public Library. Reprinted in Quinn, p. 227.

(2) Kennedy to T. W. White, April 13, 1835. See Mabbott, *Politian*, p. 58.

(3) *Letters . . . in the Valentine Museum*, p. 265.

(4) See Quinn, *A History of the American Drama from the Beginning to the Civil War*, Second Edition (1943), pp. 225-237.

(5) Howard Paul, "Recollections of Edgar Allen [sic!] Poe," *Munsey's Magazine*, VII (August, 1892), 557. Woodberry lists Mr. Paul's article as having appeared in the "Sept. 1892" number of *Munsey's*. Hervey Allen repeats the error (*Israfel*, II, 573).

(6) Killis Campbell, who does not hesitate to reject other attributions of authorship to Poe, does not exclude the possibility of this scenario from "The Poe Canon" (PMLA, XXVII, 350).

(7) Mabbott, *Politian*, p. iv. M. William Little Hughes's translation is in *Contes inédits d'Edgar Poe*, Paris, 1862, pp. 249-281.

(8) For Quinn's discussion of "Monos and Una" see his *Poe*, pp. 324-325.

(9) *The Works of Edgar Allan Poe*, edited by E. C. Stedman and G. E. Woodberry, vol. IV, p. 295.

(10) See *American Literature*, II (November, 1930), 232-235, "The Sources of Poe's 'Three Sundays in a Week,'" by Fannye N. Cherry.

(11) *Poe*, p. 233.

(12) *Works*, XIII, 73.

(13) James Southall Wilson, "About 'Politian.'" In the *Politian Papers* at the Enoch Pratt Free Library, Baltimore.

(14) *Doings of Gotham* (eds., Spannuth and Mabbott), p. 97.

(15) "The American Drama," *Works*, XIII, 36.

(16) Thus Quinn, p. 231. Mabbott claims that the wife was acquitted. For my purposes, however, this detail is not of the slightest value.

(17) *Works*, XV, 119.

(18) *Graham's Magazine*, May, 1842.

(19) *Broadway Journal*, October 4, 1845 (vol. II, no. 13, p. 190).

(20) For the sources of Poe's names in *Politian*, see Mabbott, pp. 59-61 of his edition.

(21) "Last Days of Edgar Allan Poe," *Scribner's Monthly*, XV (March, 1878), 709.

(22) *Works*, XIII, 51.

(23) *Politian*, II, 38-48.

(24) *Ibid.*, II, 52-58.

(25) *Ibid.*, II, 66-68.

(26) *Works*, XIII, 37.

(27) See Mabbott's *Politian*, "Commentary," pp. 59-79.

(28) *Poe*, p. 251.

(29) *Works*, X, 117.

(30) "Une Tragedie Inédite d'Edgar Poe," *La Revue de France*, LIV (Paris, 1925), 5. Introduction by H. R. Woestyn.

(31) *Poe*, p. 89.

(32) Postal card in *Politian Papers* (Enoch Pratt Free Library, Baltimore).

(33) *Partisan Review*, November-December, 1942, p. 460.

(34) *Works*, XI, 142. (Poe's reference was to Rufus Dawes).

(35) Scene III, 36 ff.

(36) *Israfel*, II, 445-446.

(37) *Politian*, pp. 63-64.

(38) "A Dreamer of Things Impossible," *The Academy*, LXI (September 28, 1901), 263.

(39) H. W. Wells, *The American Way of Poetry*, p. 26.

(40) Scene XI, 33-39.

(41) Valentine letters, p. 55.

(42) *La Nuova Europa*, April 15, 1945.

(43) *Contes inédits d'Edgar Poe*, pp. 263-264.

(44) See Una Pope-Hennessy, *Poe*, pp. 232-233.

(45) *Studies in Classic American Literature*, p. 100.

(46) Quoted by H. R. Woestyn in his introduction to *Politienne*. See note 30.

(47) *The Works of Lord Macaulay*, London, 1871, vol. V, pp. 10-11.

(48) See "Critical and Miscellaneous Essays. By T. Babington Macaulay," *Works*, X; "About Critics and Criticism" and "Peter Snook," XIV. For a study of Macaulay's influence on Poe, see "Edgar Poe et Macaulay," by Maurice Le Breton, in *Revue Anglo-Américaine*, XIII (October, 1935), 38-42.

(49) *Promenades Littéraires, Première Série* (Paris, 1904), p. 361.

CHAPTER III

(1) Frances Aymar Mathews, *Bachelor of Arts*, III (August-September, 1896), 328-337.

(2) Agnes M. Bondurant, *Poe's Richmond*, p. 149.

(3) *Ibid.*, p. 131.

(4) See Martin Staples Shockley, "American Plays in the Richmond Theatre, 1819-1838," *Studies in Philology*, XXXVII (January, 1940), 100-119.

(5) Howard Paul, *Munsey's*, August, 1892.

(6) *The Mind of Poe*, pp. 1-33. See also Campbell's "Poe's Reading," *University of Texas Studies in English*, V (1925), 166-196.

(7) *Selections from the Critical Writings of Edgar Allan Poe*, Introduction, p. xxxi.

(8) *Works*, XIII, 43. Also note: "Most persons think of [plot] as a simple complexity; and into this error even so fine a critic as Augustus William Schlegel has obviously fallen. . . ." — *Works*, X, 116.

(9) *Poe*, p. 116.

(10) *Burton's Gentleman's Magazine*, Vol. V, p. 282 (November, 1839).

(11) *Broadway Journal*, August 16, 1845; *Works*, XII, 226-228.

(12) Now in the Koester Collection in Baltimore. The title page reads: "Hamlet, Prince of Denmark: A Tragedy in Five Acts by William Shakespear. As Performed at the Theatre in Boston. Boston: Printed for David West and John West April, 1704."

(13) In "Metzengerstein," "The Masque of the Red Death," and "William Wilson."

(14) See Mabbott's notes to *Politian*, p. 63.

(15) "The American Drama," *Works*, XIII, 52.

(16) Review of *Poems* by William W. Lord, *Broadway Journal*, May 24, 1845; *Works*, XII, 148.

(17) Spannuth and Mabbott, *Doings of Gotham*, p. 97.

(18) *Works*, XVI, 100.

(19) Phillips, II, 1492. Quoted on the authority of Edward M. Alfriend, at one time editor of the *Southern Literary Messenger*.

(20) Karl J. Arndt, "Poe's *Politian* and Goethe's *Mignon*," *Modern Language Notes*, XLIX (February, 1934), 101-104. Note, however, the surmise of William Bryan Gates that the indebtedness to Goethe may have come through Byron ("Poe's *Politian* Again," MLN, XLVIV, 561).

(21) May, 1836; *Works*, VIII, 322.

(22) "Fifty Suggestions," *Graham's Magazine*, May and June, 1845; *Works*, XIV, 183.

(23) *Works*, XVI, 174-175.

(24) T. O. Mabbott, "The First Book Publication of Poe's 'Raven,'" *Bulletin of the New York Public Library*, XLVII (1843), 581-584.

(25) The review appears in *Works*, XII, 130-135; Dinneford's protest and Poe's reply follow, pp. 135-139.

(26) "Poe and Journalism," *English Journal*, XXI (May, 1932), 350.

(27) *Graham's*, February, 1845.

(28) Heartman and Rede, *A Census of First Editions and Source Materials by Edgar Allan Poe in American Collections*, I, 24.

(29) *Broadway Journal*, March 29, 1845; *Works*, XII, 112-121.

(30) Review of Bulwer-Lytton's *Night and Morning*, *Works*, X, 117.

(31) *Works*, XIII, 44-45.

(32) *Works*, XII, 112-121.

(33) *Broadway Journal*, April 5, 1845; *Works*, XII, 124-129.

(34) August, 1845; *Works*, XIII, 38-54.

(35) "Marginalia," *Works*, XVI, 172.

(36) *Works*, XIII, 54-73.

(37) Ostrom, *Letters of Poe*, II, 311.

(38) *Works*, Griswold ed., vol. III, p. 203.

(39) *Godey's Lady's Book*, March, 1846; *Works*, XIII, 105-125.

(40) "Marginalia," *Works*, XVI, 109-110.

(41) New York *Evening Mirror*, January 9, 1845. Also in the *Weekly Mirror*, I (January 18, 1845), 229. Reprinted with slight revision in "Marginalia," *The United States Magazine, and Democratic Review*, July, 1846 (vol. XIX, pp. 30-31).

(42) "The New Comedy by Mrs. Mowatt," *Broadway Journal*, March 29, 1845; *Works*, XII, 119.

(43) *Godey's Lady's Book*, August, 1845; *Works*, XVI, 68.

(44) See N. Bryllion Fagin, "Herman Melville and the Interior Monologue," *American Literature*, VI (January, 1935), 433-434.

(45) *Works*, XII, 120.

(46) Review of *Fashion*, *Works*, XII, 118-119.

(47) Review of *Barnaby Rudge*, *Works*, XI, 39; also see Alterton and Craig, *Representative Selections*, pp. 533-534, note.

(48) George C. D. Odell, *Annals of the New York Stage*, vol. V, p. 100.

(49) *Works*, XII, 211.

(50) *Broadway Journal*, August 2, 1845; *Works*, XII, 211.

(51) *Works*, XIV, pp. 42 and 62.

(52) Article on Robert T. Conrad in Spannuth and Mabbott, *Doings of Gotham*, p. 97.

(53) *Works*, XII, 185-186.

(54) *Ibid.*, XII, 211.

(55) *Ibid.*, XII, 212.

(56) *Ibid.*, XII, 187.

(57) *Ibid.*, XII, 129.

(58) William Doyle Hull II, *A Canon of the Critical Works of Edgar Allan Poe, with a Study of Poe as Editor and Reviewer*. Unpublished dissertation at the University of Virginia, p. 595. See also *Broadway Journal*, I (April 26, 1845), 271.

(59) *Works*, XII, 211.

(60) *Works*, XV, 17.

(61) *Works*, XII, 190.

(62) *Ibid.*, XII, 212.

(63) *Ibid.*, XII, 212.

(64) *Broadway Journal*, II (July 19, 1845), 31.

(65) *Works*, XIV, 179.

(66) *Broadway Journal*, August 2, 1845; *Works*, XII, 212.

(67) William Doyle Hull II, *op. cit.*, pp. 489 and 497.

(68) *Works*, XII, 212.

(69) *Burton's Magazine*, May, 1840; *Works*, X, 91-96.

(70) See " Marginalia," *Works*, XVI, pp. 29 and 138.

(71) " Marginalia," *Democratic Review*, November, 1844; *Works*, XVI, 8.

(72) " Marginalia," *Southern Literary Messenger*, July, 1849; *Works*, XVI, 171. The De Meyer referred to was Leopold de Meyer, who at his American début in 1845 was billed as " Imperial and Royal Pianist to the Emperors of Austria and Russia." See Odell, *Annals of the New York Stage*, V, 168.

(73) See opening paragraph of " The Island of the Fay."

(74) " Marginalia," *Works* (Griswold ed.), V, 594.

(75) " Marginalia," *Graham's Magazine*, January, 1848; *Works*, XVI, 126-127.

(76) Arnold Mulder, " American Criticism for American

Readers," *Essay Annual* — 1937 (Erich Walter, ed.), p. 124.

(77) *Works*, I, 190.

(78) George E. De Mille, *Literary Criticism in America*, p. 105.

(79) "The American Drama," *American Whig Review*, August, 1845; *Works*, XIII, 37.

(80) *Works*, XVI, 172.

(81) "Prospects of the Drama," *Broadway Journal*, April 5, 1845; *Works*, XII, 127.

(82) *Works*, XII, 185.

(83) *Ibid.*, XII, 188.

(84) *Works*, XVI, 81.

CHAPTER IV

(1) George Moore, *An Anthology of Pure Poetry*, p. 34.

(2) James Hannay, ed., *The Poetical Works of Edgar Allan Poe*, p. xxxiv.

(3) A. E. Housman, *The Name and Meaning of Poetry*, New York, 1933, pp. 8 and 36.

(4) For a convincing refutation of this claim see Killis Campbell's edition of the *Poems*, p. 171.

(5) Especially Lemonnier's *Edgar Poe et les Poètes Français*, 1932, and "L'influence d'Edgar Poe sur les conteurs Français symbolistes et décadents," *Revue de littérature comparée*, XIII (1933), 102-133; Camille Mauclair, *Le Génie d'Edgar Poe; la légende et la vérité — la methode — la pensée — l'influence en France*, 1925.

(6) John C. French, ed., *Poe In Foreign Lands and Tongues*, Baltimore, 1941. Contains: "Poe in France," by Dr. Jeanne Roselet; "Poe in Russia," by Dr. Lubov Keefer; "Poe in Germany," by Dr. Herbert Schaumann; "Poe in Spain and Spanish America," by Dr. Pedro Salinas. An earlier symposium, held in 1909 at the University of Virginia, and recorded in *The Book of the Poe Centenary* (Charlottesville, 1909), contains two excellent papers on the same subject: Dr. Alcée Fortier's summary (in French) of Poe's influence on French literature and Dr. Georg Edward's resumé of Poe's influence in Germany.

Two other studies on the same subject are P. Wächter's *Edgar Allan Poe und die deutsche Romantik* (Leipzig, 1911) and J. E. Englekirk's *Edgar Allan Poe in Hispanic Literature* (New York, 1934).

(7) John C. French, *op. cit.*, pp. 8 and 18.

(8) Robert Magidoff, "American Literature in Russia," *Saturday Review of Literature*, November 2, 1946, p. 10.

(9) French, *op. cit.*, p. 30.

(10) *Expression in America*, pp. 156 and 167.

(11) "The Laggard Art of Criticism," *College English*, VI (February, 1945), 245. For another discussion of Poe's notation of "super-rational sensation," see Edmund Wilson, *Axel's Castle*, pp. 13-19.

(12) "A Note on Poe's Method," *Studies in Philology*, XX (July, 1923), pp. 309, 304, 305.

(13) "Edgar Poe's Significance," *Critic*, II (June 3, 1882), 147.

(14) *Op. cit.*, p. 306.

(15) "Edgar Allan Poe," in *Classic Americans*, pp. 277 and 274.

(16) *Works*, XIV, 194-195.

(17) Both quotations are from *Man and Mask* by Feodor Chaliapin, Garden City, N. Y., 1932, p. 114.

(18) "The Philosophy of Composition," *Works*, XIV, 195.

(19) "Marginalia," *Works*, XVI, 67.

(20) *Works*, XIV, 204.

(21) Susan Archer Talley Weiss, "Last Days of Edgar A. Poe," *Scribner's*, XV (March, 1878), 715.

(22) H. W. Wells, *The American Way of Poetry*, p. 23.

(23) *American Prose Masters*, p. 179.

(24) *The Works of Edgar Allan Poe*, with an Introduction and a Memoir by Richard Henry Stoddard, I, 172.

(25) *Works*, I, 287.

(26) Wightman F. Melton, "Poe's Mechanical Poem," *Texas Review*, III (1917-1918), 135-137.

(27) For a summary of all these possible sources see Campbell, *Poems*, pp. 280-281.

(28) Preface, 1845; *Works*, VII, xlvii.

(29) "The Rationale of Verse"; *Works*, XIV, 220.

(30) Ostrom, *The Letters of Poe*, I, 78.

(31) "The Poetic Principle"; *Works*, XIV, 275.

(32) *Music and Edgar Allan Poe: A Bibliographical Study*, p. 82.

(33) *Music Lovers' Encyclopedia*. Compiled by Rupert Hughes. Completely Revised and Newly Edited by Deems Taylor and Russell Kerr. New York, 1939, p. 515.

(34) "Last Days of Edgar A. Poe," *Scribner's*, p. 713.

(35) See *The Oxford Anthology of American Literature*, New York, 1938, p. 1647.

(36) "Pen Portraits and Reviews," in *The Collected Works* (Ayot St. Lawrence Edition), XXIX, 235.

(37) John Phelps Fruit, *The Mind and Art of Poe's Poetry*, pp. 100-101.

(38) The text of both versions is that given by Campbell in *Poems*, pp. 68-69.

(39) Arthur Du Bois, "The Jazz Bells of Poe," *College English*, II (December, 1940), 244.

(40) *Works*, XII, 21.

(41) *Essay on Rime*, New York, 1945, p. 65.

(42) Professor Kent was the first to observe this correspondence. See *The Complete Poetical Works* with Introduction by Charles W. Kent, p. 204.

(43) "Marginalia," *Works*, XVI, 137.

(44) *Ibid.*, p. 28.

(45) *Ibid.*, pp. 138-140.

(46) See Campbell, *Poems*, p. 105.

(47) Wilson O. Clough, "The Use of Color Words by Edgar Allen [sic!] Poe," PMLA, XLV, 598-599.

(48) For a discussion of the identity of Annabel Lee see Bradford A. Booth, *College English*, VII (October, 1945), 17-19. See also Mabbott's suggestion that "Annabel Lee" contains traces of both women (*Merlin*, by Lambert A. Wilmer. Edited by Thomas Ollive Mabbott, New York, 1941, p. v).

(49) *Works*, I, 222.

(50) *Ibid.*, p. 12.

(51) Alterton and Craig, *Poe*, p. 507.

(52) See Oral S. Coad, "The Meaning of 'Eldorado,'" *Modern Language Notes*, LIX (January, 1944), 59-61.

(53) *Godey's Magazine and Lady's Book*, XXX (December, 1845), 263.

(54) G. W. Peck, " Mere Music," *The Literary World*, L (March 9, 1850), 225-226.

(55) *Poe*, p. 99.

(56) " Poe's 'Ulalume,' " *Side-Lights on American Literature*, pp. 327-342.

(57) See Quinn, *Poe*, p. 532.

(58) Emile Lauvrière, *The Strange Life and the Strange Loves of Edgar Allan Poe*, p. 302.

(59) *Muse Anthology*, p. 56.

(60) " Poe's Verse," *Interpretations of Literature*, II, 151.

(61) *Op. cit.*, p. xxxiii.

(62) See Robert Magidoff, *op. cit.*

(63) Preface to *Tales of the Grotesque and the Arabesque* (1840).

(64) *Studies in Classic American Literature*, p. 113.

(65) See Kent, *The Book of the Centenary*, p. 197.

(66) *In the American Grain*, p. 221.

(67) Vol. XI (1931), p. 56.

(68) *American Literature*, VIII, 394-395.

(69) *Op. cit.*, p. 237.

(70) " To Edgar Allan Poe, Esq.," in *Ladies and Gentlemen*, p. 258.

(71) *The Shock of Recognition*, pp. 82 and 83.

CHAPTER V

(1) *Poe's Short Stories*, p. ix.

(2) Arthur H. Quinn and Edward H. O'Neill, eds., *The Complete Poems and Stories of Edgar Allan Poe, with Selections from His Critical Writings*, New York, 1946, 2 vols.

(3) *The Development of the American Short Story*, p. 138.

(4) *Forces in American Criticism*, pp. 201-202.

(5) *American Prose Masters*, p. 222.

(6) *Works*, XVI, 28.

(7) *Works*, XI, 102-104.

(8) *Ibid.*, 108.

(9) *Book of the Poe Centenary*, p. 164.

(10) *Works*, XI, 107.

(11) *Works*, XIV, 188.

(12) *Works*, XVI, 152.

(13) *Works*, XIV, 188-189.

(14) *Ibid.*

(15) *Works*, XVI, 171.

(16) *Ibid.*, 170.

(17) *The Life and Poems of Edgar Allan Poe*, p. 124.

(18) *Works*, XIV, 188.

(19) Introduction to *Little Masterpieces: Edgar Allan Poe*, New York, 1905, p. viii.

(20) *Works*, XVI, 18.

(21) Edward J. O'Brien, *The Advance of the American Short Story*, p. 75.

(22) *The Philosophy of the Short Story*, p. 45.

(23) *Murder for Pleasure*, p. 16.

(24) W. T. Bandy, "A Source of Poe's 'The Premature Burial,'" *American Literature*, XIX (May, 1947), 167-168. Also see Joseph S. Schick, "The Origin of 'The Cask of Amontillado,'" *American Literature*, VI (March, 1934), 18-21.

(25) See Cornelia Varner, "Notes on Poe's Use of Contemporary Materials in Certain of His Stories," *The Journal of English and Germanic Philology*, XXXII (January, 1933), 77-80.

(26) *Modern Philology*, XXV (August, 1927), 105.

(27) *The Philosophy of Literary Form*, Baton Rouge, Louisiana, 1941, p. 161.

(28) Quinn, *Poe*, p. 596.

(29) Edward Shanks, *Poe*, p. 27.

(30) *The Stage Is Set*, New York, 1932.

(31) *Scenery: A Manual of Scene Design*, Stanford University and London, 1931, p. 81.

(32) *The Poetical Works of Poe*, p. xxxiii.

(33) "Edgar Allan Poe and Architecture," *Sewanee Review*, XL (January-March, 1932), 148-160.

(34) *Works*, X, 112-113.

(35) *Classic Americans*, p. 273.

(36) Whitty, *Complete Poems* . . . , p. xxvi.

(37) Louis Hartmann, *Theatre Lighting*, New York and London, 1930. See chapter entitled, "A Ghost Comes In."

(38) Wilson O. Clough, "The Use of Color Words by Edgar Allen [sic!] Poe," PMLA, XLV (June, 1930), 598-613.

(39) *Ibid.*, p. 605.

(40) *Works*, XI, 121.

(41) *Works* (Stedman and Woodberry ed.), VII, 303.

(42) Review of *Zanoni, Works*, XI, 122.

(43) Introduction to the Tales; *Works* (Stedman and Woodberry), I, 113.

(44) See Edward Hungerford, "Poe and Phrenology," *American Literature*, II (September, 1930), 209-231.

(45) Introduction to *Little Masterpieces: Poe*, New York, 1905, p. vi.

(46) "The Interpretation of 'Ligeia,'" *College English*, V (April, 1944), 365.

(47) Letter dated August 9, 1846, *Works*, XVII, 265.

(48) *Studies and Appreciations*, New York, 1900, pp. 117-118.

(49) *Poems of Poe* (Stedman and Woodberry), p. xvi.

(50) *The Critical Game*, p. 198.

(51) *Works*, XVI, 31.

(52) Lee Simonson, *op. cit.*, p. 317.

(53) *The Advance of the American Short Story*, p. 85.

(54) *Works*, XVI, 40.

(55) The Dial Press, 1946.

(56) *Op. cit.*, p. 116.

(57) *Works*, XIV, 272.

(58) "The Women of Poe's Poems and Tales," *University of Texas Studies in English*, V (1925), pp. 208-209.

(59) Charles Allen Smart, "On the Road to Page One," *Yale Review*, XXXVII (Winter, 1948), 243.

(60) *Expression in America*, p. 163.

(61) *The American Journal of Psychology*, XXXI (October, 1920), 370-402.

(62) "The Stricken Eagle," in *Muse Anthology of Modern Poetry*, p. 93.

(63) *Ibid.*, p. 89.

(64) See G. Gruener, "Notes on the Influence of Hoffman upon Poe," PMLA, XIX (1904), 1-25.

(65) Vladimir Astrov, "Dostoievsky on Edgar Allan Poe," *American Literature*, XIV (March, 1942), 73.

(66) Introduction to Tales, *Works* (Stedman and Woodberry), I, 94.

(67) *The Shapers of American Fiction*, pp. 54-55.

(68) See his review of *The Works of Edgar Allan Poe* (John H. Ingram, ed.), in *Works of Stevenson* (South Seas ed.), New York, 1925, V, 325.

(69) *On the Prose of Edgar Poe*, Publication of the Irkutsk State Pedagogical Institute, 1937. (In Russian)

(70) *The World of Washington Irving*, p. 359.

(71) Walter Blair, "Poe's Conception of Incident and Tone in the Tale," *Modern Philology*, XLI (May, 1944), 239.

CHAPTER VI

(1) Carrol D. Laverty, "Poe in 1847," *American Literature*, XX (May, 1948), 166.

(2) *Ibid.*, pp. 164-168.

(3) *Dragonwyck*, Philadelphia, 1946, p. 195.

(4) *The Saturday Review of Literature*, August 11, 1945, p. 15.

(5) See the Facsimile Edition with an introduction by Thomas Ollive Mabbott, New York, 1941.

(6) *Ibid.*, p. vi.

(7) See *Poe's Brother* edited by Hervey Allen and Thomas Ollive Mabbott, p. 32. Also see Ostrom, *Letters*, I, 44.

(8) *Poe's Brother*, pp. 53-54.

(9) *Southern Literary Messenger*, February, 1836; *Works*, VIII, 234-237.

(10) Frank H. Hosford, "A Booth Plays Poe," *Detroit Free Press*, November 24, 1895.

(11) Review in the *Baltimore Sun*, October 12, 1895.

(12) See Odell, *Annals of the New York Stage*, XIV, 733.

(13) *The Baltimore American*, October 13, 1895.

(14) In *Semiramis and Other Plays*, New York, 1909.

(15) See article by Havilah Babcock in *The State*, Columbia, S. C., March 12, 1933.

(16) November 15, 1936.

(17) Ford's Theatre program for the week of November 2, 1936.

(18) Phillips, I, 778.

(19) *Ibid.*, I, 841.

(20) See Samuel Montefiore Waxman, *Antoine and the Théâtre-Libre*, Cambridge, Mass., 1926, p. 223.

(21) See May Garretson Evans, *Music and Edgar Allan Poe*, pp. 39 and 70.

(22) Copy in the New York Public Library.

(23) For examples, see *The Bread Loaf Book of Plays* (Hortense Moore, ed.), Middleberry, Vt., 1941, and *One Hundred Non-Royalty Plays* (William Kozlenko, ed.), New York, 1940.

(24) "The Tell-Tale Heart" by Peter West, Boston, 1938; "The Tell-Tale Heart" by Pauline Phelps, Sioux City, Iowa, 1939.

(25) The Hugh Lester Offices, Hollywood, California.

(26) Malcolm Cowley, "Aidgarpo," *New Republic*, November 5, 1945.

(27) See his review of a poem by Mrs. Welby, *Works*, XIII, 131.

(28) See Arthur Ransome, *Poe*, p. 232.

(29) *The Critic*, II, 147.

(30) Walter Fuller Taylor, "Israfel in Motley," *Sewanee Review*, XLII (July-September, 1934), pp. 335, 339, 340.

(31) *American Prose Masters*, pp. 222-223.

(32) Philip Alexander Bruce, "Background of Poe's University Life," *South Atlantic Quarterly*, X, 225.

(33) *The Letters of Edgar Allan Poe*, edited by John Ward Ostrom, Cambridge, Mass., 1948, 2 vols.

(34) *Ibid.*, I, 22, and n. 23.

(35) Madeleine B. Stern, "The House of the Expanding Doors," *New York History*, XXIII (January, 1942), 49.

INDEX